Physical activity in patients with anorexia nervosa

Seasonal variation and management strategies

Tanja Hechler

Tectum Verlag
Marburg 2004

Hechler, Tanja:
Physical activity in patients with anorexia nervosa:
Seasonal variation and management strategies.
/ von Tanja Hechler
- Marburg : Tectum Verlag, 2004
Zugl.: Trier, Univ. Diss. 2004
ISBN 978-3-8288-8755-8

Tectum Verlag
Marburg 2004

To my dear parents

and to Professor Beumont's family

Acknowledgements

My sincerest appreciation goes to my Australian supervisor, Professor Pierre Beumont, for his time, efforts, patience and critical guidance throughout the course of this project. He also offered me the opportunity to work at the Department of Psychological Medicine, providing me with ideal working facilities. Moreover, he organised financial support from the Jenny Truman Memorial Fund (Medical Foundation, University of Sydney), without which part 2 of this report would not have been feasible. Throughout my stay in Sydney, Professor Beumont guided me through problems, always taking time to discuss and find solutions for small and big barriers in the process of my research. Not only that, he also supported my work by introducing me to his colleagues and researchers across the world and by enabling me to present my research at international conferences. It was with great sadness, that I learned about his passing away while attending a conference in Ravello, Italy, in October 2003. To express my gratefulness for everything he has done for me, I have dedicated this work to his family.

I would also like to thank Professor Stephen Touyz for his constant support and interest in my work. When Professor Beumont could not supervise me any longer, it was Professor Touyz who stepped in, reading drafts of my thesis and providing me with very helpful feedback and great support.

Further, I would like to acknowledge the interest and support of my German supervisor, Professor Reinhold Lässle. Through constant email-contact, he guided me through my work from Germany, providing useful feedback and critical comments.

I would also like to express my gratitude to Professor Dirk Hellhammer, who agreed to be a co-supervisor and who showed constant interest in my work. My stay at the

University of Sydney was made possible by a special agreement between the University of Trier and Sydney that Professor Hellhammer and Professor Beumont negotiated with the Vice-Chancellors of the respective universities.

Further, I am extremely grateful to all my colleagues from the Department of Psychological Medicine, i.e., Emmy Giannakopoulos, Peta Marks, Sarah Maguire and Toni Addison. It was through their help that my English improved and I settled in the Department and was thus able to conduct my research project. Their constant support, friendship, help and answers to my many questions were of inestimable value to me.

I am also very grateful to Elizabeth Rieger, who patiently read through drafts of my thesis and provided me with extremely valuable feedback and always took time to discuss my questions. Muriel Wang read through my thesis from an English point of view and made it sound English instead of 'German-English'. Louise George patiently listened to my problems and worries, providing me with supportive comments and feedback on how to proceed when encountering difficulties.

Particular thanks to Guy Plasqui from the Netherlands. My work (i.e. part 2) would not be finished if it was not for him. Through more than 500 emails, he guided me through the analysis of the Tracmor data and statistics and thus, became an inestimable value for my research and a dear friend.

I would also like to express my gratitude to Professor Klaas Westerterp. His interest in physical activity and anorexia nervosa was one of the starting points for my research project (part 2). He provided us with the Tracmors and also took time to discuss my research critically, broadening my ideas and understanding on physical activity and body composition.

I am further grateful to Professor Gail Huon who agreed to help me with part 1. It was her student, Josephine Chau, who administered the surveys to the Australian students. Professor Huon further took time to discuss my research with me and put it into a general context rather than focussing on dieting disorders.

In addition, I like to thank the therapeutic teams of the four specialised hospitals (i.e., the Royal Prince Alfred Hospital, Carlingford Day Therapy Centre, Wesley Private Hospital and Westmead Hospital) who not only allowed me to contact their patients but also gave helpful comments on how to address the patients. These were of inestimable value for the recruitment process of part 2.

Thanks as well to Sarah Giesecke, who administered the surveys to the German sample, read through the questionnaire, helped with data entry and literature search.

I also thank Professor Toro Uehara, who put me into contact with colleagues from Japan and China (part 3).

I would also like to thank Don Rowe for his help with computer programs (particularly Reference Manager).

In addition, I am grateful to Thorsten Kauder, who designed a computer program to analyse the Tracmor data.

Living in Australia for the past two and a half years would not have been possible without the financial support of the German Exchange Service (DAAD), the Christina Barz-Stiftung and the Australia-Europe Scholarship, and as such, I gratefully acknowledge their enormous contributions to my work.

My sincerest thanks go to all my participants in the three parts, i.e. the Australian and German students (part 1), the clinical specialists (part 3) and particularly, the patiens and controls (part 2) who were so committed and interested in my study. I hope it was of interest to them all and maybe even of therapeutic benefit for some.

I am indebted to my dear friends from Australia, i.e. Liz Pratley, Anne Müller, Georgie Lampe, Emmy Giannakopoulos, Louise George, Shaun Cornelius, Pascale Kippelin, Kate and Kain Swift, Anthony Modrich, Ella and Oli who showed me how to enjoy and live in Australia and thus helped me to obtain an Australian attitude when encountering difficulties (i.e. 'no worries, mate!').

Likewise, I would not have been able to enjoy my stay in Sydney as much and thus, would not have been able to complete my research had it not been through the sincere, patient and constant support and interest of my family (Elke, Gunter and Claudia Hechler) and my German friends, i.e., Klaudia Wolke, Mara Rohlfing, Corinna Stamm, Katharina Kotthoff, Silja Vocks and Volker Grüsgen. Last but not least, I am extremely grateful to Stephan Schneider, who helped me cope with the difficult part of writing the thesis through his patient and beautiful support.

Table of contents

11

Part 2:
Physical activity in patients with anorexia nervosa: Which patterns do emerge across three seasons?

14

Part 3: How do clinical specialists understand the role of physical activity in dieting disorders?

General introduction

"Whoever wishes to pursue properly the science of medicine must proceed thus. First, he ought to consider what effects each season of the year can produce; for the seasons are not all alike in both themselves and their changes." (Hippocrates)

Anorexia nervosa is a severe mental illness, which is today the third most common chronic condition in adolescent girls and young women (World Health Organisation Collaborating Centre for Mental Health and Substance Abuse, 1997). Relapse rates are high at around 15 to 25%. The role of physical activity in anorexia nervosa has recently received some attention as a factor fundamental to the pathogenesis of the disorder (Beumont, Arthur, Russell, & Touyz, 1994; Casper, 1998; Davis, Katzman, & Kirsh, 1999; Hebebrand et al., 2003). Physical activity appears to be one behaviour that worsens over time and contributes to maintaining the dieting disorder (Exner et al., 2000) via its impact on energy expenditure and on patients' pathological attitudes towards the activity of exercise (Davis, Brewer, & Ratusny, 1993). A comprehensive understanding of patients' physical activity is therefore warranted.

In contrast to a cross sectional examination of patients' activity, a seasonal analysis provides an opportunity to investigate seasonal variation (or the lack thereof) in physical activity in patients with anorexia nervosa. If physical activity varies across the seasons in patients with anorexia nervosa, as demonstrated in the general population (Matthews et al., 2001; Uitenbroek, 1993), certain seasons may represent high risk in terms of increased activity and hence a worsening of symptomatology. Treatment strategies should then be adapted accordingly.

Since the research for this thesis was conducted in Sydney, Australia, Part 1 of the report aims to determine how Australians perceive seasonal changes in physical activity, food choice and dieting and if they differ from German participants, who reside in a distinctly different climate.

In Part 2, seasonal variation of physical activity in patients with anorexia nervosa and healthy controls is examined using a multidimensional approach. Further, the relationship between physical activity and body composition variables is investigated.

The two parts aim to evaluate the following assumptions:

Assumption 1: Australians and Germans will not differ in their perception and understanding of seasonal changes in physical activity, food choice and dieting.

Assumption 2: Seasonal variation in physical activity (i.e., duration, frequency and body movement) and body composition will be detected in patiens with anorexia nervosa and a negative relationship between physical activity and body composition variables will emerge in the patient group.

In Part 3, a review of management strategies for physical activity in patients with anorexia nervosa is provided. Further, results of a survey conducted with clinical specialists on their understanding of the role of physical activity in the context of anorexia nervosa and their assessment and management strategies are presented.

For each of the three parts, a literature review directs the reader towards an understanding of the rationale behind the project's aims and hypotheses. Methods and results are presented and critically discussed, including methodological limitations and implications for future research.

In summary, the present report on 'Physical activity and anorexia nervosa: Seasonal variation and management strategies' aimed to provide a comprehensive analysis of physical activity in anorexia nervosa, including the aspect of seasonality as well as management strategies.

Reference list for general introduction

Beumont, P. J., Arthur, B., Russell, J. D., & Touyz, S. W. (1994). Excessive physical activity in dieting disorder patients: Proposals for a supervised exercise program. [Review] [48 refs]. *International Journal of Eating Disorders, 15*, 21-36.

Casper, R. (1998). Behavioral activation and lack of concern, core symptoms of anorexia nervosa? *International Journal of Eating Disorders, 24*, 381-393.

Davis, C., Brewer, H., & Ratusny, D. (1993). Behavioral frequency and psychological commitment: Necessary concepts in the study of excessive exercising. *Journal of Behavioral Medicine, 16*, 611-628.

Davis, C., Katzman, D. K., & Kirsh, C. (1999). Compulsive physical activity in adolescents with anorexia nervosa: a psychobehavioral spiral of pathology. *Journal of Nervous & Mental Disease, 187*, 336-342.

Exner, C., Hebebrand, J., Remschmidt, H., Wewetzer, C., Ziegler, A., & Herpertz, S. (2000). Leptin suppresses semi-starvation induced hyperactivity in rats: Implications for anorexia nervosa. *Molecular Psychiatry, 5*, 476-481.

Hebebrand, J., Exner, C., Hebebrand, K., Holtkamp, C., Casper, R. C., Remschmidt, H. et al. (2003). Hyperactivity in patients with anorexia nervosa and in semistarved rats: Evidence for a pivotal role of hypoleptinemia. *International Journal of Eating Disorders, 79*, 25-37.

Matthews, C. E., Freedson, P. S., Herbert, J. R., Stanek, E. J., Merriam, P. A., Rosal, M. C. et al. (2001). Seasonal variation in household, occupational, and leisure time physical activity: Longitudinal analyses from the Seasonal Variation of Blood Cholesterol Study. *American Journal of Epidemiology, 153,* 172-183.

Uitenbroek, D. G. (1993). Seasonal variation in leisure time physical activity. *Medicine and Science in Sports and Exercise, 25,* 755-760.

World Health Organisation Collaborating Centre for Mental Health and Substance Abuse (1997). Dieting Disorders. In World Health Organisation Collaborating Centre for Mental Health and Substance Abuse (Ed.), *Management of Mental Disorders. Treatment Practice Protocols* (pp. 464-525). Darlinghurst NSW: World Health Organisation Collaborating Centre for Mental Health and Substance Abuse.

Part 1:

People's perception and understanding of seasonal changes in three health-related behaviours: The role of environmental behaviours and engagement in the behaviours

Table of contents

List of tables

Publications

People's perception and understanding of seasonal changes in three health-related behaviours: The role of environmental factors and engagement in behaviours.

Tanja Hechler, Josephine Chau, Emmy Giannakopoulos, Sarah Giesecke, Gail Huon, Elizabeth Rieger, Silja Vocks.

To be submitted to the Medical Journal of Australia.

Abstract

This study aimed to examine perceived seasonal changes in three health-related behaviours: physical activity, food choice and dieting. Of interest is whether individuals from different geographical regions differ in their perception and understanding of seasonal changes in these behaviours. A semi-structured survey was administered to 121 female Australian and 109 German students aged 19 to 33 years. The majority of both Australians and Germans perceived seasonal changes in physical activity and food choice, but did not perceive changes in dieting. The two samples differed in the causes they proposed to account for perceived seasonal changes in physical activity and food choice. In particular, environmental factors were found to be significantly more important for the German participants (χ^2 $_{(df=1, N=165)}$=9.37, p=0.002). In terms of dieting behaviour, more Australians than Germans reported dieting (χ^2 $_{(1, N=230)}$=10.2, p=0.001) and perceived seasonal changes (χ^2 $_{(N=224, df=1)}$ = 8.82, p=0.005). For both Australians and Germans, dieters were less likely to perceive seasonal changes in food choice (OR=0.52; 95% CI: 0.27-1.0) and in dieting (OR=0.17, 95% CI: 0.08-0.36). The findings suggest that programmes designed to enhance physical activity across the seasons would be improved by a greater understanding of perceived seasonal changes in physical activity and people's explanations for these changes as well as how such perceptions differ depending on the geographical region. Further, the fact that dieting, once established, appears to be a stable behaviour pursued across the seasons, suggests the importance of prevention strategies.

Keywords: seasonality, physical activity, food choice, dieting, Australia, Germany

1. Overview

Seasonal variation has been investigated, particularly in the context of Seasonal Affective Disorder (SAD) and the disorder is presented in chapter 1.1.. However, behaviours have been found to vary across the seasons not only in patients suffering from SAD but also in healthy participants (chapter 1.2.). Information on seasonal variation in physical activity, food choice and dieting is essential in the context of prevention of cardiovascular diseases, obesity and dieting disorders[1]. Chapter 1.3. therefore provides a detailed overview on seasonal variation in the three health-related behaviours. To understand seasonal variation in these behaviours and the potential role of environmental factors, participants from different geographical regions being exposed to different climatic conditions have to be compared. However, studies comparing residents from the Northern and Southern Hemisphere are rare. A comparison between Australia and Germany would be particularly interesting given the different climatic conditions which characterise these two countries. Chapter 1.4. summarises studies into seasonal variation from Australia and Germany with the aim to conclude if differences between the two countries are to be expected. To draw conclusions on Australians' and Germans' perception of seasonal changes in the three behaviours, it has to be examined if they differ in their activity-levels, food choice and dieting. Chapter 1.5. therefore provides an overview of studies into physical activity, food choice and dieting in Australian and German participants. Further, although seasonal changes in behaviours have been investigated extensively from a quantitative

---

[1] Since anorexia nervosa and bulimia nervosa represent consequences of weight losing behaviour of which dieting is the principal component, the term 'dieting disorder' rather than 'eating disorder' will be used throughout this dissertation (Touyz & Beumont, 1999).

27

perspective, particularly with regards to SAD, qualitative studies focusing on people's perception and understanding of these changes are rare (chapter 1.6.). The current study therefore aimed to provide information on how a group of 121 female Australians and 109 Germans perceive and understand seasonal changes in the three health-related behaviours (chapter 1.7. and 1.8.). Methods and results are presented (chapter 2. and 3.) and critically discussed, including methodological limitations and implications for future research (chapter 4.).

1.1. Definition of seasonality and seasonal affective disorder

Hippocrates was among the first to recognise that the timing of depressive episodes can be related to the seasons, and particularly since the beginning of the 20th century, researchers have investigated the influences of seasonal changes on behaviours (for a review see (Kasper, Wehr, Bartko, Gaist, & Rosenthal, 1989b)). These environmental changes comprise, among other aspects, changes in the ambient temperature and duration and intensity of daylight (photoperiod). Variations have been observed in psychological variables such as mood, performance and personality and physiological variables such as metabolism, thermoregulation, the neuroendocrine axis and central nervous system monoamines (Lacoste & Wirz-Justice, 1989). Kasper, Wehr, Bartko, Gaist and Rosenthal (1989b) defined seasonality as the degree to which seasonal changes affect factors such as mood, energy, sleep length, appetite, food preferences or social activities. One psychological disorder, which has received particular attention in terms of seasonality is Seasonal Affective Disorder (SAD) – the periodic recurrence of major depressive disorder in consecutive autumn or winter months, with remission during summer (Rosenthal, Bradt, & Wehr, 1984). A milder form of SAD has also been characterised and is termed Subsyndromal SAD (S-SAD) (Kasper et al., 1989a).

1.2. Seasonal variation in behaviours in healthy participants

In nonclinical populations, seasonal rhythms have been studied extensively. Lacoste and Wirz-Justice (1989) provide a review on recent publications regarding behavioural, physiological and biochemical measures. It is generally accepted to perceive seasonality

29

as a dimensional variable, with the majority experiencing peaks in depressive symptoms during winter (Magnusson, 2000).

What causes seasonal variation in behaviours? Various mechanisms have been proposed to account for seasonal variation in behaviours and physiological variables, particularly, mechanisms underlying SAD. Since seasonality is understood as a dimensional variable, mechanisms underlying SAD are presented here. These can be extrapolated to the understanding of seasonal variation in behaviours in the general population.

SAD is thought to be primarily caused by lack of light in winter (Eiliv & Vidje, 2001; Magnusson, 2000). The larger photoperiod variance (variance in the duration and intensity of daylight) across the seasons at higher latitude should therefore lead to higher prevalence rates of winter SAD closer to the poles (Kjellman, 2001). A number of studies have examined whether rates of SAD and S-SAD vary with latitude. However, studies have not always found significant correlations between latitude and prevalence rates. Mersch, Middendorp, Bouhuys, Beersma and van den Hoofdakker (1999) calculated correlation between prevalence and latitude in North America and Europe. The correlation for North America was strong (r=0.70, p<0.01) and for Europe, almost significant (r=0.70, p=0.06). They concluded that if latitude was influencing prevalence, that influence was only weak and other factors have to be taken into account. In Australia, Murray and Hay (1997) found a small correlation between latitude and prevalence (r=0.10, p=0.017), thus confirming Mersch's results. Magnusson (2000) reviewed epidemiological studies of SAD and concluded that several studies have found an increasing prevalence of SAD with higher northern latitudes, while others have not. Therefore the effect of latitude is probably small.

Kjellman (2001) reviewed papers on the role of the photoperiod and concluded that the photoperiod was of importance for the onset of winter SAD. Further, studies found that people acclimatise to living at a northern location and to long dark winters. Prevalence rates for SAD were therefore higher in those who had migrated to higher latitudes (for a review see (Magnusson, 2000)). It has also been suggested that genes may influence the tendency to experience seasonal changes, but results are inconsistent (Magnusson, 2000).

Apart from environmental or biological factors, Aschoff (1981) highlighted the importance of sociocultural factors in seasonal changes in behaviours. He argues that the steady decreases in the amplitude (peak to trough distance) of behaviours suggest a decrease in the effectiveness of environmental factors or a decrease in the responsiveness. These changes are probably related to industrialisation and the increase in standard of living. Hence, sociocultural factors *"may increasingly override the influence of natural forces"* ((Aschoff, 1981), p. 486) and the *"deseasonalisation"* would be a *"denaturalisation"* caused by industrialisation. Similarly, Lacoste and Wirz-Justice (1989), despite their biological perspective, acknowledge the potential role of a conditioned behavioural response (*"winter blahs and spring irritability"*, p. 219) that may override the original physiological changes initiated by light duration and heat and cold. Persinger (1983) suggests that winter is associated with subtle but persistent reinforcement schedule shifts. Four major winter-related stimulus patterns thus influence our psychological responses during the season. These are 1) a subtle and gradual shift in the ratio of negative to positive stimuli (e.g., occurrence of travel hazards or the aversiveness of exposure to the environment), 2) stimulus redundancy (winter contains fewer alterations in stimuli such as less birds singing and smells), 3) the consequences of coerced hypoactivity due to avoiding the cold by remaining in the living area and 4) the facilitation of anxiety due to the increase in the proportion of negative stimuli.

To date, Nelson (1990) summarised the knowledge on mechanisms underlying SAD and seasonal variation in behaviours appropriately by stating that there is difficulty knowing the underlying causes of seasonal variation in human behaviour as humans are exposed to both natural and artificial environmental changes.

1.3. Seasonality in three health-related behaviours

1.3.1. Seasonality in physical activity

The Seasonal Pattern Assessment Questionnaire (SPAQ) (Rosenthal et al., 1984) aims to identify cases of SAD and S-SAD and therefore comprises items that are related to the pathophysiology of affective disorders. Seasonality however, has been demonstrated in other behaviours not necessarily related to affective disorders such as the engagement in physical activity (Dannenberg, Keller, Wilson, & Castelli, 1989; Uitenbroek, 1993; Wankel, 1988).

Physical activity is generally defined as any bodily movement produced by skeletal muscles that results in energy expenditure (Caspersen, Powell, & Christenson, 1985). Its intensity (light, moderate and vigorous), duration and frequency are assessed in standardised questionnaires (for example the 24-Hour Physical Activity Recall, (Matthews et al., 2001)). Considerable seasonal variation in physical activity has been found in several studies (Dannenberg et al., 1989; Levin, Jacobs, Ainsworth, Richardson, & Leon, 1999; Matthews et al., 2001; Uitenbroek, 1993). For example,

Matthews et al. (2001) demonstrated a complex seasonal pattern for different intensities of physical activity. They found a peak in leisure and household moderate intensity activities during July, occupational activities tended to peak in January and no seasonal variation emerged for vigorous physical activity (such as regular exercise). It can be speculated that those who obtain a regular exercise routine will maintain it despite seasonal changes in environmental variables (see also part 2, chapter 1.7.).

The findings of seasonal variation in physical activity have important implications for epidemiologic and clinical investigations of the health effects of physical activity. Overall, ischemic heart disease and cerebrovascular disease were, respectively, the first and second leading cause of death throughout the world (Booth, 2000). Seasonal variation in incidence of coronary heart disease has been attributed, among other factors, to seasonal changes in blood pressure (Matthews et al., 2001). Physical activity has been shown to favourably influence blood pressure and therefore Matthews et al. (2001) conclude that seasonal variation in physical activity may be associated with the seasonal variation in cardiovascular events through effects on risk factors of the disease. Further, Craft and Landers (1998) demonstrated in their meta-analysis an inverse association between exercise and depression, which suggests that engagement in physical activity over the year may prevent seasonal mood fluctuations. The SPAQ does not cover variation in physical activity. Studies into seasonal variation of physical activity usually used questionnaires or objective monitoring (e.g., using Caltrac; (Matthews et al., 2001)) administered repeatedly to the participants over the year. This procedure is very robust and powerful in terms of a quantitative assessment of physical activity. Particularly the study of Matthews et al. (2001) was carefully designed from an empirical-analytical perspective (Fossey, Harvey, McDermott, & Davidson, 2002) and the researchers obtained estimates of 'habitual' physical activity levels (i.e., past 12 months) rather than short-term measures. As seasonal variation of physical activity plays an important role in prevention of cardiovascular heart disease and seasonal mood changes, a qualitative rather than a quantitative assessment of seasonal changes would be beneficial in terms of understanding individuals' perception and explanation of seasonal changes in physical activity. As yet, no such studies have been undertaken.

1.3.2. Seasonality in food intake and the role of food choice

In addition to physical activity, food intake, particularly with regards to the content of the food consumed, has been shown to vary seasonally. Interest in seasonal changes in food intake has emerged from two lines of research: 1) the observation that SAD patients showed seasonal patterns in their eating behaviours, such as increased appetite, higher food intake and carbohydrate craving during winter (Kraeuchi & Wirz-Justice, 1988; Kraeuchi & Wirz-Justice, 2001) and 2) observations of seasonal variation in dietary intake (increased fat intake) and its role in the higher morbidity for cardiovascular disease and stroke during winter (Shahar et al., 1999). Seasonal variation in food intake is more common in developing countries where food is not available throughout the year (Westerterp-Plantenga, 1999). However, Van Staveren, Deurenberg, Burema, de Groot and Hautvast (1986) found less fat consumption in a group of 114 female participants from the Netherlands during summer. During winter, daily dietary fibre was higher. Shahar et al. (1999) found increased fat and sodium intake in a group of 94 male workers in Israel during winter. They discussed the potential risks associated with higher fat intake during winter such as an increase in body weight and its contribution to cardiovascular disease. Kraeuchi and Wirz-Justice (2001) reported increased total caloric intake, especially carbohydrates, in autumn in healthy participants. They argue that the excess in carbohydrate intake may not be restricted to a seasonal disturbance such as SAD but can be more generally related to depressive mood.

This suggests that it might be useful to investigate changes in food choice across the seasons. The process of food choice according to Furst, Connors, Bisogni, Sobal and Winter Falk (1996) is a complex process and incorporates not only decisions based on conscious reflection, but also those that are automatic, habitual and subconscious. They described an elaborate model of food selection, consisting of three major components: 1) life course: past influences of personal experiences and historical eras, current involvement and trends and transitions and anticipations of future events, 2) influences: ideals, personal factors, resources, social framework and food context and 3) personal system: a) values such as sensory perception, monetary considerations, convenience, health/nutrition, managing relationships and quality; and b) strategies that tended to recur and be relatively routine and simplify the task of making food choice, for example "*whatever is a good name*" (Furst, Connors, Bisogni, Sobal, & Winter Falk, 1996). Steptoe, Pollard and Wardle (1995) investigated motives for food choice and designed a questionnaire to assess the perceived importance of different factors in food choice (see 3a) values in Furst's model). These were weight control, sensory appeal, ideological reasons, health, mood, convenience, natural content, price and familiarity.

In the context of the above-mentioned observations regarding seasonal variation in food intake (particularly the observed increases in fat and carbohydrate intake during winter), it can be speculated that food choice during winter might be different from that during

35

summer. In studies of different geographical locations (e.g., in Australia, (Murray & Hay, 1997) or Switzerland (Kasper, 1991)), the majority of people felt worst during winter and best during summer. It can therefore be speculated that food choice during winter is centred around mood, such as choosing foods that enhance mood and help in coping with stress (Steptoe, Pollard, & Wardle, 1995). In summer – a season experienced as more active and entailing more socialising - food choice would be more centred upon sensory appeal, health and potentially weight loss. The SPAQ quantifies seasonal variation in appetite and certain food groups such as bread, sugar, fish and salads (Kasper, 1991). However, it does not cover an assessment of perceived changes and understanding of changes in food choice. Since variation in food intake, particularly increases in fat and carbohydrate in winter, are crucial in their contribution to cardiovascular disease, an investigation into people's perception and understanding of seasonal changes in food choice as potential causes for the variation is important. As yet, no study has investigated the perception and understanding of seasonal changes in food choice in healthy participants.

1.3.3. Seasonality in dieting behaviour

Studies into seasonal variation in dieting behaviour – defined as changes in eating habits with the intention to lose weight – are rare. Recently, Huon and Lim (2000) showed a variation in the amount of dieters and triers with the seasons in an Australian sample of 478 female adolescents (mean age=13.7). The frequency of girls who were dieting or trying to diet increased during spring and decreased during winter. According to Huon and Lim, sociocultural factors such as fashion exerting pressure on adolescent girls to be thin for summer account for the seasonal variation. Story, Neumark-Sztainer,

Sherwood, Stang and Murray (1998) observed that dieting for weight loss is a common and widespread practice among adolescents and recently, some positive impacts of dieting behaviour on psychosocial wellbeing have been investigated. In their study, they showed more healthful behaviours in adolescents with moderate dieting (i.e., girls with moderate dieting engaged in more health-promoting eating and exercise behaviour than extreme dieters or nondieters). In terms of negative outcomes, dieting is considered to play a role in the development of pathological eating and dieting disorders. Polivy and Herman (2002) recently reviewed the literature on causes for dieting disorders. They concluded that sociocultural pressure to be thin and dieting are among the factors that appear to contribute to the development of dieting disorders. Investigating the influence of sociocultural factors in a non-dieting population, Griffiths et al. (2000) showed that those people with restrained eating and dieting behaviour were more aware of social pressures (assessed with the Sociocultural Attitude towards Appearance Questionnaire, SATAQ (Heinberg, Thompson, & Stormer, 1995)). Similarly, Griffiths et al. (1999) demonstrated in a study with female anorexic, bulimic, and EDNOS patients and healthy controls that patients internalised sociocultural attitudes towards their appearance to a greater extent than healthy controls. As restrained eating may lead to full-blown eating pathology in some people (Griffiths, 2000), any factor that increases dieting behaviour in some people requires investigation.

According to the results of Huon and Lim (2000), the seasons of spring and summer might constitute one such factor. It can be assumed that dieting status would impact on the seasonal variation in dieting and the perceived pressure to be thin for summer. Considering Griffiths' results (1999; 2000), it is likely that dieters are more affected by the pressure to be thin for summer than non-dieters and hence, increase their dieting during these seasons.

An identification of 'high-risk' seasons for dieting can therefore broaden the understanding of factors that trigger dieting behaviour and can thus be integrated into the prevention of dieting behaviour and dieting disorders. Rather than assessing participants' dieting status across different seasons, a broader approach including their perceptions of changes in dieting and explanations of these changes may highlight perceived pressures for dieting behaviour across the seasons. No study has yet investigated the perception and understanding of seasonal changes in dieting in healthy participants.

1.4. Seasonality and geographic region

A comparison of seasonal changes in behaviours between residents from the Southern and Northern Hemisphere is helpful in investigating the role of geographic region in seasonality. Australia is generally perceived as a country with minimal environmental variation across the seasons. In a city like Sydney, winters are milder than in a German city like Trier and the ambient temperature rarely drops below 0°C. Since Australia is closer to the equator, the photoperiod is lower. In summer, the mean day length (sunrise to sunset) in Sydney is 822 minutes (Australian Surveying and Land Information Group, 2002) compared to 935 minutes in Trier (Sternwarte Hamburg, 2003). In winter, the mean day length is 633 minutes in Sydney and 538 minutes in Trier.

Studies into seasonality of behaviours in the Southern Hemisphere are rare (Lacoste & Wirz-Justice, 1989). In Australia, studies found that adolescent Australian girls showed seasonal variation in their dieting behaviour (Huon & Lim, 2000). Boyce and Parker (1988) found that 80 out of 138 participants form Victoria and New South Wales reported depressive symptoms associated with a particular season. Murray and Hay (1997) found seasonal variation in wellbeing, weight, physical activity, eating habits and sleep in a sample of 526 female Australians (from the eight states of Australia). Twelve percent of the sample reported that the changes in behaviours with the seasons were a problem.

To the best of our knowledge, no study has investigated differences in people's perception and understanding of seasonal changes in behaviours between residents from the Northern and Southern Hemisphere. This comparison may broaden the understanding of environmental and sociocultural factors that determine seasonal changes in behaviours. Comparisons between residents from Australia - as one nation from the Southern Hemisphere that shares a similar cultural background to European countries - and residents from Europe (that is Germany) would be particularly interesting.

The question emerges as to who would be more affected by seasonal changes: Australians or Germans. One could assume that seasonal changes in behaviours occur to a lesser degree in Australians because of the milder climate and the lower photoperiod. However, as pointed out in chapter 1.4., the effect of latitude is probably small and it is yet to be clarified to what degree the photoperiod affects people's perception and understanding of seasonal changes in behaviours. Therefore it can be hypothesised that Australians and Germans may not differ in their perception and understanding of seasonal changes in behaviours.

In conclusion, seasonal variation in behaviours has been demonstrated in both countries. No information is available on people's perception and understanding of seasonal changes in residents from Australia or Germany. Since the latitude-hypothesis is still critically debated and since seasonal variation in behaviours has been demonstrated in both countries, we expect to see no differences in the perception and understanding of Australian and German participants. If Australians from a mild climate and Germans from a more extreme climate (including the difference in hours of daylight) do not differ in their perception and understanding of seasonal changes in behaviours, we can assume that environmental factors may play a minor role.

1.5. Do Australians and Germans differ in physical activity, food choice and dieting?

In order to answer the question as to whether Australians or Germans would perceive more seasonal changes in their behaviours, it has to be clarified if Australians and Germans differ in any of the three behaviours that are investigated.

1.5.1. Differences in levels of physical activity?

To the best of our knowledge, no study has investigated differences in levels of physical activity between Australians and Germans. In Australia, Bauman and Owen (1999) summarised results from the Commonwealth Department of Sport (1984-1987, N=17053) and the NSW household survey (1996, N=3392) and found that 15% engaged in vigorous physical activity and around 33% in moderate intensity activities. The Australian Bureau of Statistics (2000) found in their 2000-survey that 54.7% of the

Australian population participated in sports activities. The highest rates for participation emerged in the age group of 18-24-year-olds, with more than 60% participating in sports. Generally, more males than females engaged in physical activities.

In Germany, Stock, Wille and Krämer (2001) investigated health behaviours of German university students (N=650, 288 males and 362 females) from 19 to 33 years of age. They found that only 21.8% were not exercising. More males than females tended to engage in vigorous exercise (> 4h/week). Twenty-two percent of the females did not exercise. In a cross-sectional study with residents from the 15 members of the European Union, Martinez-Gonzalez et al. (2001) investigated the prevalence of physical activity during leisure time. They found that in Germany (N=1159, age range 15-65 years), 29.4% stated to be inactive, 70.6% participated in leisure-time activities. Over the whole sample, rates for participation were highest for the 15-24-year-olds with 82.8% engaging in leisure-time activities. Ruetten et al. (2001) found in their study that 64.1% of participants from East Germany (N=913) and 70.1% from West Germany (N=489) aged 18 years and above reported to be physically active when asked if they did any gymnastics, physical activity or sports.

The studies are difficult to compare with regards to their assessment and definition of physical activity. Some studies simply asked whether participants participated in sports activities (Australian Bureau of Statistics, 2000; Ruetten et al., 2001) whereas others assessed self-reported hours of exercise per week (Stock, Wille, & Kramer, 2001). However, the rates of inactivity appear to be similar in the two countries with around 20-30% of the population being inactive. The age and gender of the participants are important variables that determine participation rates. From the studies, it can be concluded that particularly younger participants engage in sports activities. Males tended to show higher participation rates than females in both countries. Hence, it can be hypothesised that comparable levels of physical activity (i.e., time in moderate and hard intensity activities) will emerge in a group of females students from Australia and Germany aged 19-35 years.

1.5.2. Differences in food choice?

The Australian Institute of Health and Welfare (2002) summarises findings of studies on the health status of Australians, including health behaviours such as dietary intake and related knowledge and attitudes. Accordingly, average energy intake increased by over 10% for boys and girls aged 10-15 years, and by around 4% for adults between 1980 and 1990. The current level of saturated fat intake (37%) is above recommendations of 30%, and only 17% of the adult population met the recommendation for daily fruit intake of 300g (two serves without fruit juice). In terms of attitudes and knowledge about food intake, the report summarises that in major urban centres in Western Australia, South Australia, New South Wales and Queensland about two-thirds were able to link fat intake with heart disease. No studies investigating food choices in Australians could be found in literature search with PubMed and PsycInfo.

In Germany, Keller, Kreis and Huck (2001) reported insufficient fruit and vegetable consumption in male and female adults aged 25 to 50 years. Stehle (2000) found increased fat intake in older adults (654 males and 896 females) aged between 65 and 85 years resulting from high consumption of meat and cold meat. In students (362 males and 288 females) aged 19 to 33 years, Stock et al. (2001) found a high proportion of females making conscious efforts for healthy nutrition. Pudel und Westenhoefer (1991) summarised study results into nutrition, knowledge and motives for food choice in the population from East and West Germany assessed in 1990 (N_{East}=978, N_{West}=1936). In a cluster analysis, they found four types of food choice: 1) price-conscious with 20% of the population, 2) natural content with 30%, 3) modern gourmet, i.e., choosing food according to its sensory appeal with 25% and 4) conscious of body weight with 25%.

It has been shown that sociocultural factors impact on health behaviours with a tendency for people in poor circumstances to generally have worse health than those in advantaged conditions (Australian Institute of Health and Welfare, 2002). Education seems to play an important role in this regard.

In summary, there are no studies comparing food choices in Australians and Germans. Australians and Germans tend to show a similar food intake pattern, with too few consumption of fruits and vegetables and a too high consumption of saturated fats. Studies into factors for food choice in Germany found the following factors to be important: health, sensory appeal and natural content. Weight concerns tended to be more important in females than in males. When comparing populations, the gender and socioeconomic background have to be controlled as potential confounding variables. It can therefore be hypothesised that no differences in food choice factors will emerge in an Australian and German female student population.

1.5.3. Differences in dieting?

In Australia, dieting behaviour and its prevalence have been studied extensively and various degrees of dieting have been examined. Dependent on the degree of dieting, prevalence rates ranged from 1.6% for extreme dieting in 1785 females (age >15 years) (Hay, 1998) to 47.2% for dieting defined as 'How often have you gone on a diet (that is, limited how much you ate) in order to lose weight during the last year?' (Ball, 2002) in 14779 females aged 18 to 23 years.

Studies into prevalence of dieting in Germany are not as common, and those who investigated prevalence rates did not always specify their definition of dieting. For example, Westernhoefer (2001) surveyed his participants from East and West Germany in 1997 (N_{East}=2155, N_{West}=2130, age range: 18-96) on binge eating, restrained eating, dieting and symptoms of dieting disorders. These results were compared with a survey conducted in West Germany in 1990 (N=1773). In 1997, the sample consisted of 3318 females and 2740 males. Participants were presented a list of weight control behaviours. Dieting was included but no definition was provided. Restrained eating was defined as 'I consciously hold back at meals in order not to gain weight'. In 1997, 10.2% of the participants from West Germany and 13.3% of the ones from East Germany engaged in dieting. Around 37% in each part of Germany stated to engage in restrained eating behaviour. Stock et al. (2001) found significant gender differences in efforts for healthy nutrition and engaging in low-fat diets. More females than males reported to make high conscious efforts for a healthy nutrition (43.8% compared to 27.7%); 65.7% of the female students compared to 53.2% of the males engaged in low-fat diets. Pudel (2000) observed in his survey that around 35% of female adolescents (aged 12 to 17 years) wanted to lose weight.

To the best of our knowledge, no study has compared rates of dieting between Australians and Germans. However, Ball (2002) investigated the relationship between ethnicity and several aspects of eating and weight pathology in a community sample of young Australian females (N=14779, age range: 18-23 years). They found similar percentage of dieters, defined as 'How often do you go on a diet to lose weight?', in

44

participants from an Australian and European background: 47.2% for Australians and

45.1% for Europeans.

The studies into prevalence rates of dieting are difficult to compare due to the use of

different definitions for dieting. The study of Ball (2002) suggests similar rates of

dieting in Australian and European females, however these females were all assessed

while living in Australia.

Despite these difficulties, percentage rates tended to be similar in Australian and

German studies when applying a mild definition of dieting, around 30-40% reported

dieting or restrained eating. Therefore it can be hypothesised that a similar percentage of

Australian and German students will engage in mild dieting behaviour defined as

changing one's eating habits with the intention to lose weight.

1.6. Assessment of seasonal changes in behaviours: The need for qualitative research

Seasonal changes in behaviours are usually assessed by specially designed

questionnaires, such as the Seasonal Pattern Assessment Questionnaire (SPAQ)

(Rosenthal et al., 1984), recently reviewed by Magnusson (1996). The SPAQ was

originally designed and used as a first line screening instrument, and the index cases

were subsequently interviewed and diagnosed clinically.

As pointed out above, it is still an ongoing discussion as to whether environmental

and/or sociocultural factors influence seasonal changes in human behaviours. It seems

therefore essential to understand the individual's experience of these changes in terms

of whether they perceive seasonal changes in their behaviours and, if so, the

explanations they offer for such changes.

As pointed out previously, seasonality is defined as the degree to which seasonal changes affect criteria such as mood, energy, sleep length, appetite, food preferences or the wish to socialise with others (Kasper et al., 1989b). Taking a qualitative rather than a quantitative approach (e.g., the SPAQ) in which people's everyday theories that guide their behaviour and potential behaviour changes across the seasons would be examined, can broaden the understanding of seasonality. Consequently, it has been shown in other areas, (for example qualitative research into patients' perspectives on taking medications (Buston, Parry-Jones, Livingston, Bogan, & Wood, 1998)), that knowledge of people's theories can be implemented into programmes that attempt to modify behaviours.

Modifying activity patterns over the year (i.e., maintaining physical activity) is crucial in obesity prevention and prevention of coronary heart disease (see chapter 1.3.1.). Thus, in the context of seasonal variation in physical activity, knowledge on whether a person observes his/her own activity to change from one season to the next and knowledge on the person's understanding of these seasonal changes may be useful and be implemented into programmes to enhance physical activity over the year. For example, if people perceive environmental factors as major causes to prevent them from engaging in physical activities, programmes can address these perceived barriers by informing on alternative indoor-activities. If people however, perceive mood factors as determining their activity levels, programmes need to include psychoeducation on the beneficial effects of physical activity on mood alterations.

The same applies for people's perception of seasonal changes in food choice and dieting. Specifically, knowledge on how people perceive their food choice to change across the seasons and how they explain these changes can be utilised in programmes for obesity prevention. Thus, if people, for example, perceive food choice to vary across the seasons, mainly caused by mood fluctuations, programmes need to inform participants on alternative coping strategies to deal with seasonal mood swings.

In terms of dieting, prevention of severe dieting is important and understanding of factors that may trigger engagement in severe dieting is therefore warranted. If people, for example, perceive sociocultural pressures to be thin for summer and increase their dieting behaviour accordingly, programmes need to challenge and counteract these motives for dieting.

1.7. Summary

In summary, the majority of studies that have investigated seasonal variation in behaviours adopted a quantitative approach (Fossey et al., 2002). The qualitative assessment of people's perception and understanding of seasonal variation in their behaviours provides a powerful tool in understanding people's theories of behaviour changes across the seasons. Perception of seasonal changes is thereby defined as descriptions on how a person perceives his/her own behaviour to change from one season to the next. People's understanding of seasonal variation in their behaviour is defined as the explanations people offer for the perceived seasonal changes in the behaviours.

Behaviours such as physical activity, food intake and dieting have been shown to vary seasonally but are not fully covered in the assessment of seasonality with common questionnaires such as the SPAQ. Seasonal variation in physical activity has been associated with seasonal variation in blood pressure and is thus related to cardiovascular heart disease (Matthews et al., 2001; Uitenbroek, 1993; Wankel, 1988).

Seasonal variation in food intake, particularly increased fat and carbohydrate intake during winter has been linked to the higher morbidity of cardiovascular diseases during winter. Links between food intake and underlying mood states, hence highlighting the role of motives for food choice have been discussed. People's perception and understanding of seasonal variation in food choice however, has not been investigated.

In the context of dieting disorders, dieting with the intention to lose weight is considered as one risk factor for developing unhealthy eating habits or even symptoms of a dieting disorder. Prevention of dieting is thus encouraged and any factor that triggers dieting needs to be explored. It has recently been shown that dieting behaviour varies across the seasons with sociocultural factors, such as the pressure to be thin for summer, probably accounting for this variation. Only one study thus far has investigated seasonal variation in dieting. If however, certain seasons present 'high-risk' seasons for dieting, particularly in those who are already dieting and hence, are more influenced by sociocultural pressures, an understanding of changes in dieting across the seasons and explanation for these changes become crucial in the prevention of dieting.

Comparisons of the perception of seasonal changes in behaviours between residents from the Southern and Northern Hemisphere are rare. A comparison between Australia and Europe (that is, Germany) is particularly interesting. This comparison provides insight into the role of changes in environmental variables for people's perception and understanding of seasonal changes in behaviours. Theories for seasonal changes in the three behaviours of Australian and German residents may be integrated into prevention programmes for cardiovascular heart disease, obesity and dieting behaviour.

1.8. Aims and hypotheses

The current study aimed to provide preliminary information on the perception and understanding of seasonal changes in three health-related behaviours in a female Australian (N=121) and German sample (N=109). The behaviours covered were physical activity, food choice and dieting. With a specially designed questionnaire, the Brief Survey on Perception of Seasonal Changes (BSPSC, see Appendix A and B), participants were asked about their engagement in physical activity, food choice and dieting behaviour. Further qualitative descriptions of perceived changes between winter and summer and causes for the changes were assessed. The BSPSC was administered to both groups during the winter-season in the respective country – July/ August for the Australian sample, December for the German sample – thus minimising the influence of the season on answers in the questionnaire.

It was hypothesised that there would be no differences in levels of physical activity, food choice and dieting behaviour between the two groups. It was also expected that there would be no differences between the two samples in terms of their perception and understanding of seasonal changes in the three behaviours. It was further hypothesised that participants' characteristics such as engagement in hard intensity physical activity and dieting would predict if they perceive seasonal changes in behaviours. Participants' perception and understanding of seasonal changes in physical activity, food choice and dieting might be integrated in programmes for enhancement of regular physical activity, prevention of obesity and dieting behaviour.

1.9. Hypotheses

1. Physical activity, food choice and dieting in an Australian and German participants

1.1. Physical activity (defined as estimated time in moderate and hard intensity activities) will not differ between students in Australia and Germany.

1.2. No differences are expected in the motives for food choice of the Australian and German participants.

1.3. No differences are expected in the frequency of dieters between the Australian and German participants (with dieting defined as changes in eating habits with the specific intention to lose weight).

2. Perception and understanding of seasonal changes in physical activity, food choice and dieting

2.1. The Australian and German samples will not differ in terms of the number of participants who notice seasonal changes in their physical activity, food choice and dieting.

2.2. The Australian and German sample will notice similar seasonal changes in the three health-related behaviours.

2.3. The Australian and German sample will identify similar causes for the perceived seasonal changes in the three health-related behaviours.

3. The perception of seasonal changes in the three behaviours will be associated with the time spent in hard intensity activities and dieting behaviour.

2. Methods

2.1. Design

In this study a cross-sectional design was used to assess participants from Australia and Germany. Perception of seasonal changes in physical activity-levels, food choices and dieting behaviour were assessed with a brief survey (Brief Survey on Perception of Seasonal Changes, BSPSC, see Appendix A and B) specially designed for this study.

2.2. Participants

One hundred and twenty-one female first-year psychology students from Australia (aged 17-32 years) and 110 students from Germany (aged 19-39 years) participated in the study. One German participant had to be excluded as she stated to have been diagnosed with major depression resulting in a sample size of 109. Both groups (Australia - Germany) were assessed during the season of winter in the respective country (i.e., July/August for the Australian group and November/December for the German group), thus minimising the influence of the season on answers in the questionnaire. The analyses included only female participants as studies have shown that females react more sensitively to seasonal changes than males (Lacoste & Wirz-Justice, 1989). The total sample size was N=230.

2.2.1. Australian sample

The BSPSC was administered to first-year psychology students of the University of New South Wales (UNSW, Australia) while they were participating in a study into "The effect of magazine exposure on women's mood and body image" (Chau, 2003). One hundred and thirty-five participants aged 17-32 years were initially contacted for Chau's study and filled in the BSPSC. One hundred and twenty-one of those were female. Of those, 111 were integrated in Chau's study. Demographic data of the 111 female participants were collected. Separate demographics could not be collected with the BSPSC, however information regarding ethnic background and means for age, weight and height of the Chau-sample (n=111) were obtained (91.7% of the sample of the present study). Demographics are summarised in table 1.

2.2.2. German sample

The German sample originally consisted of 144 first-year psychology students from the University of Trier. One hundred and ten were female. Of these, one had to be excluded due to a diagnosis of major depression. The age range was 19-39 years. Students were recruited during a statistic lecture. A research assistant administered the survey and explained its structure. Demographic data were obtained through a brief demographic questionnaire assessing (see Appendix C) age, gender, marital status, body weight (kg) and height (m). The table 1 summarises the demographic data for participants from Australia and Germany.

Table 1: Demographic data of the Australian and German sample

	Australian sample		German sample	Total sample
N	121		109	230
Age in years				
Mean ± SD	19.7 ± 2.4^1		21.1 ± 2.9	20.4 ± 2.7
Range	17-32		19-39	17-39
N (%) of participants with European background	$54\ (48.6)^2$		106 (97.2)	160 (69.6)
N (%) of participants with Asian background	$57\ (47.1)^2$		2 (1.8)	59 (25.6)
N (%) of participants from other countries (Iran)	0		1 (0.9)	1 (0.4)
	For Whites	For Asians		
Body weight (kg)				
Mean ± SD	56.4 ± 8.7	48.5 ± 7.42^3	59.7 ± 8.2^4	$54.9 \pm ?^{25}$
BMI				
Mean ± SD	21.9 ± 2.7	19.9 ± 2.2^3	$20.7^4 \pm 2.5$	$20.8 \pm ?^{25}$
Marital status % (N)				
Single	[6]		83.5 (91)	[6]
Married				
De facto			16.5 (18)	

[1] N=120, one Australian participant did not answer the question.
[2] Data from UNSW-study (N=111) (Chau, 2003).
[3] For Australian participants with Asian background (n=57).
[4] N=107, two German participants did not answer the question.
[5] Computed as mean from three body weight values for whites, Asians and Germans.
[6] Not assessed in UNSW-study.

2.3. Measures and procedure

2.3.1. The Brief Survey on Perception of Seasonal Changes (BSPSC)

The BSPSC (see Appendix A and B) was designed to assess perception of seasonal changes in three behaviours: physical activity, food choice and dieting. The English version was translated into German by the first author. The German version of the

53

questionnaire was then sent out to five German psychologists to validate its translation before administering it to the participants.

The participants were asked to briefly describe their activity-levels, with physical activity subdivided into three categories of intensity (light, moderate and hard). Definitions of the categories were taken from the 24-hr Physical Activity Recall by Matthews et al. (2001). Examples of activities in the three intensities are displayed in table 2.

Table 2: Three intensity categories of physical activity (Matthews et al., 2001)

Light intensity activities	standing, slow walking and carrying light objects
Moderate intensity activities	walking at a normal pace, working with moderate effort
Hard intensity activities	vigorous physical work, jogging, swimming (laps)

For each of the categories, participants were asked to estimate how many days per week and how many hours per day they spent in the respective intensity-category and what type of activity they engaged in. In a dichotomous question, participants were asked if they perceived any changes in their activity-levels across the seasons during the past five years (yes/no).

Regarding the assessment of food choice, items were taken from the Food Choice Questionnaire (FCQ; (Steptoe et al., 1995)). The factor 'ideological reasons' was taken from a questionnaire of Lindeman and Stark (1999) who extended the FCQ. Nine factors that influence food choice were listed and briefly described. These were: 1) weight control, 2) sensory appeal, 3) ideological reasons, 4) health, 5) mood, 6) convenience, 7) natural content, 8) price and 9) familiarity.

Participants were asked to rank the factors from 1 to 9 (1=most applicable, 9=least applicable). Similar to the physical activity-questions, participants were then asked whether they perceived any changes in their food choice (yes/no; dichotomous variable) across the seasons during the past five years.

Dieting was assessed as a dichotomous variable asking participants if they had currently changed their eating habits with the specific intention to lose weight (adapted from Strong and Huon (1997)). They were asked if they had noticed any changes in their dieting behaviour across the seasons during the past five years (dichotomous variable).

An open question-format was used to assess participants' perception of seasonal changes (i.e., description of the perceived changes in physical activity, food choice and dieting) during winter and summer. The two most extreme seasons were chosen to make a comparison easier. Further participants wrote down what they thought was causing the changes across the seasons (i.e., their understanding of the perceived changes). These two open questions were analysed by identifying units of meaning (UOM; (Maykut & Morehouse, 1994)), defined as units that were understandable without additional information). Participants could be assigned to more than one UOM. All UOMs were transcribed and coded by the first author (TH).

To assess the reliability of the coding procedure, two independent judges in Australia and two in Germany were asked to recode some of the questionnaires. For the Australian sample, 16 questionnaires for changes in physical activity and causes for these changes (13% of the data), 12 for changes in food choice and causes for these changes (9.9% of the data) and 11 for changes in dieting and causes for these changes (9.0% of the data) were reanalysed by the judges. The small numbers resulted due to the fact that not all participants answered all questions. Booth, Owen, Bauman and Goren (1995) pointed out that reliability is inflated when no-responses are included. Therefore only complete questionnaires were rated by the judges.

Agreement rates between the coding of the first author and the two independent judges were calculated as a percentage. Means in percentage were computed for the rates of the two judges for each of the UOMs. Due to the small numbers of rated questionnaires, kappa coefficients were not computed. The results are presented in table 3.

For the Australian judges, agreement rates between the original rater and the judges ranged between 50.1% (for change in physical activity: winter decrease-summer increase) to 100.0% (for change in physical activity: winter increase-summer decrease and change in dieting: winter increase-summer decrease). For the majority of UOMs (19 of 21), the agreement rates were higher than 70%. Despite lower agreement rates for three UOMs (physical activity: winter increase-summer decrease, food choice: content of food and amount of food), differences between the Australian and German samples in these UOMs were described and analysed. The difference in agreement rates for the UOMs will be critically reviewed in the discussion.

Two independent German judges recoded questionnaires from the German sample, namely 10 questionnaires (9.1% of the data) for physical activity and food choice and nine questionnaires for dieting (69.2% of the data, since n=13 who answered the question on changes in dieting). The agreement rates between the original rater and the German raters ranged between 60.0% and 100.0%. Only three out of 21 UOMs received an agreement rate below 80%. These were mood and motivation as a cause for change in physical activity, mood and social situation as a cause for changes in food choice and mood and social situation as a cause for changes in dieting. Table 3 provides a list, a brief description of the identified UOMs and the agreement rates for the Australian and German judges.

Table 3: Units of meanings and agreement rates between original rater and independent judges

	Agreement rates for 2 Australian judges Mean %	Agreement rates for 2 German judges Mean %
UOMs for perceived changes in physical activity		
Winter decrease-summer increase		
For statements referring to a decrease in activity during winter and an increase during summer; regarding general physical activity, different intensities (hard) and exercising	50.1	80.0
Winter increase-summer decrease		
For statements referring to an increase in activity during winter and a decrease during summer, regarding general physical activity, moderate intensity activities and work-related activities	100.0	95.0
Outdoors versus indoors activities		
For statements referring to change in the type of activity and its context such as swimming, beach-activities during summer and squash and gym-activities during winter	71.9	90.0
UOMs for perceived causes of changes in physical activity		
Environmental variables		
For statements referring to weather conditions such as lack of sunshine, high/low ambient temperature, rain and reduced amount of daylight	71.9	90.0
Mood and motivation		
For statements referring to mood states that prevent from the engagement in activities such as feeling tired, lazy, depressed and exhausted and statements referring to motivation levels such as feeling less energetic, motivated and a lack of interest in activity during winter	81.3	60.0
Time management and life-style		
For statements referring to changes in life-style that impact on time-management such as holiday-time during summer, working hours, increase in commitments, different group of friends and decline in sports participation since studying	93.8	95.0
Appearance		
For statements referring to changes in activity due to physical appearance such as losing weight for summer; possibility to hide appearance in winter clothes; clothing fashion which forces to lose weight during summer	90.6	100.0
Organised sports		
For statements referring to types of sport that do or do not fluctuate across the seasons such as frisbee and swimming	87.6	100.0
UOMs for perceived CHANGES in food choice		
Content of food		
For statements referring to the content of food such as fatty and sugary food during winter, healthy food and more liquid during summer	58.4	85.0
Amount of food		
For statements referring to the amount of food such as increase in food intake during winter, decrease in food intake during summer	58.4	85.0
Temperature of consumed food		
For statements referring to the temperature of the consumed food such as warm food during winter (soups, "cooked things") and cold foods during summer (ice-cream, cold drinks)	79.2	100.0

UOMs for perceived CAUSES of changes in food choice		
Environmental variables For statements referring to weather conditions and their impact on food choice such as attracted to large hot meals in winter to deal with the cold; eating what keeps one warm; food as coolant during summer; temperature as influencing factor for appetite	79.2	85.0
Availability of foods For statements referring to availability of foods during the seasons such as greater variety of fruits during summer	95.8	100.0
Mood and social situation For statements referring to mood states and social situations influencing food choice such as worse mood during winter leading to less healthy eating; "winter makes one feel lazy so the eating gets lazy"; "in summer more outgoing to cafes and restaurants"	75.0	75.0
Activity and weight loss For statements referring to activity level and weight loss causing changes in food choice such as being not as active during winter and hence, "snacking more"; "like to look slim in swimming costume"	95.8	95.0

UOMs for perceived CHANGES in dieting		
Winter decrease -summer increase in dieting For statements referring to an increase in dieting during summer; "more difficulties to diet during winter, when it is cold"; "more control over dieting during summer"; "more weight fluctuations during winter"; "harder to lose weight during winter"	80.9	100.0
Winter increase– summer decrease in dieting For statements referring to more conscious eating and dieting during winter; more relaxed during summer; "thinner and skinnier during winter"	100.0	94.5

UOMs for perceived CAUSES for changes in dieting		
Appearance For statements referring to appearance such as constant shedding of weight for summer clothes; "one is seen more during summer"; "can't hide in clothes"; "more body-conscious during summer at beach"; "want to look good, slim during summer"	90.9	88.9
Environmental variables For statements referring to weather changes that make dieting harder during certain seasons such as "in summer, one can just get away with eating less but drinking lots of liquid"	77.4	88.9
Mood and social situation For statements referring to mood states and social situations influencing dieting behaviour such as less social interactivity in winter and thus, less body conscious; summer, more time spent at the beach; sunshine and better weather has impact on mood and as a consequence on eating habits	95.5	77.8
Activity and exercise For statements referring to activity level that change during the seasons and thus affect dieting such as more exercise in summer; "when one is not out exercising there is more chance to eat"	86.3	88.9

2.3.2. Procedure

Australian participants filled in the BSPSC as part of participation in a study into "The effect of magazine exposure on women's mood and body image" (Chau, 2003). The German sample filled in the BSPSC during a statistic lecture. A research assistant administered the survey and explained its structure. Participants in both countries were given 15 minutes to fill in the survey.

2.4. Completion

Missing data occurred most frequently for the FCQ-questions. Participants either filled in one number only or they selected the same numbers for several categories. Subdividing the sample into the two countries resulted in 18.2% (n=22) missing values for food choice for the Australian sample and 22.9% (n=25) for the German sample. Missing data also occurred when answering the question on changes in dieting. Some participants who did not engage in dieting behaviour left out the question. Thus, 3.3% (n=4) participants of the Australian sample and 2.8% (n=3) participants of the German sample did not answer the question on changes in dieting.

2.5. Environmental variables in Sydney and Trier

Environmental data from weather stations from each country were obtained. For Sydney, the Bureau of Meteorology supplied the information on the following weather station for the year 2002: Sydney Observatory Hill (latitude 53°, 51', 39''S; longitude 151°12'18''E; elevation 39.0m). For Trier, the Deutscher Wetterdienst supplied information for the weather station: Trier-Petrisberg (latitude 49°44'N; longitude 06°39'E; elevation 265.0m). Means per months for ambient temperature (°C), cloud cover (oktas) and precipitation (mm) are presented in table 4.

Table 4: Environmental data for Sydney and Trier for the year 2002

City		Jan	Feb	Mar	Apr	May	Jun	Jul*	Aug*	Sep	Oct	Nov	Dec#
Sydney	Temp	23.5	22.2	22.0	20.4	16.1	13.9	13.2	14.7	17.6	19.6	21.3	21.7
	CC	4.2	5.7	4.9	4.0	3.7	3.5	2.4	2.8	2.5	3.4	4.4	4.3
	Prec	98.4	348.2	45.4	68.4	92.8	28.4	24.2	19.8	21.8	5.8	31.8	75.0
Trier	Temp	0.9	6.2	6.8	9.4	13.7	18.2	18.0	18.4	13.6	9.8	7.8	3.8
	CC	6.3	6.0	5.1	4.4	5.7	5.0	5.2		4.3	6.2	6.8	6.8
	prec	31.2	127.5	61.9	40.4	52.2	39.7	55.6	105.4	32.7	108.6	97.2	

Temp: Ambient temperature (°C)
CC: cloud cover (oktas; where 8 oktas means total cloud cover and 0 oktas clear sky)
Prec: Precipitation (mm)
* Time point Australian sample was administered the survey.
# Time point German sample was administered the survey.

In Australia, the change in ambient temperature from winter to summer was plus 8.5°C (mean ambient temperature in July 13.2 °C, mean ambient temperature in December 21.7°C). In Germany, a temperature change of plus 14.6°C was experienced from winter to summer. During winter, the average temperature in Australia was 14.0°C compared to 1.0°C in Germany. In summer, Australians experienced an average temperature of 22.9°C compared to 18.2°C in Germany. Highest precipitation (in mm) occurred in Australia during summer (February), in Germany during winter (February). Data on duration of daylight (difference in hours between sunrise and sunset) for Australia were obtained from the Australian Surveying and Land Information Group (2002). For Germany, the Sternwarte Hamburg (2003) provided the necessary information. Since Australia is closer to the equator, the photoperiod is lower. In summer, the mean day length (sunrise to sunset) in Sydney is 822 minutes compared to

935 minutes in Trier. In winter, the mean day length is 633 minutes in Sydney and 538 minutes in Trier.

2.6. Statistical procedures

Australians' and Germans' physical activity level, motives for food choice and dieting were described using mean (± SD) and frequency tables. For differences between the two countries in the time spent in different intensities of physical activity, independent t-tests (two-tailed) and Sharpened Bonferroni to account for multiple comparisons were computed. For differences in food choice factors and dieting (categorical variables), Chi-square tests were computed.

Differences between Australian and German respondents in the UOMs for changes in physical activity, food choice and dieting and in the UOMs for reasons for the perceived changes were tested with Chi-square tests. Alpha levels of .05 (*) and .01 (**) were used for all statistical tests.

A seasonality score (perception of changes in behaviour: 1=yes, 2=no) was computed indicating whether participants were affected by the seasons. Seasonality was thereby defined as perceiving changes across the seasons in at least one of the three behaviours. A logistic regression was computed with seasonality as the dependent variable and amount of time spent in hard intensity activities (hrs per day) and dieting (yes, no) as predictors.

Further logistic regressions were computed to predict the perception of seasonal changes in a) physical activity (1=yes, 2=no), b) food choice (1=yes, 2=no) and c) dieting (1=yes, 2=no), using the same predictors as above (i.e., time in hard intensity activities and dieting).

Statistical analyses were performed using SPSS for Windows (version 10.0).

3. Results

The characteristics of the samples are described in table 1 (see chapter 2.2.). An independent t-test (two-tailed) revealed a significant age difference between the groups ($t_{(227)}$= -3.8, p<.01). Australian participants were on average two years younger than German participants. The difference in age emerged due to different educational systems. In Germany, students spend nine years at high school before commencing study at university compared to eight years in Australia. Despite the age difference, these two groups were similar in that they had just started studying psychology at a university.

3.1. Physical activity, food choice and dieting behaviour in Australian and German participants

3.1.1. Physical activity

Australian participants chose transport chores such as walking as the main type of light and moderate intensity activity (light: 60 of 110, 54.5%; moderate: 107 of 119, 89.9%) and jogging (35 of 113, 31.0%) and swimming (10 of 113, 8.8%) as the main hard intensity-activities. Twenty-six percent (30 of 113) of the Australian participants did not engage in any hard intensity activities. Australian participants (n=118) reported spending on average 3.8 hours (SD=3.1) per day in light intensity activities, 3.1 hours (SD=2.8, N=119) in moderate intensity activities and 1.2 hours (SD=1.2, n=117) in hard intensity activities.

Similarly, the majority of the German sample named walking as their main light (42 of 87, 48.3%) and moderate activity (62 of 88, 70.5%). Thirty-four percent (29 of 85) of

63

the sample engaged in jogging as a hard-intensity activity, 14.1% (n=12) in swimming and 12.9% (n=11) in working activities (eg as a waitress). Twelve percent (13 of 109) stated not to engage in any hard activity. German participants reported spending on average 5.6 hours (SD=3.9, n=105) in light, 4.1 hours (SD=3.2, n=106) in moderate and 1.3 hours (SD=1.1, n=104) in hard intensity activities per day.

The two groups differed significantly in the reported amount of time per day (hours/day) spending in light intensity activities ($t_{(221)}$ = -3.79, p<0.01) and in moderate intensity activities ($t_{(223)}$ = -2.52, p=0.01). Australians reported spending less time in light and moderate intensity activities compared to Germans. Similarly, when comparing the groups with regard to the engagement in hard intensity activities (yes/no), more Germans than Australians reported engaging in hard intensity activities (Chi-square $_{(df=1, N=230)}$=6.95, p=0.008). That is, 88.1% of the German sample compared to 74.4% of the Australian sample stated to engage in hard intensity activities.

3.1.2. Food choice

Eighteen percent (n=22) of the Australian participants had missing data on the food-choice questions resulting in a sample size of 99. For these, the following hierarchy for the three factors selected as most applicable emerged: sensory appeal (n=45, 45.5%), health (n=19, 19.2%) and convenience (n=12, 12.1%). Weight control was selected by nine percent of the sample (n=9). Fourteen percent (n=14) selected one of the remaining factors. The results are presented in table 4.

For the German sample, 22.9% (n=25) did not fill in the food-choice questions correctly resulting in a sample size of n=84. For these, the following food choice factors-hierarchy for the three factors selected as most applicable emerged: sensory appeal (n=33, 39.3%), health (n=18, 21.4%) and convenience (n=10, 11.9%). Weight control was chosen by nine percent (n=8) of the German sample and 17.9% (n=15) selected one of the remaining factors (see table 5).

As eight cells had a sample size smaller than 5 (see table 5), only four food choice factors were analysed in a Chi-square analysis for differences between the Australian and German sample. The factors were summarized in one categorical variable with four categories. Participants fell in category 1 if they chose sensory appeal as most applicable, in category 2 if they chose health, category 3 if they chose convenience and category 4 if they chose weight concerns. No significant differences between Australians and Germans emerged regarding the number of participants selecting the four motives for food choice (Chi-square $_{(df=3, N=154)}$=0.46, p=0.93). The majority of participants from both countries chose sensory appeal as the most important food choice factor, followed by health and convenience. Around 10% of female participants in each country selected their food on the basis of weight control concerns (see table 5).

Table 5: Factors for food choice selected by Australian and German participants

Factors for food choice	Australian sample (n=99)	German sample (n=84)
	n (%)	
Sensory appeal[1]	45 (45.5)	33 (39.3)
Health[1]	19 (19.2)	18 (21.4)
Convenience[1]	12 (12.1)	10 (11.9)
Weight control[1]	9 (9.1)	8 (9.5)
Familiarity	5 (5.1)	
Price	3 (3.0)	4 (4.8)
Mood	4 (4.0)	3 (3.6)
Natural content	1 (1.0)	4 (4.8)
Ideological reasons	1 (1.0)	5 (6.0)

[1] Included in Chi-square test.

3.1.3. Dieting

Thirty-five percent (n=41) of the Australians reported to currently engage in dieting behaviour. Fifteen percent (n=17) of the German sample were currently dieting. A significant group difference emerged for dieting behaviour (Chi $_{(1, N=230)}$=10.2, p=0.001). Significantly more Australians than Germans indicated that they engaged in dieting behaviour. The results are presented in table 6.

Table 6: Dieters and non-dieters in Australia and Germany

Currently dieting	Australian	German sample n (%)	Chi-square	p-level
Yes	41 (33.9)	17 (15.6)	10.2	0.001**
No	80 (66.1)	92 (84.4)		
Total	121	109		

** p<0.01

3.2. Perception and understanding of seasonal changes in physical activity, food choice and dieting

3.2.1. Physical activity and perception of seasonal changes

Seventy-four percent (n=89) of the Australian participants perceived a change in their physical activity across the seasons. Of the German sample, 71.6% (n=78) indicated a perceived change in activity-levels. A Chi-square-test showed no group-differences in the perception of seasonal changes in physical activity (Chi-square $_{(1, N=230)}$=0.12, p=0.74). In both countries, the majority of participants tended to notice a change in their activity-level across the seasons (see table 7).

Table 7: Perception of seasonal changes in physical activity

	Australians n=121	Germans n=109	Chi-square	p-level
Change in physical activity across seasons? n (%)				
Yes	89 (73.6)	78 (71.6)	0.12	ns
No	32 (26.4)	31 (28.4)		

3.2.1.1. Perceived changes in physical activity across the seasons

Four UOMs were identified (see table 3). These were winter decrease-summer increase, winter increase-summer decrease, outdoors versus indoors activities and miscellaneous factors such as a perceived decrease in activity-levels with age. Missing data occurred for 27.3% (n=33) of the Australian and 29.4 % (n=32) of the German sample resulting in 165 participants who answered the question.

When looking at the number of participants who mentioned the four UOMs, the majority of Australians noticed either a decrease in their physical activity-levels during winter and an increase during summer (n=46, 52.3%) or described changes in the type of physical activity (n=26, 29.5%), changing from outdoor to indoor activities (e.g., beach activities during summer, squash and gym during winter).

Sixty-six percent (n=51) of the German participants noticed decreases in their activity-levels during winter and an increase during summer. Ten percent (n=8) noticed a change in the type of activity, from indoor-activities during winter to outdoor-activities during summer. Nine percent (n=7) observed an increase in activity-levels during winter and a decrease during summer.

Significantly more Australians than Germans experienced differences in the type and context of physical activity (indoors versus outdoors, Chi-square $_{(df=1, N=165)}$ =9.21, p=0.002). There was a trend for more German participants to perceive a decrease in their activity-level during winter (Chi-square $_{(df=1, N=165)}$ =3.30, p=0.07). Table 8 summarises the findings.

Table 8: Which seasonal changes in physical activity do Australians and Germans perceive?

UOMs for perceived changes in physical activity [1]	Australian sample n=88	German sample n=77	Chi-square	p-level
	n (%) who mentioned the respective UOM			
1. Winter decrease-summer increase	46 (52.3)	51 (66.2)	3.30	0.07
2. Winter increase-summer decrease	9 (10.2)	7 (9.1)	0.06	ns
3. Outdoors versus indoors activities	26 (29.5)	8 (10.4)	9.21	0.002**
4. Others	3 (3.4)			#

**p<0.01
No Chi-square computed due to small sample size.
[1] For definition of UOMs, see table 3.

3.2.1.2. Perceived causes for changes in physical activity across the seasons

Six UOMs for perceived causes of changes in physical activity across the seasons were identified. These were: weather, mood and motivation, time management and life-style, appearance, organised sports and other factors such as illnesses (see table 3). The sample size was N=165, of these 88 (72.7%) were Australians and 77 (70.6%) were Germans.

Environmental variables were the most frequently named cause of a change in physical activity among the Australian sample (n=46, 52.3%), including among other factors a change in ambient temperature (n=11, 12.5%) or the amount of daylight (n=6, 6.8%). Twelve percent (n=11) did not specify how they perceived environmental factors to impact on their levels of physical activity.

Mood and motivation were the second most frequently named cause (n=28, 31.8%). For instance, feeling less energetic and experiencing a lack of interest were reported to result in a decrease in physical activity during winter.

Eighteen percent (n=16) reported factors such as time-management (e.g., working hours or increase in commitments).

Seventy-five percent (n=58) of the German sample considered environmental variables as the main factor impeding on activity-levels. Factors mentioned were among others change in hours of daylight (n=17, 22.1%), changes in ambient temperature (n=14, 18.2%) and lack of sunshine during winter (n=8, 10.4%). Thirty-two percent (n=25) did not specify how they perceived environmental variables to impact on their activity-levels. The second most frequently mentioned cause was mood and motivation (n=15, 19.2%). Four percent (n=3) stated that time-management impacted on activity-levels.

Significant differences emerged in the amount of participants who mentioned environmental variables as a major cause for changes in physical activity. More Germans than Australians saw themselves affected by environmental variables (Chi-square $_{(df=1, N=165)}$=9.37, p=0.002).

Further, a trend for differences in the amount of participants considering mood and motivation as an important factor emerged, with more Australians than Germans tending to have their physical activity levels affected by mood and motivational changes across the seasons (Chi-square $_{(df=1, N=165)}$ =3.24, p=0.07). Also, more Australians than Germans reported that differences in their activity-level were due to life-style changes and differences in their time-management (Chi-square $_{(df=1, N=165)}$ =9.17, p=0.002). However, since the cell-size for Germans was less than five, these results are only indicative of a significant group-difference. Table 9 summarises the findings.

Table 9: How do Australians and Germans explain seasonal changes in physical activity?

UOMs for perceived causes for change in physical activity [1]	Australian sample n=88 n (%) who mentioned the respective UOM	German sample n=77	Chi-square	p-level
1. Environmental variables	46 (52.3)	58 (75.3)	9.37	0.002**
2. Mood and motivation	28 (31.8)	15 (19.5)	3.24	0.07
3. Time management and life-style	16 (18.2)	3 (3.9)	9.17	0.002**&
4. Appearance	6 (6.8)	1 (1.3)		#
5. Organised sport	3 (3.4)			#
6. Others	1 (1.1)	5 (6.4)		#

** p<0.01
& cell size <5
# No Chi-square computed due to small sample size.
[1] For definition of UOMs, see table 3.

3.2.2. Food choice and perception of seasonal changes

Sixty-one percent (n=61) of the Australian sample and 51.2% (n=43) of the German sample perceived changes in their food choice across the seasons. In a Chi-square analysis, no difference emerged regarding the number of participants who perceived seasonal changes in food choice in the two samples (Chi $_{(1, N=230)}$ =0.88, p=0.35). In both countries, the majority of participants perceived a seasonal change in their food choice (see table 10).

Table 10: Perception of seasonal changes in food choice

Perception of seasonal changes in food choice?	Australian sample n=121 n (%)	German sample n=109 N (%)	Chi-square	p-level
Yes	74 (61.2)	60 (55.0)	0.88	ns
No	47 (38.8)	49 (45.0)		

3.2.2.1. Perceived changes in food choice across the seasons

Three UOMs were identified for perceived changes in food choice across the seasons. These were content of food, amount of food, and temperature of consumed food (see table 3). One hundred and thirty-one participants answered the question. Of these, 74 (56.5%) were Australians and 57 (52.3%) were Germans.

The majority of Australians (n=46, 62.2%) noticed changes in the content of food across the seasons (e.g., consumption of fatty and sugary food during winter, and healthy food and liquids during summer). Changes in the temperature of the food were perceived by 41.9% (n=31) of the sample, i.e., consumption of hot foods such as soups during winter and cold foods such as ice-cream during summer.

Of the German sample, 80.7% (n=46) noticed changes in the content of food across the seasons. Changes in the temperature of foods was the second most frequently perceived change in food choice (n=13, 22.8%).

In Chi-square analyses, significant differences emerged for the UOM 'content of food'. More Germans mentioned a change in the content of food across the seasons such as eating more fatty food during winter (Chi-square $_{(df=1, N=131)}$ =5.29, p=0.02). Further, significantly more Australians noticed a change in the temperature of the food they were consuming in that more hot foods were consumed during winter and cold foods during summer (Chi-square $_{(df=1, N=131)}$ =5.26, p=0.02). Table 11 displays the results.

Table 11: Which seasonal changes do Australians and Germans perceive in food choice?

UOMs for perceived changes in food choice [1]	Australian sample n=74	German sample n=57	Chi-square	p-level
	n (%) who mentioned the respective UOM			
1. Content of food	46 (62.2)	46 (80.7)	5.29	0.02*
2. Amount of food	11 (14.9)	4 (7.0)	1.96	ns[s]
3. Temperature of consumed food	31 (41.9)	13 (22.8)	5.26	0.02*

*p<0.05
[s] Cell size <5
[1] For definition of UOMs, see table 3.

3.2.2.2. Perceived causes for changes in food choice across the seasons

Five UOMs were identified for perceived causes of changes in food choice across the seasons. These were 1) environmental variables, 2) availability of foods, 3) mood and social situation, 4) activity and weight loss and 5) other factors such as biological explanations (e.g., the belief that the body needs more energy during winter). One hundred and twenty-eight participants (55.4%) answered the question, of those 71 (55.5%) were Australian and 57 (44.5%) German.

Environmental variables (such as dealing with the cold with hot food during winter) were mentioned by 64.8% (n=46) of the Australian sample. Seventeen percent (n=12) did not specify how they perceived environmental variables to impact on their food choice. Mood states as a relevant cause for changes in food choice was mentioned by 12.7% (n=9), while 4.2% (n=3) mentioned social situations as responsible for food choice changes (e.g.,, going to cafés more often during summer). Together with other life-style aspects (e.g., not wanting to spend extensive time with cooking over hot stoves during summer), the UOM mood and social situation combined were relevant for 18.3% (n=13) of the Australian sample. Fifteen percent (n=11) named other causes such as lesser activity during winter (which in turn would lead to more snacking during winter) or the desire to look slim for summer (which would result in a decrease in eating during summer). Fourteen percent (n=10) attributed changes in their food choice to the availability of foods during the seasons for example greater ranges of fruits during summer.

Similarly, environmental variables were named by the majority of German participants, followed by the availability of foods that impacted on food choice, mood and social situations and other factors (see table 3). Five percent (n=3) reported that they changed their food choice across the seasons due to weight concerns.

Results from the Chi-square analyses showed that a similar amount of Australians and Germans mentioned causes for changes in food choice such as 'environmental variables', 'availability of foods' and 'mood and social situation'. The results are displayed in table 12.

Table 12: How do Australians and Germans explain seasonal changes in food choice?

UOMs for perceived causes for changes in food choice [1]	Australian sample n=71	German sample n=57	Chi-square	p-level
	n (%) who mentioned the respective UOM			
1. Environmental variables	46 (64.8)	30 (52.6)	1.94	ns
2. Availability of foods	10 (14.1)	13 (22.8)	1.63	ns
3. Mood and social situation	13 (18.3)	11(19.3)	0.02	ns
4. Activity and weight loss	11(15.5)	3 (5.3)	3.40	0.07[&]
5. Others (biology, health, sensory appeal)	7 (9.9)	7 (12.3)	0.19	ns

[&] cell size <5
[1] For definition of UOMs, see table 3.

3.2.3. Dieting and perception of seasonal changes

Twenty-eight percent (33 of 117) of the Australian participants perceived changes in their dieting behaviour across the seasons compared to 12.3% (13 of 106) of the German participants. Significantly more Australians than Germans perceived changes in dieting behaviour across the seasons (Chi $_{(1, N=223)}$ =8.63, p=0.003, see table 13).

Table 13: Perception of seasonal changes in dieting behaviour

	Australian sample n=117	German sample n=106	Chi-square	p-level
Perception of seasonal changes in dieting behaviour? n (%)				
Yes	33 (28.2)	13 (12.3)	8.63	0.003**
No	84 (71.8)	93 (87.7)		
** p<0.01.				

3.2.3.1. Perceived changes in dieting behaviour across the seasons

Two UOMs for perceived changes in dieting behaviour across the seasons were identified. These were 1) winter decrease in dieting and summer increase and 2) winter increase in dieting and summer decrease (see table 3). Forty-four (19.0%) participants answered the question on changes in dieting behaviour, 31 were Australians (70.5%) and 13 Germans (29.5%).

The majority of both Australians (77.4%) and Germans (76.9%) perceived an increase in their dieting behaviour during summer and a decrease during winter. No significant group differences emerged in the number of participants mentioning the respective UOMs. Table 14 shows the results.

74

Table 14: Which seasonal changes do Australians and Germans perceive in dieting behaviour?

UOMs for perceived changes in dieting behaviour [1]	Australian sample n=31 n (%) who mentioned the respective UOM	German sample n=13	Chi-square	p-level
1. Winter decrease and summer increase in dieting	24 (77.4)	10 (76.9)	0.01	ns
2. Winter increase and summer decrease in dieting	5 (16.1)	1 (7.7)	0.55	ns[&]

[&] Cell size <5.
[1] For definition of UOMs, see table 3.

3.2.3.2. Perceived causes for changes in dieting across the seasons

Four UOMs were identified for perceived causes for changes in dieting behaviour across the seasons. These were 1) appearance, 2) environmental variables, 3) mood and social situation, and 4) activity and exercise (see table 3). Forty-two (18.2%) participants answered the question. Of these, 32 (76.2%) were Australians and 10 (23.8%) Germans.

Of the 32 Australians, 31.3% (n=10) perceived appearance as the major cause for changes in dieting across the seasons. Comments such as "one is seen more during summer" and "can't hide in clothes" characterised this UOM. Twenty-five percent (n=8) perceived environmental variables as impacting on changes in dieting across the seasons. (e.g., in summer, "one can just get away with eating less but drinking lots of liquid"). Twenty-two percent (n=7) mentioned mood and social situation. For example, 6.3% (n=2) of the participants reported that sunshine would affect their mood and their mood states would in turn impact on their dieting habits. Regarding social situation, participants mentioned that due to less social interaction during winter, they felt less body-conscious, which in turn resulted in less dieting. Nine percent (n=3) referred to changes in activity-levels (e.g., a drop in exercise during winter), which would then lead to "more time to eat".

Sixty percent (n=6) of the Germans perceived appearance as the major cause for changes in dieting. Forty percent (n=4) mentioned environmental variables and its impact on dieting. Twenty percent (n=2) attributed changes in dieting to changes in mood and social situation and another 20.0% (n=2) mentioned changes in activity-levels that would lead to changes in dieting.

Overall, Australians and Germans named similar reasons for changes in dieting behaviour across the seasons such as 'environmental variables', 'changes in mood and social situation' and 'changes in activity and exercise'. There was a trend for Germans to mention 'appearance'-related issues more frequently than Australians as an important cause for changes in dieting across the seasons (Chi-square $_{(df=1, N=42)}$ =2.67, p=0.10). The results are summarised in table 15.

Table 15: How do Australians and Germans explain seasonal changes in dieting behaviour?

UOMs for perceived causes for changes in dieting behaviour [1]	Australian sample n=32 n (%) who mentioned the respective UOM	German sample n=10	Chi-square	p-level
1. Appearance	10 (31.3)	6 (60.0)	2.67	0.10
2. Environmental variables	8 (25.0)	4 (40.0)	0.84	ns[&]
3. Mood and social situation	7 (21.9)	2(20.0)	0.02	ns[&]
4. Activity and exercise	3 (9.4)	2 (20.0)	0.82	ns[&]

[&] Cell size <5.
[1] For definition of UOMs, see table 3.

3.3. Predicting perception of seasonal changes in physical activity, food choice and dieting

Overall 194 participants (84.3%) perceived seasonal changes in their behaviours, while 36 (15.7%) did not. Of the ones who perceived changes, 106 (46.1%) were Australian and 88 (38.3%) were German. No differences emerged between the two countries in the amount of participants indicating to perceive seasonal changes in their behaviours (Chi-square $_{(df=1, N=230)}$ =2.05, p=0.15).

3.3.1 Predicting the perception of seasonal changes in physical activity

None of the two predictors (i.e., time in hard intensity activities and dieting) was associated with the perception of seasonal changes in physical activity (yes/no; all coefficients with p>0.05). Perception of seasonal changes in physical activity occurred independent of the time spent in hard intensity activities and dieting behaviour.

3.3.2. Predicting the perception of seasonal changes in food choice

Perception of seasonal changes in food choice (yes/no) was associated with the current dieting status. Specifically, the odds of perceiving seasonal changes in food choice are 0.52 times less for those who were dieting (95% CI: 0.27-1.0).

3.3.3. Predicting perception of seasonal changes in dieting behaviour

Perception of seasonal changes in dieting behaviour (yes/no) was associated with the current dieting status. Specifically, the odds for perceiving seasonal changes in dieting are 0.17 less for those who were dieting (95%CI: 0.08-0.36). Also, time spent in hard intensity activities (hours per day) was a significant predictor of perception of seasonal changes in dieting behaviour. The odds for perceiving seasonal changes in dieting were 0.52 times less for those participants who reported spending more time in hard intensity activities (95%CI: 0.32-0.83).

4. Discussion

4.1. Summary of major findings

As expected, Australians and Germans perceived seasonal changes in physical activity and food choice but not in dieting behaviour. Contrary to the hypothesis, both groups differed in some of the perceived changes and named causes for the changes, particularly with regards to the role of environmental factors. As hypothesised, dieting status was associated with the perception of seasonal changes in two of the three behaviours, i.e., dieters were less likely to perceive seasonal changes in food choice and dieting. Further, those who reported exercising were less likely to perceive seasonal changes in dieting.

4.2.1. Physical activity

4.2.1.1. Summary of findings on physical activity and perception of seasonal changes

Australian participants reported spending less time in light and moderate intensity activities compared to German participants. Similarly, fewer Australians than Germans reported engaging in hard intensity activities. As predicted, the majority of participants from both countries perceived changes in their physical activity across the seasons. Significantly more Australians than Germans described changes in the type of activity and its context (i.e., changing from indoor to outdoor activities during summer), whereas more Germans than Australians tended to perceive a decrease in their activity level during winter and an increase during summer. For the German sample, environmental factors were the predominant cause for changes in physical activity, being reported by 74% of these participants. Only 19% of the Germans considered changes in mood states as important factors. In contrast, only half of the Australian sample attributed changes in their activity to environmental factors, with the remaining half comprised of those who considered mood and motivation as important factors and those who perceived changes due to time-management and life-style factors. Dieting status and physical activity (hard intensity activities) were not associated with the perception of seasonal changes in physical activity.

4.2.1.2. Discussion of findings on physical activity

Contrary to the hypothesis, Australian and German female participants were found to differ in their reported levels of physical activity, with Germans reporting higher activity levels in terms of time spent in light and moderate intensity activities and engagement in hard intensity activities.

Differences between the Australian and German samples in terms of activity levels may have been contributed to by the fact that 51.7% of the Australian sample were from an Asian background (see table 1). Investigating activity-levels in the general population in China (Tianjin), Hu et al. (2002a) found that 67% of females claimed that they did not engage in leisure-time physical activities. This percentage is higher than those found in Westernised countries; for example, in both Europe (representative sample with approximately 1000 adults aged 15 and upwards selected from each member state; (Martinez-Gonzalez et al., 2001)) and the United States (N=105,853 respondents in 50 states aged 18 and above; (US Department for Health and Human Services, 1997)) only 27% reported not engaging in leisure-time physical activities. These results suggest that engaging in leisure-time physical activity is not common in Asian populations. Hu et al.

(2002a) assumed that it is due to heavy work burdens and lack of time that Chinese people do not engage in leisure-time activities. Further, Chinese people spend more time in commuting physical activity since China is the largest bicycle-using country in the world (Hu et al., 2002b). Hence, lower reported levels of physical activity, particularly exercise, in the Australian sample might have resulted from these cultural differences. In the current study, the influence of ethnicity could not be investigated. Future studies need to broaden the understanding of cultural differences in engagement of physical activity and its impact on perception of seasonal changes.

The finding that the majority of participants perceived seasonal changes in physical activity is in accordance with findings from previous studies into seasonality and physical activity (Dannenberg et al., 1989; Matthews et al., 2001; Uitenbroek, 1993; Wankel, 1988). These studies have consistently demonstrated increases in people's physical activity during spring/summer and decreases during autumn/winter. The current study extends these findings in that, apart from changes in quantity of activities, participants also perceived changes in the quality and type of physical activities, particularly in the Australian sample. Compared to Trier, the city of Sydney appears to offer a variety of outdoor sports and activities. Such differences in the opportunity to engage in a variety of activities may lead to people perceiving changes particularly in the type of activity. Conclusions from the identified UOMs and potential differences between the two groups need to be drawn carefully. Agreement rates particularly for the UOM 'winter decrease-summer increase' were low (50.1%). Therefore future studies need to incorporate a more comprehensive assessment of people's perception of seasonal changes in physical activity. Given that, better agreement rates might be obtained and hence, differences between Australians and Germans can be identified with greater certainty.

The study also extends previous findings in that it provides a preliminary investigation into people's explanations for the observed changes in physical activity across the seasons. Environmental factors such as changes in ambient temperature and hours of daylight were named as causes for changes in activity-levels, particularly from German participants. This result supports the contention that environmental changes induce changes in activity-levels (Matthews et al., 2001). Germans encounter more extreme changes in environmental factors (see chapter 2.5.). It can therefore be assumed that dependent on the climate people live in, environmental factors are perceived as more or less important for changes in physical activity. The finding that Germans and Australians differed in the number of participants selecting environmental factors as a cause for changes in activity supports this notion.

In the current study, more Australians than Germans perceived mood and motivation as important causes for changes in physical activity. It might be speculated that motivation as a cause for changes in physical activity might play a more important role in participants from an Asian background where physical activity is perceived as less important, than for people coming from an ethnic background where physical activity is part of the culture they live in which again calls for future studies to investigate the role of ethnic background on the perception of seasonal changes in activity-levels.

Neither of the predictors (i.e., engagement in hard intensity activities and dieting behaviour) was found to predict perception of seasonal changes in physical activity in the sample. This result failed to replicate findings from Matthews et al. (2001) who showed that particularly those participants without an exercise-routine demonstrated variation in their activity levels across the seasons. It was therefore expected that the amount of hard intensity activity would be associated with the perception of seasonal changes in physical activity. In the current study, 74% of the participants who reported engaging in hard intensity activities reported perceiving seasonal changes in activity-levels. The present study differed from Matthews' study in that it focussed on people's perception rather than a quantitative assessment of physical activity across the seasons. It is interesting to note that a quantitative assessment of physical activity did not find seasonal changes in people with an exercise-routine, whereas a qualitative assessment found that people perceive seasonal changes. Hence, exercisers might not change the quantity of their activity-levels across the seasons as demonstrated by Matthews et al. (2001) but they might differ the context of exercising (e.g., indoor vs. outdoor activities). Further, people seem to be aware of these changes despite the complexity of the cognitive task of recalling physical activities (Baranowski, 1988). The fact that exercisers notice changes in their activity-levels across the seasons might also hint at their efforts to keep up their activity-level by changing the context of their physical activity. A compensation of decreased moderate intensity activities in winter by increases in exercise behaviour has recently been suggested by Plasqui and Westerterp (2004). They found in a study into seasonal variation in physical activity energy expenditure with 25 Dutch participants (15 females and 10 males), that those participants who were highly active tried to compensate for decreases in moderate intensity activities in winter by sports activities. It remains to be clarified if exercisers not only compensate for drops in physical activity in winter through increases in their exercise but also through adapting their exercise to the climate in the respective seasons, e.g., changing from outdoor to indoor activities.

It was expected that dieting behaviour would impact on the perception of seasonal changes in physical activity. Dieters were assumed to be more affected by sociocultural pressure to be thin for summer (Griffiths, 2000; Huon & Lim, 2000) and would therefore perceive more seasonal changes in their activity-levels, for example increases in activity-levels during spring and summer to lose weight. The current study did not find an association between dieting status and perception of seasonal changes in physical activity. Regardless of the dieting status, the majority (more than 70%) did perceive seasonal changes in their activity-levels. Perception of seasonal changes in physical activity therefore seems to be a strong phenomenon that occurs regardless of differences in people's behaviours such as dieting. This finding converges with results of studies into seasonality in physical activity (Dannenberg et al., 1989; Levin et al., 1999; Matthews et al., 2001; Uitenbroek, 1993). Uitenbroek (1993) therefore concluded that the extent of seasonality in physical activity for exercise is quite exceptional. If this seasonality in physical activity is caused by environmental factors such as the photoperiod (Kjellman, 2001) or by conditioned response to the winter season as suggested by Persinger (1983) remains to be clarified.

In terms of programmes to enhance physical activity over the year, the preliminary results suggest that factors such as the climate the participants live in as well as their ethnic background must be incorporated into programmes. In Germany, a focus on providing indoor activities to overcome the perceived influence of environmental factors as a barrier to physical activity might be important. In Australia, mood and motivation as barriers to continuous engagement in physical activity need to be addressed. Strategies such as psychoeducation on the link between engagement in physical activity and its positive impact on seasonal changes in mood (Craft & Landers,

1998; Uitenbroek, 1993) might be effective. If people understand that engagement in physical activity helps them to overcome lower mood states during winter, they might become motivated to continue activity during the winter months. Future studies need to expand on people's theories for seasonal changes in physical activity, particularly with regard to the influence of living in different climates, the role of differing ethnic backgrounds and the stages of dieting.

4.2.2. Food choice

4.2.2.1. Summary of findings on food choice

The majority of participants from both countries chose sensory appeal as the most important food choice factor, followed by health and convenience. Around 10% of female participants in each country selected their food on the basis of weight control concerns. As predicted, the majority of participants from both countries perceived changes in their food choice across the seasons. Regarding perceived changes in food choice, more Germans than Australians indicated a change in the content of their food (e.g., more sugary and fattening food during winter) whereas more Australians than Germans observed changes in the temperature of the foods they were choosing across the seasons (e.g., warm foods during winter, cold food and drinks during summer). Despite these differences in the perceived changes, Australians and Germans listed similar reasons for changes in food choice. The majority perceived environmental variables as the main factor. Availability of foods and mood and social situation were reported as relevant causal factors by approximately 20% of the sample. Dieting status was associated with the perception of seasonal changes in food choice in that dieters were less likely to perceive seasonal changes in food choice.

4.2.2.2. Discussion of findings on food choice

As predicted, no differences in participants' perceived motives for food choice emerged between Australians and Germans. This finding suggests that females of a comparable age and educational status demonstrate similar motives for their food choices despite a different cultural background. Consistent with previous studies in Germany (Pudel & Westenhoefer, 1991) and the United Kingdom (Steptoe et al., 1995), young females in the present study chose their food according to its sensory appeal, health factors and convenience and weight loss strategies.

The finding that the majority of the participants perceived seasonal changes in their food choice converges with studies into seasonal variation in food intake (Kraeuchi & Wirz-Justice, 2001; Shahar et al., 1999; Van Staveren, Deurenberg, Burema, de Groot, & Hautvast, 1986). These studies found increased caloric intake, particularly fat and carbohydrate intake during autumn and winter. Compared to the perception of seasonal changes in physical activity found in the current study, fewer participants noticed changes in their food choice across the seasons (61.2% of the Australian sample and 54.5% of the German sample). This finding is in line with observations that seasonal changes in food choice or food intake are more pronounced in developing countries where food availability changes throughout the year (for a review see (Westerterp-Plantenga, 1999)).

The current study extends the understanding of seasonality of food choice in that, besides the content of the foods, participants also described changes in the temperature of foods, particularly in the Australian sample. This finding contradicts lay-assumptions that Australians are not affected by seasonal changes in environmental factors such as ambient temperature. Despite the less extreme temperature fluctuations between winter and summer in Sydney compared to Trier (see chapter 2.5.), more Australians than Germans reported changes in the temperature of foods (i.e., warm foods during winter and cold drinks during summer). It is possible that the higher summer temperatures in Sydney (where temperatures can reach up to 45°C), result in greater changes in the selection of food on the basis of temperature during summer. In Germany, ambient temperature during summer rarely exceeds 30°C. Further, the fact that the majority of houses in Sydney are not equipped with central heating may account for the need to warm oneself up with hot foods. Hence, the observation that more Australians noticed a change in the temperature of their food may be explained by the greater importance of food as a cooling and warming method during summer and winter, respectively. These findings need to be explored in future studies to highlight the role of perception of environmental factors on changes in food choice and other behaviours.

Approximately 20% in each group (Australians: 18.3%; Germans: 19.3%) mentioned mood and social situation as causal factors for changes in food choice. This finding supports the assumption of Kraeuchi and Wirz-Justice (2001) who argued that the excess in carbohydrate intake during autumn may be related to depressive moods. It has been shown that, regardless of the geophysical location, people experience seasonal mood fluctuations. Kasper (1991) found that 43.2% of a sample from the northern United States felt worst during January and February. Murray and Hay (1997) found that for the majority of the 526 Australian females (60.8%), winter was associated with feeling worst, gaining weight and being inactive. Kraeuchi and Wirz-Justice (2001) suggested that in SAD patients a real 'metabolic demand' for glucose could underlie the characteristic carbohydrate craving during their winter depression. Therefore the increased carbohydrate consumption could be seen as a form of self-medication. It is not known if individuals who experience seasonal fluctuations in their mood states would be affected by similar symptoms albeit to a lesser degree. Understanding people's food choices during the seasons and the role of seasonal changes in mood states may help to counteract increases in food intake during the winter months and potentially to prevent increases in obesity during winter (Shahar et al., 1999).

The finding that around 20% (14.1% of the Australian and 22.8% of the German sample) considered the availability of foods as an important cause for changes in food choice is in accordance with Fursts' model (1996) on the process of food choice. They found that people noted that the availability of certain foods varied with the season and adapted their food choice accordingly.

It is of interest that dieters in the present study were less likely to perceive seasonal changes in their food choice. Dieting with the intention to lose weight therefore seems to be associated with an inflexible food choice that does not vary across the seasons. Dieters are primarily focussed on selecting foods to control body weight. Further, Lindeman and Stark (2000) investigated food choice motives in distressed (n=22) and healthy dieters (n=44). They found that dieters who displayed dieting disorder attitudes appreciated the pleasure of eating significantly less than the healthy dieters. In addition, distressed dieters used food choice as an expression of identity in that they selected food more in terms of their personal ideologies (i.e., values, world views and philosophy of life). Accordingly, these motives and the intention to lose weight will override any perception of seasonal changes in food choice and may be indicative of the rigidity of the dieting behaviour.

4.2.3. Dieting

4.2.3.1. Summary of findings on dieting

Significantly more Australians than Germans reported dieting behaviour (33.9% compared to 15.5%). Contrary to the hypothesis, significantly more Australians than Germans perceived changes in their dieting behaviour across the seasons (28.2% Australians compared to 12.1% Germans). Concerning changes in dieting, Australians and Germans observed similar changes across the seasons with the majority describing an increase in dieting during summer and a decrease during winter. In both groups, appearance-related issues such as increased body-consciousness were named as causing the changes in dieting behaviour. Environmental variables, changes in mood and social situation and changes in activity and exercise were reported by fewer participants. Time spent in hard intensity activities and dieting were associated with the perception of seasonal changes in dieting. Specifically, those participants who reported spending more time in hard intensity activities were less likely to perceive seasonal changes in dieting. In addition, dieters were less likely to perceive seasonal changes in dieting.

4.2.3.2. Discussion of findings on dieting

It is of interest that more Australians than Germans reported engaging in dieting behaviour. In the current study, dieting was defined as changing one's eating habits with the intention to lose weight and thus formed a mild definition of dieting. The higher percentage of Australian dieters might result from the surroundings they live in. Sydney is a city surrounded by beaches where outdoor activities and beach culture are an essential part of daily living. It can be speculated that sociocultural pressures to be thin are of greater importance in such an environment than in a city like Trier without any beaches and beach-culture.

Residing in different climates might further account for the differences in dieting between Australians and Germans. This finding is in line with studies into the impact of ambient temperature on dieting disorder pathology. Sloan (2002), for example, found in her study in 59 female students from Florida and 69 students from Pennsylvania that residing in a warm weather climate was associated with increased dieting disorder pathology. She argued that residing in a warm climate may result in it being nearly impossible to avoid warm weather clothing, such as shorts, skirts and bathing suits. Since Sydney has a warmer climate than Trier, differences in dieting between Australians and Germans might be related to differences in the climates.

Also, 47.1% of the Australian sample were from an Asian background and coming from an Asian background has recently been connected to higher risk of developing eating dysfunctions (Wildes, Emery, & Simons, 2001). In their meta-analysis, Wildes et al. (2001) found that Asians (living in Western countries) tended to show higher levels of dietary restraint, weight and dieting concerns. According to the authors, Asian women living in Western countries may feel additional pressure to be thin due to their inability to meet other white beauty standards, such as fair skin and blonde hair.

Only one study has previously investigated seasonal changes in dieting behaviour. Huon and Lim (2000) analysed 478 adolescent girls who reported an absence of dieting at the commencement of the study. Over the course of two years, the number of dieters increased during spring and decreased during winter. The result of the current study demonstrates that the majority of the participants did not perceive seasonal changes in dieting behaviour. Likewise, of those who reported dieting, the majority did not perceive seasonal changes in their dieting behaviour. Dieting therefore appears to be a behaviour perceived as stable across seasons. This finding contradicts with the results from Huon and Lim (2000). One explanation might relate to the age difference of the two samples. The mean age in the current study was 19 years for the Australian participants and 21 years for the German participants compared to a mean age of 13 years in the sample of Huon and Lim. The adolescents had not started dieting at the commencement of the study. Hence, it can be speculated that the initiation of dieting behaviour might co-occur with the spring or summer season when sociocultural pressures to be thin are at their peak. Once dieting behaviour is established (e.g., in student populations), variation of dieting across the seasons is not perceived but it appears to be a stable behaviour. Prevention strategies for dieting behaviour should address perceived pressures to be thin across the seasons and develop strategies to counteract increases in commencement of dieting during spring and summer.

In the current study, of those who perceived seasonal changes in dieting the majority observed increases in dieting during spring/summer and decreases during winter. Likewise, the majority attributed changes in dieting to appearance factors such as being more body-conscious during summer, being more exposed and thus increasing efforts to lose weight. Here, perceived sociocultural pressures rather than environmental factors seem to impact on perceived changes in dieting behaviour. Spring and summer constitute seasons associated with particular pressures to lose weight and may lead to an increase in dieting during summer as already demonstrated by Huon and Lim (2000).

Time spent in hard intensity activities was associated with the perception of seasonal changes in dieting. Specifically, those participants who reported spending more time in hard intensity activities were less likely to perceive seasonal changes in dieting. Studies into seasonal variation in physical activity demonstrated no seasonal variation for vigorous intensity activities such as exercise (Matthews et al., 2001). Plasqui and Westerterp (2004) have argued that active people may try to compensate for drop in moderate intensity activities during winter by sports (i.e., hard intensity) activities. It can be speculated that those who exercise regularly are characterised by attitudes and motives (such as the pursuit of fitness), which account for the lack of seasonality in exercise. These attitudes may also trigger continuous dieting behaviour across the seasons and override perception of seasonal changes in dieting behaviour.

4.3. Methodological concerns

The present study had several limitations. These can be subdivided into a) assessment-related limitations, b) problems that came up while conducting the study, and c) limitations due to differences in the climate between Sydney and Trier.

4.3.1. Assessment-related limitations

In the current study, hard intensity activities were defined as vigorous physical work, jogging, swimming (laps) and participants were required to report the types of activities they engaged in and estimate the time they spent in these activities. A major problem with self-reports of physical activity is that they require participants to fulfil a highly complex cognitive task (Baranowski, 1988) comprised of attending to the activity of concern, detecting the level of intensity of the activity in a manner approximating the understanding of the investigator, and estimating the duration spent in the critical activities. Therefore recall effects might have impacted on participants' answers in the current study. Due to the shortness of the BSPSC and the pilot character of the study, no recall aids for example using a segmented day form, thus dividing the day into three segments which helps subjects to remember sequentially over the day (Sallis, 1997) could be implemented. Therefore the accuracy of the self-reported time spent in physical activity might be questionable.

Dieting was defined as a change in eating habits with the intention of losing weight. An assessment of the degree of dieting (Strong & Huon, 1997) was not included. It is possible that dependent on the dieting status, seasonal variation in dieting or other behaviours are perceived. Specifically, chronic dieters would be expected to perceive less seasonal changes as an indication of their rigidity of dieting and the related attitudes (Lindeman & Stark, 1999; Lindeman & Stark, 2000). Future studies should incorporate an assessment of the stages of dieting and determine its influence on the perception of seasonal changes in physical activity, food choice and dieting.

Some of the identified UOMs particularly for changes in food choice had low agreement rates. For example, agreement between the original rater and the two Australian raters were 58.4% for the content of food-UOM and 58.4% for the amount of food-UOM whereas an agreement of 79.2% was obtained for the last UOM. It an be speculated that the UOMs for changes in food choice are overlapping, for example eating warmer foods during winter obviously is related to a change in the content of the foods. Further, agreement rates were low for mood and social situation as perceived causes for changes in the three health-related behaviours, indicating that this UOM was not clearly defined. Future studies employing factor analysis may be helpful in identifying more distinct and comprehensible UOMs.

The current study aimed to assess people's perception and understanding of seasonal variation in three health-related behaviours. It was not assessed, if these seasonal changes were perceived as problematic. Future studies incorporating the degree to which participants perceive themselves as being affected by seasonal changes (e.g., using the SPAQ) may highlight differences in people's perception and understanding of seasonal changes. It can be assumed that people who perceive the changes as problematic would identify mood-related factors as causal factors for changes in their behaviours, whereas people who do not perceive the changes as problematic may explain changes with changes in environmental factors.

4.3.2. Problems that came up while conducting the study

The BSPSC was designed as a one-page survey that was incorporated in the assessment of Chau's study (2003). It was therefore not possible to assess demographic variables for the Australian sample. The current study therefore lacks information on differences in the perception of seasonal changes between participants from a different ethnic background (e.g., from an Asian background). Prevalence rates of SAD have shown to be similar in Asian and Caucasian samples (for a review see (Mersch, Middendorp, Bouhuys, Beersma, & van den Hoofdakker, 1999)), however thus far, no study has investigated people's perception and explanation for seasonal changes in an Asian and Caucasian sample.

Further, Australian participants took part in a study into 'The effect of magazine exposure on women's mood and body image' (Chau, 2003) and might therefore have been susceptible for the issue of dieting compared to the unselected group from Trier. Differences in the amount of dieters might have resulted due to the selection of the group (i.e., the assumption that those who participate in studies in the area of body image may be prone to dieting behaviour) rather than real differences between Australians and Germans.

4.3.3. Limitations due to differences in the locations

The current study compared an Australian sample from Sydney with a German sample from Trier and was thus, one of the first studies to compare residents from the Northern and Southern Hemisphere in their perception of seasonal changes in behaviours. However, the geographical location of Sydney and Trier as in coast-climate versus inland-climate may have impacted on people's perception. To identify differences in the perception and understanding of seasonal changes between Australians and Germans, influence of climatic factors should be minimised. Hence, future studies should compare residents from similar locations in both countries (e.g., comparing residents from Sydney to residents from Hamburg). Also, when participants in both countries reside in a city surrounded by beaches the impact of sociocultural pressures on the perception of seasonal changes, particularly in physical activity and dieting, can be further investigated.

4.4. Conclusion and future directions

The current study extended knowledge regarding the perception and understanding of seasonal variation in three health-related behaviours in a female Australian and German sample. Australians and Germans perceived seasonal changes, particularly in levels of physical activity. They mentioned different explanations for these changes that call for different intervention strategies to enhance physical activity across the seasons. Food choice was perceived to vary to a lesser degree than physical activity. While Germans attributed changes mostly to environmental factors, more Australians than Germans mentioned mood-related factors as causal factors. It remains to be clarified in future studies, if this finding is indicative of Australians being more negatively affected by seasonal changes and thus selecting food to cope with seasonal mood fluctuations. Those who were dieting were less likely to perceive seasonal changes in their food choice and dieting, presumably reflecting the rigidity of their dieting. It can be speculated that there is a negative relationship between the severity of dieting and the perception of seasonal changes in behaviours. In future studies, cultural differences regarding the perception and understanding of seasonal changes in physical activity, food choice and dieting should be investigated. It is of interest if people from cultures where physical activity is part of daily living compared to people from cultures where engagement in leisure-time physical activity is small, differ in their perception of seasonal changes. Further, differences in the perception of seasonal changes in food choice and dieting between Asian and Caucasian participants may broaden the understanding of cross-cultural differences in dieting behaviour and the impact of dieting on perception of seasonal changes.

5. Reference list

Aschoff, J. (1981). Annual rhythms in man. In J.Aschoff (Ed.), *Handbook of Behavioral Neurobiology. Vol.4: Biological Rhythms* (pp. 475-487). New York: Plenum Press.

Australian Bureau of Statistics (2000). *Participation in sport and physical activities.* Canberra: Australian Bureau of Statistics.

Australian Institute of Health and Welfare (2002). *Australia's health 2002: The eight biennial health report of the Australian Institute of Health and Welfare.* Canberra: Australian Institute of Health and Welfare.

Australian Surveying and Land Information Group (2002). *Sunrise and sunset for Sydney.*

Ball, K. (2002). Body weight, body image, and eating behaviours: Relationships with ethnicity and acculturation in a community sample of young Australian women. *Eating Behaviors, 3,* 216.

Baranowski, T. (1988). Validity and reliability of self report measures of physical activity: An information-processing perspective. *Research Quarterly, 59,* 314-327.

Bauman, A. & Owen, N. (1999). Physical activity of adult Australians: epidemiological evidence and potential strategies for health gain. [Review] [69 refs]. *Journal of Science & Medicine in Sport, 2,* 30-41.

Booth, M., Owen, N., Baumann, A., & Gore, C. J. (1995). *Active and inactive Australians. Assessing and understanding levels of physical activity.* Canberra: Department of the Environment, Sport and Territories.

Booth, M. (2000). Assessment of physical activity: An international perspective. *Research Quarterly for Exercise & Sport, 71,* 114-120.

Boyce, P. & Parker, G. (1988). Seasonal affective disorder in the Southern Hemisphere. *American Journal of Psychiatry, 145,* 96-99.

Buston, K., Parry-Jones, W., Livingston, M., Bogan, A., & Wood, S. (1998). Qualitative research. *British Journal of Psychiatry, 172,* 197-199.

Caspersen, C. J., Powell, K. E., & Christenson, G. M. (1985). Physical activity, exercise, and physical fitness: Definitions and distinctions for health-related research. *Public Health Reports, 100,* 126-131.

Chau, J. (2003). *The effect of magazine exposure on women's mood and body image.*

Craft, L. L. & Landers, D. M. (1998). The effect of exercise on clinical depression and depression resulting from mental illness: A meta-analysis. *Journal of Sport and Exercise Psychology, 20,* 339-357.

Dannenberg, A. L., Keller, J. B., Wilson, P. W., & Castelli, W. P. (1989). Leisure time physical activity in the Framingham Offspring Study. Description, seasonal variation, and risk factor correlates. *American Journal of Epidemiology, 129,* 76-88.

Eiliv, L. & Vidje, H. (2001). Responses to the Seasonal Pattern Assessment Questionnaire in different seasons. *American Journal of Psychiatry, 158,* 316-318.

Fossey, E., Harvey, C., McDermott, F., & Davidson, L. (2002). Understanding and evaluating qualitative research. *Australian & New Zealand Journal of Psychiatry, 36,* 717-732.

Furst, T., Connors, M., Bisogni, C. A., Sobal, J., & Winter Falk, L. (1996). Food choice: A conceptual model of the process. *Appetite, 26,* 247-266.

Griffiths, R. A., Russell, J., Schotte, D., Thornton, C., Touyz, S., & Varano, P. (1999). Sociocultural attitudes toward appearance in dieting disordered and nondieting disordered subjects. *European Eating Disorders Review, Vol 7,* 193-203.

Griffiths, R. A. (2000). Restrained eating and sociocultural attitudes to appearance and general dissatisfaction. *European Eating Disorders Review, Vol 8,* 394-402.

Hay, P. (1998). The epidemiology of eating disorder behaviors: an Australian community-based survey. *International Journal of Eating Disorders, 23,* 371-382.

Heinberg, L. J., Thompson, J. K., & Stormer, S. (1995). Development and validation of the sociocultural attitudes towards appearance questionnaire. *International Journal of Eating Disorders, 17,* 81-89.

Hu, G., Pekkarinen, H., Haenninen, O., Yu, Z., Tian, H., Guo, Z. et al. (2002a). Physical activity during leisure and commuting in Tianjin, China. *Bulletin of the World Health Organization, 80,* 933-938.

Hu, G., Pekkarinen, H., Hanninen, O., Yu, Z., Guo, Z., & Tian, H. (2002b). Commuting, leisure-time physical activity, and cardiovascular risk factors in China. *Medicine & Science in Sports & Exercise, 34,* 234-238.

Huon, G. & Lim, J. (2000). The emergence of dieting among female adolescents: Age, body mass index, and seasonal effects. *International Journal of Eating Disorders, 28,* 221-225.

Kasper, S., Rogers, S. L., Yancey, A., Schulz, P. M., Skwerer, R. G., & Rosenthal, N. E. (1989a). Phototherapy in individuals with and without subsyndromal seasonal affective disorder. *Archives of General Psychiatry, 46,* 837-344.

Kasper, S., Wehr, T. A., Bartko, J. J., Gaist, P. A., & Rosenthal, N. E. (1989b). Epidemiological findings of seasonal changes in mood and behavior. *Archives of General Psychiatry, 46,* 823-833.

Kasper, S. (1991). *Jahreszeit und Befindlichkeit in der Allgemeinbevoelkerung.* Berlin: Springer.

Keller, S., Kreis, J., & Huck, C. (2001). Fuenf am Tag? Motivationale und psychosoziale Aspekte des Obst- und Gemueseverzehrs. *Zeitschrift für Gesundheitspsychologie, 9,* 87-98.

Kjellman, B. F. (2001). The photoperiod. In T.Partonen & A. Magnusson (Eds.), *Seasonal affective disorder: Practice and research* (pp. 163-168). Oxford: University Press.

Kraeuchi, K. & Wirz-Justice, A. (1988). The four seasons: food intake frequency in seasonal affective disorder in the course of a year. *Psychiatry Research, 25,* 323-338.

Kraeuchi, K. & Wirz-Justice, A. (2001). Carbohydrate intake. In T.Partonen & A. Magnusson (Eds.), *Seasonal affective disorder: Practice and research* (pp. 197-200). Oxford: University Press.

Lacoste, V. & Wirz-Justice, A. (1989). Seasonal variation in normal subjects: An update of variables current in depression research. In N.E.Rosenthal & M. C. Blehar (Eds.), *Seasonal affective disorders and phototherapy* (pp. 167-229). New York: Guilford Press.

Levin, S., Jacobs, D. R. Jr., Ainsworth, B. E., Richardson, M. T., & Leon, A. S. (1999). Intra-individual variation and estimates of usual physical activity. *Annals of Epidemiology, 9,* 481-488.

Lindeman, M. & Stark, K. (1999). Pleasure, pursuit of health or negotiation of identity? Personality correlates of food choice motives among young and middle-aged women. *Appetite, 33,* 141-161.

Lindeman, M. & Stark, K. (2000). Loss of pleasure, ideological food choice reasons and eating pathology. *Appetite, 35,* 263-268.

Magnusson, A. (1996). Validation of the Seasonal Pattern Assessment Questionnaire (SPAQ). *Journal of Affective Disorders, 40,* 121-129.

Magnusson, A. (2000). An overview of epidemiological studies in seasonal affective disorder. *Acta Psychiatrica Scandinavica, 101,* 176-184.

Martinez-Gonzalez, M. A., Varo, J. J., Santos, J. L., De Irala, J., Gibney, M., Kearney, J. et al. (2001). Prevalence of physical activity during leisure time in the European Union. *Medicine & Science in Sports & Exercise, 33,* 1142-1146.

Matthews, C. E., Freedson, P. S., Herbert, J. R., Stanek, E. J., Merriam, P. A., Rosal, M. C. et al. (2001). Seasonal variation in household, occupational, and leisure time physical activity: Longitudinal analyses from the Seasonal Variation of Blood Cholesterol Study. *American Journal of Epidemiology, 153,* 172-183.

Maykut, P. & Morehouse, R. (1994). *Beginning qualitative research. A philosophic and practical guide.* London: The Falmer Press.

Mersch, P. P. A., Middendorp, H. M., Bouhuys, A. L., Beersma, D. G. M., & van den Hoofdakker, R. H. (1999). Seasonal affective disorder and latitude: A review of the literature. *Journal of Affective Disorders, 53,* 35-48.

Murray, G. W. & Hay, D. A. (1997). Seasonal affective disorder in Australia: is photoperiod critical? *Australian & New Zealand Journal of Psychiatry, 31,* 279-284.

Nelson, R. J., Badura, L. L., & Goldman, B. D. (1990). Mechanisms of seasonal cycles of behavior. *Annual Review of Psychology, 41,* 81-108.

Persinger, M. A. (1983). Winter blahs and spring irritability: The chronic but subtle behavioral operations. *Perceptual & Motor Skills, 57,* 494-496.

Plasqui, G. & Westerterp, K. R. Seasonal variation in total energy expenditure, physical activity and physical fitness in Dutch young adults. *Obesity Research*, (in press).

Polivy, J. & Herman, C. P. (2002). Causes of eating disorders. *Annual Review of Psychology, 53*, 187-213.

Pudel, V. & Westenhoefer, J. (1991). *Ernaehrungspsychologie. Eine Einfuehrung*. Göttingen: Hogrefe.

Pudel, V. (2000). Essverhalten und Ernährungszustand von Kindern und Jugendlichen - eine Repräsentativerhebung in Deutschland. In Deutsche Gesellschaft für Ernährung (Ed.), *Ernährungsbericht 2000* (pp. 115-145). Frankfurt/Main: Henrich Verlag.

Rosenthal, N. E., Bradt, G. H., & Wehr, T. A. (1984). *Seasonal Pattern Assessment Questionnaire*. Bethesda Md: National Institute of Mental Health.

Ruetten, A., Abel, T., Kannas, L., von Lengerke, T., Luschen, G., Diaz, J. A. et al. (2001). Self reported physical activity, public health, and perceived environment: results from a comparative European study. *Journal of Epidemiology & Community Health, 55*, 139-146.

Sallis, J. F. (1997). Seven-day physical activity recall. *Medicine & Science in Sports & Exercise, 29 Supplement*, 89-103.

Shahar, D. R., Froom, P., Harari, G., Yerushalmi, N., Lubin, F., & Kristal-Boneh, E. (1999). Changes in dietary intake account for seasonal changes in cardiovascular disease risk factors. *European Journal of Clinical Nutrition, 53,* 395-400.

Sloan, D. M. (2002). Does warm weather climate affect eating disorder pathology? *International Journal of Eating Disorders, 32,* 240-244.

Stehle, P. (2000). Ernährung älterer Menschen. In Deutsche Gesellschaft für Ernährung (Ed.), *Ernährungsbericht 2000* (pp. 147-176). Frankfurt/Main: Henrich Verlag.

Steptoe, A., Pollard, T. M., & Wardle, J. (1995). Development of a measure of the motives underlying the selection of food: The Food Choice Questionnaire. *Appetite, 25,* 267-284.

Sternwarte Hamburg (2003). *Sonnendaten für ein Jahr-Trier.*

Stock, C., Wille, L., & Kramer, A. (2001). Gender-specific health behaviors of German university students predict the interest in campus health promotion. *Health Promotion International, 16,* 145-154.

Story, M., Neumark-Sztainer, D., Sherwood, N., Stang, J., & Murray, D. (1998). Dieting status and its relationship to eating and physical activity behaviors in a representative sample of US adolescents. [see comments.]. *Journal of the American Dietetic Association, 98,* 1127-1135.

Strong, K. G. & Huon, G. (1997). The development and evaluation of a staged-based Dieting Status Measure (DiSM). *Eating Disorders: The Journal of Treatment and Prevention, 5,* 97-104.

Touyz, S. & Beumont, P. J. (1999). Anorexia nervosa: New approaches to management. *Modern Medicine of Australia, June,* 95-110.

Uitenbroek, D. G. (1993). Seasonal variation in leisure time physical activity. *Medicine and Science in Sports and Exercise, 25,* 755-760.

US Department for Health and Human Services (1997). Guidelines for School and Community Programs to promote lifelong physical activity among young people. *Morbidity and Mortality Weekly Reports, 46,* 1-36.

Van Staveren, W. A., Deurenberg, P., Burema, J., de Groot, L. C. P. G., & Hautvast, J. G. A. J. (1986). Seasonal variation in food intake, pattern of physical activity and change in body weight in a group of young adult Dutch women consuming self-selected diets. *American Journal of Clinical Nutrition, 10,* 133-145.

Wankel, L. M. (1988). Exercise adherence and leisure activity: Patterns of involvement and interventions to facilitate regular activity. In R.K.Dishman (Ed.), *Exercise adherence. Its impact on public health* (pp. 369-396). Champaign, Illinois: Human Kinetics Books.

Westenhoefer, J. (2001). Prevalence of eating disorders and weight control practices in Germany in 1990 and 1997. *International Journal of Eating Disorders, 29,* 477-481.

Westerterp-Plantenga, M. S. (1999). Effects of extreme environments on food intake in human subjects. [Review] [38 refs]. *Proceedings of the Nutrition Society, 58,* 791-798.

Wildes, J. E., Emery, R. E., & Simons, A. D. (2001). The roles of ethnicity and culture in the devlopment of eating disturbances and body dissatisfaction: A meta-analytic review. *Clinical Psychology Review, 21,* 521-551.

6. Appendices

6.1. Appendix A: Brief Survey on Perception of Seasonal Changes- English version

1.) Please, put in the table below how many days per week and hours per day you do engage in the following intensities of **activity** and the main type of activity you do engage in:

Intensity of activity	Days per week	Hours per day	Main type of physical activity
Light activities (eg standing, slow walking, carrying light objects)			
Moderate activities (walking at a normal pace, working with moderate effort)			
Hard activities (eg vigorous physical work, jogging, swimming (laps))			

Have you noticed any changes in your physical activity levels over the seasons (looking over the last 5 years)?
❏ Yes   ❏ No
If yes, what changes in what intensity of physical activity did you notice in each season?

Winter	What do you think is causing these changes?
Summer	

2.) In general, which of the following options best describes your **choice of food**? Please, rank the following options from 1 to 9, 1 being most applicable to you, 9 being least applicable.

❏ Weight control (eg It is important to me that the food I eat on a typical day is low in calories)	❏ Convenience (eg It is important to me that the food I eat is easy to prepare)
❏ Sensory appeal (eg It is important to me that the food I eat on a typical day has a pleasant taste)	❏ Natural Content (eg It is important to me that the food I eat contains natural ingredients.)
❏ Ideological reasons (eg Because of my view of the world, there are some foods, which are inappropriate for me.)	❏ Price (eg It is important to me that the food I eat is cheap.)
❏ Health (eg It is important to me that the food I eat keeps me healthy.)	❏ Familiarity (eg It is important to me that the food I eat is familiar.)
❏ Mood (eg It is important to me that the food I eat helps me cope with my life.)	

Have you noticed any changes in your food choice over the seasons (looking over the past 5 years)?

❏ Yes   ❏ No
If yes, what changes have you noticed in which season?

Winter	What do you think is causing these changes?
Summer	

3.) Do you currently engage in **dieting** (consider dieting to mean any change in your eating habits performed with the specific intention to lose weight)?

❑ Yes   ❑ No

Have you noticed any changes in your dieting over the seasons (looking over the past 5 years)?

❑ Yes   ❑ No

If yes, what changes have you noticed in which season?

	What do you think is causing these changes?
Winter	
Summer	

Thank you very much for your help.

6.2. Appendix B: Brief Survey on Perception of Seasonal Changes-German version

1.) Bitte, kreuzen Sie unten in der Tabelle an, wie viele Tage pro Woche und Stunden pro Tag Sie in den folgenden **Aktivitätsniveaus/-intensitäten** aktiv sind. Bitte, geben Sie auch Ihre jeweilige Hauptaktivität fuer jede dieser Kategorien an:

Aktivitätsniveau	Anzahl an Tagen/Woche	Stunden/Tag	Hauptaktivität
Leichte Aktivitäten (z.B. aufrecht stehen, langsam gehen, leichte Gegenstände tragen)			
Mittlere Aktivitäten (z.B. im normalen Tempo gehen, mit mittlerer Anstrengung arbeiten)			
Harte Aktivitäten (z.B. anstrengende körperliche Arbeit, joggen, schwimmen (Bahnen))			

Haben Sie irgendwelche Veränderungen in Ihrem Aktivitätsniveau in den verschiedenen Jahreszeiten (in den letzten 5 Jahren) bemerkt?

❑ Ja   ❑ Nein

Wenn ja, welche Veränderungen in welcher Aktivitätsintensität haben Sie in welcher Jahreszeit bemerkt?

Winter	Was verursacht Ihrer Ansicht nach diese Veränderungen?
Sommer	

2.) Welche der unten aufgelisteten Gründe beschreibt am besten die Auswahl Ihrer **Nahrungsmittel**? Bitte, numerieren Sie die angegeben Möglichkeiten von 1 bis 9, so dass 1 die Option darstellt, der Sie am ehesten zustimmen und 9 diejenige, der Sie am wenigsten zustimmen.

❑ Gewichtskontrolle (z.B. Es ist wichtig für mich, dass das Essen, das ich an einem gewöhnlichen Tag zu mir nehme einen geringen Kaloriengehalt besitzt)	❑ Bequemlichkeit (z.B. Es ist wichtig für mich, dass das Essen, das ich an einem gewöhnlichen Tag zu mir nehme einfach zuzubereiten ist)
❑ Sinnesanregung (z.B. Es ist wichtig für mich, dass das Essen, das ich an einem gewöhnlichen Tag zu mir nehme einen angenehmen Geschmack besitzt)	❑ Natürlicher Inhalt (z.B. Es ist wichtig für mich, dass das Essen, das ich an einem gewöhnlichen Tag zu mir nehme natürliche Bestandteile enthält)
❑ Ideologische Beweggründe (z.B. Wegen meiner Weltanschauung gibt es einige Lebensmittel, die für mich nicht adäquat sind)	❑ Preis (z.B. Es ist wichtig für mich, dass das Essen, das ich an einem gewöhnlichen Tag zu mir nehme günstig ist)
❑ Gesundheit (z.B. Es ist wichtig für mich, dass das Essen, das ich an einem gewöhnlichen Tag zu mir nehme mich gesund hält)	❑ Vertrautheit (z.B. Es ist wichtig für mich, dass das Essen, das ich an einem gewöhnlichen Tag zu mir nehme mir vertraut ist)
❑ Stimmung (z.B. Es ist wichtig für mich, dass das Essen, das ich an einem gewöhnlichen Tag zu mir nehme mir dabei hilft, mit meinem Leben zurecht zukommen)	

Haben Sie irgendwelche Veränderungen in Ihrer Nahrungsauswahl in den verschiedenen Jahreszeiten (in den letzten 5 Jahren) bemerkt?

❑ Ja   ❑ Nein

Wenn ja, welche Veränderungen in Ihrer Nahrungsmittelauswahl haben Sie in welcher Jahreszeit bemerkt?

Winter	Was verursacht Ihrer Ansicht nach diese Veränderungen?
Sommer	

3.) Halten Sie im Augenblick **Diät** (Diät = eine Veränderung in Ihren Essgewohnheiten, die mit der Absicht vollzogen wird, Gewicht zu verlieren)?
❑ Ja   ❑ Nein

Haben Sie irgendwelche Veränderungen in Ihrem Diätverhalten in den verschiedenen Jahreszeiten (in den letzten 5 Jahren) bemerkt?
❑ Ja   ❑ Nein
Wenn ja, welche Veränderungen in Ihrem Diätverhalten haben Sie in welcher Jahreszeit bemerkt?

Winter	Was verursacht Ihrer Ansicht nach diese Veränderungen?
Sommer	

Vielen Dank für Ihre Hilfe.

6.3. Appendix C: Demographic data of the German sample

DEMOGRAPHISCHE DATEN

Die folgende Tabelle enthält Angaben zu Ihren demographischen Daten, sowie zu Gewicht und Groesse. Bitte, füllen Sie die Tabelle vollständig aus. Vielen Dank für Ihre Hilfe.

Code		
Geschlecht	❏ weiblich	❏ männlich
Geburtsdatum		
Alter		
Studienfach		
Semesteranzahl		
Familienstand	❏ Ledig ❏ Verheiratet ❏ Unverheiratet mit Partner	❏ Geschieden ❏ Verwitwet
Staatsangehörigkeit		
Groesse (in m)		
Gewicht (in kg)		

Part 2:

Physical activity in patients with anorexia nervosa: Which patterns emerge across three seasons?

Table of contents

List of tables

List of figures

Publications and Conference Presentations

Conferences

Physical activity across two seasons: A prospective study in anorexia nervosa patients and healthy controls. Tanja Hechler, Pierre Beumont, Reinhold Laessle, Guy Plasqui, Stephen Touyz, Klaas Westerterp.

Oral presentation at the Asian Pacific Eating Disorder Congress, Melbourne (Australia), November 2002.

Physical activity in patients with anorexia nervosa: Is there a seasonal variation? Tanja Hechler, Pierre Beumont, Reinhold Laessle, Guy Plasqui, Stephen Touyz, Klaas Westerterp.

Poster presentation at the Eating Disorder Research Society Meeting, Ravello (Italy), October 2003.

Is there a 'high-risk seasons' for physical activity in patients with anorexia nervosa? Tanja Hechler, Pierre Beumont, Reinhold Laessle, Guy Plasqui, Stephen Touyz, Klaas Westerterp.

Oral presentation at the International Conference on Behavioural Medicine, Mainz (Germany), August 2004.

Publication

Physical activity in anorexia nervosa: Which patterns do emerge across the seasons?

Tanja Hechler, Pierre Beumont, Reinhold Laessle, Guy Plasqui, Stephen Touyz, Klaas Westerterp.

Article to be submitted to the International Journal of Eating Disorders.

Abstract

Aims: The overall aim of this study was to investigate physical activity patterns in patients with anorexia nervosa (AN) and healthy controls across three seasons using a multidimensional approach. It was aimed to detect seasonal variation in physical activity (i.e., duration and body movement) and body composition and to explore the relationship between physical activity and body composition variables in the two groups.

Method: Physical activity of patients and controls was assessed during autumn (April, May), winter (July, August) and spring/summer (November, December). The sample size for autumn, winter and spring/summer was 28 (11 patients and 17 controls), 39 (17 patients and 22 controls) and 34 (14 patients and 20 controls) respectively. Activity-levels were quantified through the Seven-Day Physical Activity Recall (7-PAR in hrs/d) and objective monitoring (triaxial accelerometer in counts/min). Body composition was assessed using dual-energy X-ray absorptiometry (DEXA). Sinusoidal models were used to estimate the peak-to-trough amplitude and phase of the activity and body composition variables.

Results: Time spent in moderate intensity activity (MOD in hrs/d) showed a seasonal variation in patients (p=0.01) and a trend for a variation in controls (p=0.10), with a maximum in spring/summer and a minimum in winter. In the patient group, the number of patients engaging in strenuous activities (SA in hrs/d) in spring/summer was higher compared to controls. Body movement (in counts/min) tended to vary across the seasons in controls (p=0.10) with a maximum in autumn and a minimum in spring/summer. No seasonal variation emerged in patients and their body movement was significantly higher than that of controls ($F_{1,41}=5.5$, p=0.024). Body composition variables (i.e., body weight, percentage body fat (%BF), and FFM (in kg)) increased across the seasons in the patient group. In the control group, FFM varied across the season (p=0.01) with decreases during winter and increases during spring/summer. A trend for a significant negative correlation between body movement (i.e., high intensity body movement) and %BF emerged in the patient group only (r=-.29, p=0.08).

Conclusions: The fact that body movement was constantly increased and tended to negatively correlate with patients' %BF demonstrates the need to integrate physical activity as a standard component into the treatment of AN. Seasonality of physical activity (i.e., in moderate intensity activities and exercise) has to be recognised and implemented into treatment. That is, clinicians need to be aware of increases in patients' activity-levels particularly during spring/summer, probably triggered by increased obligatory attitudes towards exercise during winter. Energy costs of this increase in activity need to be determined to investigate impacts on body composition variables and if necessary, adapt energy requirements in this season.

1. Overview

Anorexia nervosa (AN) is today the third most common chronic condition in female adolescents and young women (World Health Organisation Collaborating Centre for Mental Health and Substance Abuse, 1997) (chapter 1.1.). Thus, any factor that maintains or worsens symptoms of the disorder has to be explored, so that its management can be integrated into treatment. Overactivity is such a factor and has recently been recognised as fundamental to the pathogenesis of AN (Beumont, Arthur, Russell, & Touyz, 1994; Davis, Katzman, & Kirsh, 1999; Katz, 1996; Thien, Thomas, Markin, & Birmingham, 2000) (chapter 1.2.). However, a clear definition of overactivity is still lacking. Chapter 1.3. therefore provides and overview of definition and assessment of physical activity in the general population. Chapter 1.4. summarises recent research into physical activity and AN, thereby examining different components of physical activity such as exercise, motivation and commitment to exercise and restlessness. In the context of physical activity in general and particularly, in patients with AN, an understanding of the impact of activity on body composition variables is essential. Chapter 1.5. provides basics on body composition such as assessment tools and chapter 1.6. summarises studies into physical activity and body composition in the general population and in patients with AN. As the review shows, physical activity impacts on body composition variables. To complicate things further, engagement in physical activities has been found to vary across the seasons with considerable seasonality (Uitenbroek, 1993) (chapter 1.7.). Seasonality (i.e., the degree to which seasonal changes affect factors such as mood, energy, sleep length, appetite, food preferences or social activities) has recently been investigated in the context of AN (chapter 1.7.3.). These studies demonstrated the importance to investigate and understand seasonal variation in AN and the potential impact of environmental factors (e.g., ambient temperature) on behaviours related to the dieting disorder. However, no study has investigated seasonal variation in components of physical activity in AN. The current study therefore aimed to scrutinize seasonal variation in physical activity in patients with AN and healthy controls (chapter 1.9. and 1.10.). Methods and results are presented (chapter 2. and 3.) and results are critically discussed, including methodological limitations and implications for future research (chapter 4.).

1.1. Clinical presentation of anorexia nervosa

Patients with AN adopt restricted eating patterns and excessive dieting and hence, AN is best described as a dieting rather than an eating disorder (Touyz & Beumont, 1999). The World Health Organisation (WHO) (1997) specifies three main characteristics: 1) deliberate loss of weight achieved by strict dieting and avoidance of food or other weight loss tactics such as excessive exercise, 2) excessive fear of obesity and weight gain and 3) associated physical dysfunctions (e.g., amenorrhea, hypothermia, osteoporosis). Further, psychological symptoms such as depression, loss of concentration, preoccupation with thoughts of food, anxiety and irritability are either caused directly by starvation or may be independent and/or premorbid. The current diagnostic criteria for AN defined by the American Psychiatric Association (DSM-IV, (American Psychiatric Association, 1994)) are displayed in table 1.

Table 1: Diagnostic criteria for AN

A.	Refusal to maintain body weight at or above a minimally normal weight for age and height (e.g., weight loss leading to maintenance of body weight less than 85% of that expected; or failure to make expected weight gain during period of growth, leading to body weight less than 85% of that expected).
B.	Intense fear of gaining weight or becoming fat, even though underweight.
C.	Disturbance in the way in which one's body weight or shape is experienced, undue influence of body weight or shape on self-evaluation, or denial of the seriousness of the current low body weight.
D.	Postmenarchal females, amenorrhea i.e., the absence of at least three consecutive menstrual cycles. (A woman is considered to have amenorrhea if her periods occur only following hormones, e.g., estrogen administration).
Specify type	
	Restricting type: during the current episode of anorexia nervosa, the person has not regularly engaged in binge-eating or purging behaviour (i.e., self-induced vomiting or the misuse of laxatives, diuretics, or enemas).
	Binge-Eating/ Purging type: during the current episode of anorexia nervosa, the person has regularly engaged in binge-eating or purging behaviour (i.e., self-induced vomiting or the misuse of laxatives, diuretics, or enemas).

Most frequently, female adolescents and young women develop the disorder (90 – 95% (World Health Organisation Collaborating Centre for Mental Health and Substance Abuse, 1997)) and AN is today the third most common chronic condition in adolescent girls and young women. Regarding its course and prognosis, approximately 70% of patients with AN return to the normal range of body weight within about six months of intervention and approximately 20% develop a chronic form of the illness (Beumont, Russell, & Touyz, 1993). Relapse rates of 15 to 25% are high. Studies indicate a mortality rate of almost 20% at a 20 year follow-up (World Health Organisation Collaborating Centre for Mental Health and Substance Abuse, 1997), suggesting that most patients who retain chronic preoccupations with weight and food experience serious physical morbidity.

1.2. Overactivity in patients with anorexia nervosa: The need for a clear definition

Historically, Gull (1874) and Lasègue (1964) commented on the high levels of physical activity of patients with AN as early as 1874. Until the 1980s however, research into physical activity and AN was lacking and the attitude prevailed that physical activity was an interesting but seemingly unimportant symptom in AN (Epling, Pierce, & Stefan, 1983). Yet, for a number of patients excessive exercising has been found to precede the dieting disorder (Davis, Fox, Cowles, Hastings, & Schwass, 1990; Davis, Kennedy, Ravelski, & Dionne, 1994; Kron, Katz, Gorzynski, & Weiner, 1978) and recovered patients have been found to still overexercise (Windauer, Lennerts, Talbot, Touyz, & Beumont, 1993). Accordingly, overactivity has recently been recognised as fundamental to the pathogenesis of AN (Beumont et al., 1994; Davis et al., 1999; Katz, 1996; Thien et al., 2000). Most anorexic patients present with overactivity and it is almost as characteristic as the dietary restriction and is equally difficult to modify (Birmingham & Beumont, 2004).

Although the phenomenon of overactivity (Birmingham & Beumont, 2004; Kron et al., 1978) has been recognised in patients with AN, and excessive exercise is mentioned as an additional weight loss strategy in the diagnostic criteria for AN (American Psychiatric Association, 1994; World Health Organisation Collaborating Centre for Mental Health and Substance Abuse, 1997), clinical consensus as to how to define overactivity is still lacking (Davis, Brewer, & Ratusny, 1993a; Herrin, 2003; Katz, 1996). Similarly, assessment of physical activity in patients with AN is less clear compared to that in obese patients and assessments are often only conducted at the beginning of treatment (Shelton & Klesges, 1995). Some researchers, such as Kron, Katz, Gorzynski, and Weiner (1978), have defined overactivity in terms of quantity of exercise. Recent definitions have followed this approach in specifying the amount, duration and type of exercise (Davis & Fox, 1993b). Birmingham and Beumont (2004) described two different components of physical activity in patients and were thus broadening the definition of overactivity. The two components were 1) deliberate exercise to burn calories (strenuous exercising, burning calories during daily activities or walking) and 2) restlessness with sleep disturbance. Davis, Brewer and Ratusny (1993a) added obsessionality to these components, highlighting the pathological and obligatory aspects of patients' attitude (e.g., continuing to exercise despite physical exhaustion). Beumont, Arthur, Russell and Touyz (1994) suggested the following subdivision of physical activity components: 1) excessive exercising, 2) restless

128

hyperactivity and 3) contrived activity (to maximise energy expenditure during daily activities).

In summary, overactivity is considered as fundamental to the pathogenesis of AN, although a clear definition is still lacking. A subdivision into different components of physical activity, such as overexercising, restlessness and commitment to exercise has been suggested by some. Hence, an overview of the construct of physical activity and its assessment in the general population may help to clarify what is meant by overactivity in AN.

1.3. Physical activity

1.3.1. Definition of physical activity and exercise

Physical activity is described as a complex phenomenon insofar as everyone performs physical activities in different contexts of daily life to varying degrees of intensity. It is generally defined as any bodily movement produced by skeletal muscles that results in energy expenditure (Caspersen, Powell, & Christenson, 1985). Assessment tools therefore often express physical activity in terms of energy expenditure. The focus on energy expenditure results from the fact that human beings obey the law of conversation of energy and must fuel all activity by extracting energy from food (Montoye, Kemper, Saris, & Washburn, 1996). However, due to its complexity, researchers have come up with various criteria to categorise physical activities apart from energy expenditure components. Table 2 lists some of these categorisations.

Table 2: Categorising the construct of physical activity

Name of criterion	Defined as	Categories of physical activity
Intensity (Blair, 1995; Levine, Eberhardt, & Jensen, 1999; Montoye, 2000; Montoye et al., 1996; Westerterp, 1999a)	Rate of energy expenditure (EE) a) Physical activity EE (PAEE)=0.9 – Total EE (TEE) – Sleeping EE (SEE) b) Physical activity level (PAL)=TEE/ Resting metabolic rate (RMR) c) nonexercise activity thermogenesis (NEAT) If level of exercise activities is constant over time, then NEAT=0.9*TEE – (RMR+PAL)	NEAT Light Moderate Vigorous
Volitional and nonexercise activities (Levine et al., 1999)	Volitional exercise (sport and fitness-related activities) Nonexercise activities (of daily living, fidgeting, spontaneous muscle contractions)	Volitional exercise Nonexercise activities
Duration (Caspersen et al., 1985; Montoye et al., 1996)	Time spent in an activity - Hours per day - Minutes per day -	
Frequency (Bassett, 2000; Montoye et al., 1996)	Times per week or year the participant engaged in an activity	
Domains (Booth, 2000; Sallis, 1997)	Domains or contexts, in which the activity takes place	Leisure time Gardening or yard work Household Transport or moving Occupational
Circumstances and motivation (Montoye et al., 1996; Ryan, 1998)	Physical activity as an intentional behaviour, in which people engage because of various motivations such as intrinsic motivation (enjoyment) or extrinsic motivation (improve physical appearance).	Intrinsic motivation (enjoyment, competence) Extrinsic motivation (appearance)
Static and dynamic (Westerterp, 1999a)	Static activities such as weight-lifting Dynamic activities such as body movement (walking)	Static Dynamic
Strength and flexibility (Prochaska, Sallis, Sarkin, & Calfas, 2000; Sallis, 1997)	Strength activities such as pushups, pull-ups Flexibility activities such as stretching, Yoga	Strength Flexibility

Physical activity does not equal exercise or vice versa. Exercise is a subcategory of physical activity, which results in energy expenditure; the more vigorous the activity, the higher the expenditure. Exercise is often performed during leisure-time, conducted several times per week or year for a specified duration of time. People who exercise do so because of varying motivations, for example the motivation to lose weight or to cope with stress. Exercise is further planned, structured and repetitive (Caspersen et al., 1985).

Understanding of the various components of physical activity, particularly the differentiation between exercise and physical activity, is essential when determining relationships between different aspects of physical activity and health measures such as body composition (Ekelund et al., 2001). This is particularly important in the context of AN.

1.3.2. Assessment of physical activity

Physical activity is a multidimensional construct (Bassett, 2000) consisting of energy expenditure, temporal information, type of activity and qualitative aspects such as motivation. Therefore, a multimethod approach of assessment is usually recommended when assessing physical activity under free-living conditions (Shelton & Klesges, 1995). Various measures of physical activity have been developed and are subdivided into the following categories in order of expense, difficulty and intrusiveness (Booth, Owen, Baumann, & Gore, 1995):

1. Calorimetry: estimates of physical activity energy expenditure (PAEE) through the doubly labelled water method or direct/ indirect calorimetry

2. Physiological markers that correlate with physical activity such as heart rate monitoring or assessment of body composition

3. Behavioural observation

4. Mechanical or electronic motion sensors such as pedometers or accelerometers

5. Dietary measures: if body weight remains stable, energy expenditure will be equal to energy intake. Thus, by measuring weight and energy intake, energy expenditure can be estimated.

6. Self-report measures such as interviews, questionnaires or surveys.

None of the available measures comprehensively satisfies the criteria of a 'good' measurement such as being valid, reliable, sensitive to change, non-reactive and acceptable to the respondent and administrator (Booth et al., 1995). However, two types of measures are recommended for use in clinical and epidemiological studies, namely motion sensors and self-report measures (Blair, 1995). As a complete review of physical activity assessment methods is beyond the scope of this chapter (for reviews see (Booth et al., 1995; Freedson & Miller, 2000; Montoye et al., 1996; Sallis & Saelens, 2000)), only these two types of measurement will be briefly presented in terms of a) description, b) components of physical activity that are assessed, c) examples, and d) advantages and limitations.

1.3.2.1. Self-report measures

a) Description: Self-report measures are self-administered or interview-administered recall methods, which require participants to recall their activities over a particular period of time. Formats include questionnaires, activity logs or diaries, and proxy reports (typically used to assess young children) (Sallis & Saelens, 2000).

b) Components of physical activity: Dependent on the recall method used, temporal information such as frequency and time spent in various intensities of activity (duration) are assessed. Further, energy expenditure can be estimated with the use of metabolic equivalent units (MET= ratio of energy expended in kilojoules divided by resting metabolic rate (RMR)). Energy expenditure rates are obtained by classifying the activity by its MET-value and multiplying this by the time spent in the activity and by body weight (for details see (Sallis, 1997)). Also, self-report measures usually cover activities from different domains of daily life such as leisure-time, household and occupational activities.

c) Examples: An example of a reliable and validated (against the doubly labelled water method) self-report measure is the Seven-Day Physical Activity Recall (7-PAR; see (Sallis, 1997) for details).

d) Advantages and limitations:

The advantages of self-report measures include the fact that they are inexpensive, feasible for large populations, non-reactive, allow for the possibility of assessing various components of physical activity, and are generally acceptable to both the respondent and administrator (Montoye et al., 1996; Sallis & Saelens, 2000).

Limitations of self-report measures (Montoye et al., 1996; Sallis & Saelens, 2000) are the social desirability bias, which may lead to over- (or under-) reporting of physical activities, the high complexity of recalling physical activities (see (Baranowski, 1988)), inaccuracies arising from different understandings of physical activity and exercise between the administrator and respondent, and the fact that energy expenditure is estimated through METs.

1.3.2.2. Motion sensors: Triaxial accelerometers

a) Description: Motion sensors are mechanical or electronic devices that detect acceleration of a limb or the trunk, depending on where they are attached to the body (Freedson & Miller, 2000). The rationale for the use of motion sensors lies in the definition of physical activity in terms of body movement, hence the dynamic property of physical activity (see table 2). All body movement entails accelerations and decelerations, and acceleration is assumed to be directly proportional to the muscular forces and therefore is related to energy expenditure (Freedson & Miller, 2000; Meijer, Westerterp, Verhoeven, Koper, & ten Hoor, 1991). There are different types of motion sensors ranging in complexity and cost from pedometers to uniaxial and triaxial accelerometers. Uniaxial accelerometers assess acceleration in one plane (usually vertical) whereas triaxial accelerometers measure acceleration in three different planes: vertical, horizontal and mediolateral. Results are still inconsistent as to which of the two monitors assesses physical activity more accurately (Freedson & Miller, 2000; Leenders, Sherman, Nagaraja, & Kien, 2001). However it seems reasonable that a three-dimensional monitor would be more accurate in capturing a greater proportion of free-living activity than a single-plane monitor. The focus here will therefore be on triaxial accelerometers.

b) Components of physical activity: Triaxial accelerometers primarily capture the body movement component of physical activity, usually measured in counts in each plane and a vector magnitude over a specified time period (Freedson & Miller, 2000). Some triaxial accelerometers are able to estimate total and physical activity energy expenditure in kcal, using a predicted equation to

134

estimate RMR incorporating age, stature, body mass and gender as independent variables (e.g., the TriTrac). It is however, recommended that the output be analysed as counts of body movement since there may be significant errors with the prediction of point estimates of energy expenditure (Freedson & Miller, 2000; Leenders et al., 2001).

c) Examples: Motion sensors are a relatively new measure of physical activity, with the first descriptions of measuring acceleration emerging in the early 1970s (Meijer et al., 1991). Hence, only two triaxial accelerometers have been developed so far –TriTrac (Hermokinetics, Inc.Madison. WI) and Tracmor (Philips Research, Eindhoven, the Netherlands) - and only one of them – the TriTrac – is commercially available.

d) Advantages and limitations:

The use of triaxial accelerometers enables objective measurement of physical activity that is unobtrusive due to their small sizes. Further, the costs are in a feasible range and temporal information and estimates of energy expenditure can be obtained (in TriTrac) (Freedson & Miller, 2000; Montoye et al., 1996) under free-living conditions.

Limitations of accelerometers emerge due to the fact that not all of the energy is reflected in acceleration or deceleration of the body mass (for example carrying a backpack or weights; (Montoye et al., 1996)). Further, in validation studies against the doubly labelled water method, the triaxial accelerometer (TriTrac) underestimated energy expenditure (Leenders et al., 2001).

1.3.2.3. Conclusion regarding assessment of physical activity

To assess physical activity, a multimethod approach is needed. In clinical studies, the use of self-report measures and motion sensors has been recommended (Blair, 1995). Accordingly, subjective and objective data can be collected. The combination of the two methods helps overcome some of the limitations of each of the methods allows for both subjective and objective data to be collected. For example, the collection of objective data can prevent social-desirability biases. Data from the accelerometer should be registered as body movement rather than energy expenditure. As Bassett (2000) pointed out, *"it is desirable to have information on all dimensions of physical activity, rather than simply a global measure of energy expenditure"* (p. 31). Therefore assessing physical activity with a self-report measure such as the 7-PAR and use of a triaxial accelerometer does not provide valid estimates of energy expenditure, but enables the researcher to obtain comprehensive and reliable information on the patterns of physical activity under free-living conditions.

1.4. Physical activity in patients with anorexia nervosa

The following chapter reviews studies into different components of physical activity in patients with AN. The components selected were exercising (i.e., overexercising, motivation for physical activity and commitment to exercise) and restlessness.

1.4.1. Exercise in patients with anorexia nervosa

Even though Gull (1874) commented on patients' physical activity, observations of increased exercise behaviour in patients with AN were not published until the 1970s. Concurrent with the increasing cultural interest in distance running (Yates, Leehey, & Shisslak, 1983), studies into overexercising in patients with AN emerged (Kron et al., 1978; Touyz, Beumont, & Hook, 1987; Yates et al., 1983). For example, Kron et al (1978) investigated the frequency of exercisers in 33 patients with AN and showed that 25 patients could be classified as hyperactive (i.e., patients manifested a day-to-day level of physical activity that was greater than that of most of their peers and involved some form of strenuous daily exertion).

Davis et al. (1997) conducted a study into the exercising history of patients with AN and bulimia nervosa (BN) during and prior to the onset of their disorder. They found that a majority of patients with AN (81%, 63 out of 78) were exercising excessively during an acute phase of the disorder. Further, significantly more patients with AN were involved in sports and exercise rather than dieting prior to the onset of the disorder (56% and 35%, respectively).

The frequency and intensity of exercise behaviour in some of the patients (for case reports see (Beumont et al., 1994; Touyz et al., 1987)), particularly commitment to the activity of exercise, shows similarities to the phenomenon of exercise dependence defined by De Coverley Veale (1987). The criteria for exercise dependence are displayed in table 3.

Table 3: Criteria of exercise dependence

A	Narrowing of repertoire leading to a stereotyped pattern of exercise with a regular schedule once or more daily
B	Salience with the individual giving increased priority over other activities to maintaining the pattern of exercise
C	Increased tolerance to the amount of exercise performed over the years
D	Withdrawal symptoms related to a disorder of mood following the cessation of exercise schedule
E	Relief or avoidance of withdrawal symptoms by further exercise
F	Subjective awareness of a compulsion to exercise
G	Rapid reinstatement of the previous pattern of exercise and withdrawal symptoms after a period of abstinence

Exercise in patients with AN has therefore been investigated in terms of the quantity of exercising (Davis & Fox, 1993b; Kron et al., 1978; Touyz et al., 1987) and in terms of a qualitative aspect: the commitment to exercise (Davis & Fox, 1993b; McLaren, Gauvin, & White, 2001; Mond, Hay, Rodgers, Owen, & Beumont, 2004).

1.4.1.1. Overexercising in patients with anorexia nervosa

Several suggestions for a definition of overexercising in patients with AN have been proposed (e.g., (Davis & Fox, 1993b; Kron et al., 1978)). Davis and Fox (1993b) for example, defined excessive exercising or overexercising as exercising at least six times a week for at least one hour per session in one of the following activities: swimming, bicycling, running, skating, home exercises, dance classes, aerobic or weight training. Several studies have investigated the frequency of overexercisers in patients with AN, with a review of these studies reporting prevalence estimates ranging from 33% to 100% (Katz, 1996). The large range in the frequency estimates of overexercisers results from different patient groups that were investigated and different definitions of overexercising. A clear definition of overexercising in terms of the quantity of exercising, such as the one suggested by Davis and Fox (1993b) is in line with the definition of exercise in the general population and can be assessed using self-reports or objective monitoring. Since excessive exercising has deleterious effects for patients with AN (see detailed review in part 3, chapter 1.2.), agreement on what is meant by overactivity in terms of exercising and how it is assessed is crucial.

1.4.1.2. Motivation for physical activity and commitment to exercise in patients with anorexia nervosa

Motives for physical activity are subdivided into intrinsic or extrinsic motives according to their focus (Ryan, 1998) (see table 2). Behaviours that are performed for the satisfaction one gains from engaging in the activity itself (e.g., desire to have fun) are classified as intrinsic motives. Behaviours that are performed in order to obtain rewards that are separate from the behaviour itself (e.g., desire to improve physical appearance) are classified as extrinsic motives. Frederick (1994) investigated relationship between motives for physical activity and the type of activity in a group of 376 adults (241 females, 134 males, one participant sex unknown) with a mean age of 39. They found that motives for physical activity differed systematically as a function of activity type. Specifically, fitness activities (i.e., running, weight lifting, Yoga) were associated with higher levels of appearance-related motivation. Further, they found that a focus upon external attributes such as appearance was associated with anxiety and depression.

Likewise, Mond, Hay, Rodgers and Beumont (2004) conducted a study with the aim of identifying those aspects of exercise behaviour that were most closely associated with dieting disorders. They found that among other factors the extrinsic motivation for exercise was a predictor of dieting disorder psychopathology in a community sample of 232 women aged 18 to 45 years.

Commitment to exercise describes the cognitive or psychological aspect of exercise (McLaren et al., 2001) and relates to criteria F of exercise dependence (De Coverley Veale, 1987) (see table 3), the subjective awareness of a compulsion to exercise. For patients with AN, Davis et al. (1993a) defined commitment to exercise as the degree to which feelings of well-being are influenced by exercising, the degree to which adherence to exercise is maintained in the face of various adverse conditions and the extent to which one's exercise regimen interferes with social commitments. Patients describe feeling an increasingly strong compulsion to be physically active even when they no longer enjoy it – indeed even when the process becomes painful and exhausting (Davis et al., 1999). All pleasurable and recreational activities are sacrificed to maintain the exercise regimen. Davis et al. (1997) demonstrated that patients who were classified as excessive exercisers (n=91) reported more obligatory and pathological attitudes to the activity of exercise than moderately active patients.

The commitment to exercise has been investigated regarding the relationship between physical activity and dieting disorder psychopathology (Mond et al., 2004). Specifically, items of the Commitment to Exercise Scale (CES; (Davis et al., 1993a)) (such as 'feeling guilty after missing an exercise session') were significantly associated with both dieting disorder pathology and poorer quality of life (Mond et al., 2004).

Further, Strober, Freeman and Morrell (1997) demonstrated that a compulsive drive to exercise at the time of discharge had a substantial effect on earlier time to relapse.

In summary, excessive exercise in patients with AN is not only defined as an increased frequency of exercising in a specified period of time but also in terms of various psychological aspects, namely an extrinsic motivation for physical activity and the commitment to exercise characterised by pathological and obligatory attitudes towards

140

the activity of exercise. Since studies have demonstrated deleterious effects of extrinsic motivation and the commitment to exercise (see part 3, chapter 1.2.3.1.), assessment of physical activity in AN should include these psychological aspects.

1.4.2. Restlessness in patients with anorexia nervosa

Restlessness is best defined as nonexercise activity as suggested by Levine, Eberhardt and Jensen (1999). They divided physical activity thermogenesis into volitional exercise (sports and fitness-related activities) and nonexercise activity thermogenesis (NEAT; see table 2). NEAT is the thermogenesis that accompanies physical activities such as fidgeting, spontaneous muscle contraction, and maintaining posture when not recumbent.

The phenomenon of restless hyperactivity in patients with AN is considered the most striking form of physical activity. Beumont et al. (1994) described it as follows: *the patient finds it difficult to keep still even for a short period, and becomes noticeably distressed if constrained to do so* (p.27). Even when weight decreases to the extent that exercising cannot be continued, restless hyperactivity is still present (Beumont et al., 1994). Katz (1996) described the phenomenon similarly, adding that the diffuse restlessness is almost invariably associated with progressive insomnia.

Nonexercise activities or fidgeting behaviour have been observed in clinical studies (Beumont et al., 1994; Davis et al., 1999), and the phenomenon of activity-based anorexia (ABA) (Epling & Pierce, 1996), where animals increase their activity (e.g., wheel-running) despite a reduction in food intake and body weight (for details see part 3, chapter 1.4.3.), has been applied to the understanding of restlessness in patients with AN.

However, the assessment of restlessness in patients with AN has proven to be difficult. As pointed out by Levine et al. (1999), nonexercise activities are non-volitional and therefore difficult to assess with self-report measures. The doubly labelled water method constitutes the gold-standard to assess the NEAT, but the cost of ^{18}O is considerable (Montoye et al., 1996). Also, analysis of samples is expensive and total energy expenditure over a specified time period is measured, such that no information is obtained on the pattern of physical activity (Bassett, 2000).

Even though studies into energy expenditure of patients with AN (Frey et al., 2000; Pirke, Trimborn, Platte, & Fichter, 1991; Platte et al., 1994) have acknowledged the role of NEAT and its potential impacts on resistance to weight gain, only two studies have explicitly dealt with nonexercise activities in AN. Bouten, van Marken Lichtenbelt and Westerterp (1996) used the doubly labelled water method and accelerometry in a patient (n=11) and an age-matched and gender-matched control group (n=13). They did not find differences in activity-levels monitored with the Tracmor and daily physical activity level (PAL) between the groups. But they found a relationship between AN patients' activity and BMI: the lower the BMI (<17.5) the more time patients spent in low level daily activity (defined as <900 counts*min $^{-1}$; PAL<1.60; activities such as standing, lying), while the higher the BMI (>17.5), the more time patients spent in high level daily activity (defined as >1150 counts * min $^{-1}$; PAL>1.85).

Exner et al. (2000) assessed the subjective experience of motor restlessness in 30 patients with AN (26 females, 4 males). They examined the relationship between experienced motor restlessness and leptin levels in AN. Leptin is a hormone mainly synthesised in adipocytes from where it is secreted in the blood stream. Serum levels of leptin correlate with BMI and even more so with the percentage body fat (%BF).

Accordingly, during the acute stage of AN when patients are at their lowest weight, leptin levels decrease and are below the reference range of age-matched and younger BMI-matched controls (for a review see (Hebebrand et al., 2003)). During therapeutically induced weight gain, leptin levels increase and in some cases even surpass the reference range. Exner et al. (2000) assessed motor restlessness at three time points: 1) at admission in the emaciated state, 2) after serum leptin levels for the first time surpassed the 25th percentile of a gender-dependent reference range formed by healthy controls matched for BMI and 3) upon attainment of maximum leptin levels measured during inpatient treatment. Utilising self-reports of the patients, they found that patients experienced less motor restlessness with increases in leptin levels.

In summary, restlessness in patients with AN has been frequently observed in the clinical context and is considered the most striking component of physical activity. Yet despite its importance, empirical investigations of restlessness in AN are lacking. However, studies in the general population that linked NEAT with resistance to weight gain demonstrate the need to understand nonexercise activities in patients with AN and its potential impact on resistance to weight gain.

1.4.3. Summary on physical activity in patients with AN

Few studies have investigated various aspects of physical activity in patients with AN. It can be expected that a study in patients with AN comprising assessment of exercise, motivation for physical activity, commitment to exercise, restlessness and time spent in various intensities of physical activity will find higher levels of exercising in the patient group compared to healthy participants. It can further be predicted that patients will demonstrate more extrinsic motivation for engaging in physical activities (i.e., engaging in activities with the intention to improve physical appearance). Commitment to exercise will be higher in patients than in healthy participants, hence, patients will display attitudes such as continuing to exercise in the face of an illness. They will also experience more restlessness, such as fidgeting and the inability to sit still. No study has investigated patients' time spent in moderate intensity activities. Moderate intensity activities are defined as similar to how the participant feels when walking at a normal pace (Sallis, 1997). From the current literature, it can be concluded that patients rather increase exercise behaviour and fidgeting movements than their time spent in moderate intensity activities. Therefore no differences between patients and healthy participants would be expected.

1.5. Physical activity and body composition

Physical activity can be assessed using direct measures such as self-reports and motion sensors or indirect measures such as body composition which are highly correlated with physical activity (Shelton & Klesges, 1995). The relationship between physical activity and body composition has been extensively investigated in the context of obesity prevention, since numerous beneficial effects of regular engagement in physical activity, particularly exercise, have been demonstrated (for a review see (Tremblay, Doucet, & Imbeault, 1999)). In patients with AN, refusal to maintain body weight at or above a minimally normal weight for age and height is one of the diagnostic criteria in the DSM-IV (American Psychiatric Association, 1994) (see table 1). Weight restoration is one of the most important goals in treatment (Probst, Goris, Vandereycken, & Van Coppenolle, 2001). Hence, several studies have investigated body composition and body composition changes in patients with AN (Birmingham et al., 1996; Frey et al.,

2000; Orphanidou, McCargar, Birmingham, & Belzberg, 1997; Polito, Cuzzolaro, Raguzzini, Censi, & Ferro-Luzzi, 1998; Probst, Goris, Vandereycken, & Van Coppenolle, 1996).

Here, the focus is on physical activity and its impact on body composition. Some studies have investigated this relationship in patients with AN and are reviewed in chapter 1.6.2.. However, the relationship between physical activity and body composition in patients with AN can only be understood, if the construct of body composition is clearly defined.

1.5.1. Definition and assessment of body composition

It is important to distinguish between body weight and body composition. While body weight is simply the mass of the body, obtained by weighing a person on a scale (Wilmore, 1995), body composition represents the net result of metabolic processes and the contribution of ingested nutrients (Heymsfield, Allison, Heshka, & Pierson, 1995). The human body can be divided into multiple components and these components can be organised into five levels of increasing complexity. These levels are the atomic level, molecular, cell-level, tissue level and whole-body level (for details see (Ellis, 2000; Heymsfield et al., 1995)). Most research is currently based on methods designed to evaluate molecular-level components. One of the most important models of the molecular level is the two-compartment model, that divides body weight into the sum of fat and fat-free body mass. Fat-free mass (FFM) thereby constitutes of the remaining components, i.e., water, protein, and various minerals (Ellis, 2000; Heymsfield et al., 1995).

Regarding the methods of estimating fatness, no direct methods exist that evaluate components such as total body fat in vivo (Heymsfield et al., 1995). All body composition methods are therefore indirect and are based on measurement of various properties such as body density. Two methods –assessment of body mass index and dual energy X-ray absorptiometry (DEXA) - will be presented in terms of a) description, b) components of body composition assessed and c) advantages and limitations.

1.5.1.1. Body mass index

a) Description: For computing one of the most widely used weight-stature index (Quetelet's body mass index (BMI)), body weight is assessed in kilograms (kg) using weighing scales, preferably a beam balance which is calibrated in kilograms and tenth of kilograms. Height is assessed in meters (m) using stadiometers. BMI is then computed as BMI=kg/m².

b) Components of body composition: BMI provides estimates of body mass that are independent of stature (Heymsfield et al., 1995).

c) Advantages and limitations:

Assessment of body weight and height is safe and easy to perform. In addition, Heymsfield et al. (1995) reported reliability coefficients for weight and height assessment approximating 1.0.

Body weight reflects the body mass, but it does not provide information on different components of body composition. Regarding the BMI, it has been found to correlate well with other measures of fatness but had weak discriminant validity (Heymsfield et al., 1995). Further, in anorexic patients, Birmingham,

146

Muller and Goldner (1998) listed several problems with weight assessment: weight was confounded by fluid loading, constipation, surreptitious weights that the patient might insert in clothing, heavy clothing and fluid shifts secondary to vomiting, diuretic and laxative abuse and renutrition.

1.5.1.2. Dual energy X-ray absorptiometry

a) Description: At the molecular level, DEXA is generally considered as one of the most accurate techniques for estimating the fat component of body composition in healthy individuals (Heymsfield et al., 1995) as well as in anorexic patients (Orphanidou et al., 1997). DEXA relies on the differential X-ray attenuation of tissues to provide estimates of bone mineral and fat. DEXA-systems emit X-rays at two different energies. As the X-rays pass through tissues, they are attenuated in relation to the specific tissue's mass attenuation coefficient. The soft tissues differ in their attenuation of X-rays due to variation in elemental composition. These soft tissue differences in X-ray attenuation at the two energies allow further resolution of soft tissues into fat and fat-free soft tissues.

b) Components of body composition: Most DEXA systems allow for whole-body or regional estimates of fat, fat-free soft tissue, and bone mineral mass and density (Heymsfield et al., 1995).

c) Advantages and limitations:

    Reliability of DEXA is generally excellent (0.97-0.99) (Heymsfield et al., 1995). In validity studies, DEXA compared favourably with fat estimates from neuron activation analysis, underwater weighing, and total body water assessment (Heymsfield et al., 1995). Orphanidou et al. (1997) concluded from their

147

findings in anorexic patients that DEXA appeared to be a valid measurement for defining body composition changes in re-fed AN patients.

However, DEXA estimates are thickness dependent, with systematic errors appearing in fat estimates and the costs for a DEXA system are high.

1.5.1.4. Conclusions regarding assessment of body composition

In the context of physical activity and AN, body composition needs to be assessed accurately, and assessment of both %BF and FFM are needed to analyse impacts of physical activity. BMI therefore does not seem to be an adequate measure of body composition, whereas DEXA appears to be a useful tool.

1.6. Review of the relationship between physical activity and body composition in patients with AN

Understanding the relationship between physical activity and body composition variables in AN is essential for the treatment of the disorder. In the general population, studies have investigated this relationship, particularly in the context of obesity prevention. Three reviews and one study into NEAT are presented. These results form a useful frame for investigating the relationship in AN.

1.6.1. Relationship between physical activity and body composition in the general population

The relationship between physical activity and body composition has been investigated extensively in the context of obesity prevention. The assumption prevails that a continuous engagement in physical activity will impact favourably on body composition variables. Recent research suggests that the goal of obesity reduction programmes should be to maximise fat loss and reduce loss in FFM (Ballor & Poehlman, 1994). There are definite advantages of the conservation of FFM: FFM is highly related to daily energy expenditure and is an important determinant of daily energy needs. Further, FFM is related to the ability to perform daily activities requiring strength and/or muscular endurance (Ballor & Poehlman, 1994).

In their meta-analysis, Ballor and Poehlman (1994) included 46 studies and aimed to determine how various factors (i.e., exercise training, gender and physical characteristics) influence the composition of diet-induced weight loss. They found that in both males and females, body weight, fat mass and % BF lost did not differ between participants of interventions using dietary restriction only and those including exercise training together with dietary restriction. Exercise training did reduce the amount of FFM lost. Hence, they concluded that exercise training and dietary restriction result in a greater conservation of FFM, while body weight, fat mass and %BF were reduced similarly in dietary intervention and dietary and exercise intervention combined.

Garrow and Summerbell (1995) included 28 publications in their meta-analysis and aimed to determine if physical training conserved FFM in overweight men and women during weight loss. They found that aerobic exercise alone caused a weight reduction of 3kg in 30 weeks in men and 1.4kg in 12 weeks in women, with little effect on FFM.

Resistance exercise had little effect on weight loss but increased FFM about 2kg and 1kg in men and women, respectively. When weight loss of 10kg is achieved by diet and exercise combined the expected loss of FFM is less, than weight loss achieved by diet alone in both males and females. They concluded that exercise, in particular resistance training, increases FFM in participants on an adequate diet.

Westerterp and Goran (1997b) analysed 22 different data sets including average daily metabolic rate (ADMR), basal metabolic rate (BMR), age and body fatness to examine the relationship between physical activity and body fatness, correcting for age. Physical activity was quantified by adjustment of ADMR for BMR (PAL=ADMR/BMR). In a regression analysis, age explained three to seven percent and five to 20% of the variation in % BF in females and males, respectively. Adding PAL to the model raised the explained variation in %BF in males but not in females. They concluded that exercise is not an effective modality to reduce body fat in females unless accompanied by restriction of energy intake.

Levine and Jensen (1999) investigated the thermogenic adaptation to resist weight gain despite overeating in 16 nonobese adults (12 males, 4 females, aged 25-36 years). They underwent measures of body composition (DEXA) and energy expenditure (doubly labelled water method) before and after eight weeks of supervised overfeeding by 1000 kcal/day. The level of exercise activities was kept constant over time and nonexercise activity thermogenesis (NEAT) was thus calculated by subtracting BMR from TEE. They demonstrated that NEAT proved to be the principal mediator of resistance to fat gain with overfeeding. The average increase in NEAT over the eight weeks accounted for two-thirds of the increase in daily energy expenditure.

In summary, the studies differed in their focus. While Ballor and Poehlman (1994) and Garrow and Summerbell (1995) aimed to determine how factors such as exercising influence body composition following diet-induced weight loss, Westerterp and Goran (1997b) aimed to predict variation in %BF with age and PAL. Finally, Levine and Jensen (1999) focussed on the impact of NEAT on the resistance to gaining fat during overfeeding. Despite these differences, the following conclusions can be drawn regarding the relationship between physical activity and body composition: Physical activity impacts on body composition variables in both males and females. It appears that exercise training (particularly resistance training) and an adequate diet combine to impact favourably on body composition (i.e., a reduction in fat mass and a conservation of FFM). Physical activity (i.e., PAL) did not predict %BF in females as shown by Westerterp and Goran (1997b). They pointed out that females and males differ in body fat distribution in that males tend to have more abdominal fat and abdominal fat has been shown to be more responsive to exercise interventions. Hence, gender differences in terms of the impact of physical activity on body composition variables (in particular %BF) can be expected. It further appears that not only exercise activities but also nonexercise activities such as standing, walking and fidgeting impact on energy expenditure and on body composition variables.

1.6.2. Relationship between physical activity and body composition in patients with AN

Clinical descriptions of AN patients' activity patterns have suggested that activity develops from being organised, planned and structured at the beginning (see chapter 1.4.2.) to becoming more intensified, driven and titrated against caloric intake over the course of the dieting disorder (Beumont et al., 1994). With further weight loss, patients tend to experience a diffuse restlessness where they experience progressive insomnia (Katz, 1996) and are unable to sit still. Accordingly, in AN where weight loss is prominent it is assumed that the loss in body composition variables triggers increased physical activity in terms of restlessness (Casper, 1998).

This relationship has been observed in animals, and the paradigm of activity-based anorexia (ABA) (Epling & Pierce, 1996) has evoked extrapolation from findings in animals to human AN (for a review on animal models in the context of AN see (Beumont, 1984)). Routtenberg and Kuznesof (1967) first described the paradoxical finding that rats whose food intake was restricted, increased wheel-running and in fact, continued to increase wheel-running despite a further decrease in food intake, resulting in death. A number of studies have replicated this finding (for reviews see (Hebebrand et al., 2003; Sherwin, 1998)).

In AN patients, studies into energy expenditure (Frey et al., 2000; Pirke et al., 1991; Platte et al., 1994) found no significant differences in total energy expenditure between emaciated patients and controls, and the authors discussed the role of physical activity energy expenditure, particularly nonexercise activity thermogenesis.

It remains unknown as to how much loss of body weight or %BF must occur to trigger increased restlessness in patients with AN. There is a dearth of research investigating this relationship using sophisticated methods to assess physical activity and body composition. Only three studies aimed to investigate the relationship in AN patients (Bouten, van Marken Lichtenbelt, & Westerterp, 1996; Exner et al., 2000; Falk, Halmi, & Tryon, 1985). Falk, Halmi and Tyron (1985) assessed 20 hospitalised female patients using actometers (wristwatch) placed at patients' wrists and ankles. They found a

152

positive relationship between percentage of target weight and average wrist activity (r=.81, p<0.01) and between percentage target weight and average ankle activity (r=.76, p<0.01).

In contrast, Bouten et al (1996) used the doubly labelled water method and accelerometry for the assessment of physical activity. They found a relationship between AN patients' activity and BMI: the lower the BMI the more time patients spent in low level daily activity, while the higher the BMI (>17.5), the more time patients spent in high level daily activity (for details see chapter 1.4.2.). No such relationship emerged in the control group.

Exner et al. (2000) (see also chapter 1.4.2.) assessed the subjective experience of motor restlessness in 30 patients with AN (26 females, 4 males) and demonstrated decreased experienced motor restlessness over the course of treatment. They did not provide data on body composition variables. Since leptin levels correlate with BMI and %BF, it can be assumed that these variables increased in the patients over the course of the assessment. Hence, their results on motor restlessness hint at a negative correlation between motor restlessness and body composition variables (i.e., the lower the body composition, the more motor restlessness).

1.6.3. Summary on the relationship between physical activity and body composition in patients with AN

In summary, clinical observations, results from animal studies, results from Bouten et al (1996) and Exner et al. (2000) suggest a negative correlation between restless hyperactivity and body composition variables in patients with AN, while Falk et al. (1985) suggested a positive relationship. To further clarify the relationship, more studies are needed incorporating a longitudinal design as well as sophisticated assessment tools for both physical activity (including various components) and body composition.

1.7. Seasonal variation in physical activity

Apart from being a multidimensional construct with impacts on body composition, physical activity has been found to vary considerably across the seasons in studies with healthy participants. Research into seasonal variation in physical activity emerged in the context of obesity prevention and the prevention of cardiovascular heart disease. Since consistent participation in physical activity appears to be required for optimal health, seasonal variation in physical activity needed to be identified and addressed in intervention and health promotion efforts designed to increase activity-levels in the general population (Matthews et al., 2001a).

1.7.1. Studies into seasonality in physical activity

Studies into seasonality of physical activity in the general population have been primarily conducted in the Northern Hemisphere and have implemented various study designs (cross-sectional surveys and longitudinal designs) and measures of physical activity. To illustrate the different designs and methods, eight studies investigating seasonality in physical activity are summarised. Table 4 provides an overview of the studies. Each entry includes citation of the study, geographical location, type of study, information on participants, assessment of physical activity, statistics used and results.

Table 4: Eight studies into seasonality in physical activity

	Type of study	Participants	Physical activity assessment	Statistics	Results
(Zahorska-Markiewicz & Markiewicz, 1984) Poland	Longitudinal study Assessment once per month over a one-year period	N=18 (21-30 years) F=9 M=9	Exercise metabolic rate (EMR) when cycling on a cyclic ergometer (60W) with indirect calorimetry	Paired t-tests between all possible pairs of months Single cosinor-method, in which 360°= 1 year	Circannual rhythm for EMR Low EMR during exercise in summer
(Dannenberg, Keller, Wilson, & Castelli, 1989) Massach., U.S.A.	Cross-sectional survey Framingham Offspring Cycle 2	N=3360 (20-69 years) F=1762 M=1598	Self-report Time spent in specific activities Estimates of MET Physical activity index (including occupational)	Analyses of seasonal variation were based on the month in which the participants were administered the questionnaire; no further specification	Based on weekly activity reports, both men and women tended to be more active in summer than in winter; difference between the seasons emerged for a) number of activities b) time spent in activities c) METs
(Uitenbroek, 1993) Scotland	Cross-sectional survey	N=16486 (18-60 years) F=9284 M=7202	Self-report Engagement in exercise Number of times they exercised for at least 20min 2 groups according to exercise (yes/no) and according to amount of exercise	Cosinor analysis: in a regression analysis a sinoid seasonal term was fitted to the data	Peak for those who reported exercising at least once a week occurred around mid-July; for those who exercised more a week earlier Seasonality was statistical significant with an amplitude of 9.2. Seasonal variation in activities like walking and swimming but not in jogging/running and keep-fit exercise.
(U.S.Department of Health and Human Services, 1997) United States 50 states	Cross-sectional survey	N=105,853 (18+ years)	Self-report Participation in exercise or activities other than regular job duties Classification into active/inactive	Monthly variation in prevalence of inactivity	High prevalence rates of inactivity during the winter months
(Levin, Jacobs, Ainsworth, Richardson, & Leon, 1999) Columbia,	Longitudinal study 14 clinic visits spaced 26 days apart SAFE study	N=77 (21-59 years) F=28 M=49	Self-report Four-Week History Physical Activity Survey (FWJ) Physical Activity Recall (PAR; two	Month of the year as fixed effect; coefficients were used to estimate seasonal patterns in	Higher levels of physical activity were reported in the warmer months (FWH; PAR; Caltrac) for the group mean Adding month of the year to the model (mixed model) reduced the intra-individual

155

U.S.A.			weeks) Accelerometry Caltrac	these mean levels and to note changes in intra- individual variance by accounting for month	variance by 7.0% for FWH, 4.2% for PAR and 5.2% for Caltrac
(Matthews et al., 2001a) Massach., U.S.A.	Longitudinal study Five assessments during 12-month period	N=580 (mean age 48) F=280 M=300	Self-report 24-hour recall (household, occupational, leisure time; MET) For subsample: accelerometry Actillume monitor Exercise and sports participation	Modelling of longitudinal data with assumption that the seasonal pattern over one year had a 12-month periodicity and that high and low levels of physical activity occurred 6 months apart Amplitude and phase of a cosine curve	Summertime increase in combined moderate leisure and household activities No seasonal variation in vigorous leisure time activity Total light activity peaked in January Those who were obese or sedentary reported smaller summer-related increases in leisure time activities in comparison with leaner and more active counterparts Actillume monitor: Similar seasonal pattern with peaks in activity in late spring
(Goodwin, Pearce, Taylor, Read, & Powers, 2001) United Kingdom	3-year prospective cross-seasonal study	N=46 (M) Two different age-groups N=25 elderly (70-82 years) N=21 young (20-30 years)	accelerometry Gaehwiler, counts/min	Paired t-tests for within-group data	Physical activity in the older group was higher in winter than in summer No seasonal difference in the younger group
(Plasqui & Westerterp, 2004b) The Netherlands	Longitudinal study 2 assessments	N=25 (20-30 years) F=15 M=10	Doubly labelled water method (PAL and AEE)	ANOVA repeated measures	No difference in TEE; PAL was higher in summer and the difference was higher for men.

Massach.= Massachusetts
F=females, M=males.

All but one study (U.S.Department of Health and Human Services, 1997) was conducted in the Northern Hemisphere. Of the eight studies, seven found seasonal variation in various components of physical activity. Only one study reported no seasonal variation in body movement in young participants (Goodwin et al., 2001). Seven studies found increases in physical activity components during spring/summer and decreases during winter. Only one study found increases in exercise metabolic rate during winter (Zahorska-Markiewicz & Markiewicz, 1984). Various components of physical activity were investigated ranging from exercise behaviour (Uitenbroek, 1993) to body movement (Goodwin et al., 2001) and PAL (Plasqui & Westerterp, 2004b). The majority of studies (n=5) found seasonal variation in leisure-time physical activities, particularly moderate intensity activities. Three studies demonstrated seasonal variation in body movement assessed with accelerometers (Goodwin et al., 2001; Levin et al., 1999; Matthews et al., 2001a).

Only one study included differences in activity-levels between weekdays and weekends. Matthews et al. (2001a) found generally higher household and leisure-time physical activities during weekends and the amplitude of the seasonal variation appeared to be greater on these days.

In summary, the overview shows that seasonality in physical activity seems to be a robust phenomenon that has been demonstrated for various components of physical activity in various populations across countries, particularly from the Northern Hemisphere. Integrating differences between weekdays and weekends in the analysis, provides more detailed information on how engagement in physical activity varies across the seasons and the days of the week.

1.7.2. Seasonality in physical activity and its relationship with body composition

Seasonal variation in physical activity has been studied not only due to the relationship between physical activity and cardiovascular diseases (Matthews et al., 2001a) but also due to a similar seasonal pattern in physical activity and body composition. However, results regarding seasonal variation in physical activity and body composition are inconsistent.

In a prospective study with 140 female participants from the Netherlands, Van Staveren, Deurenberg, Burema, de Groot and Hautvast (1986) found that mean body weight tended to decrease in summer with an amplitude of 0.2 kg. Since they did not find a seasonal variation in energy intake but fluctuations in physical activity, they concluded that physical activity may have been a causal factor for the fluctuations in body weight. Similarly, Westerterp (2001b) demonstrated in his case-study where he assessed body weight in one man over a three-year period, that body weight fluctuated across the seasons and a negative correlation with ambient temperature emerged. He concluded that the most likely candidate for seasonal changes in energy expenditure (and thus, body weight) was physical activity.

Shimamato, Aadachi and Tanaka (2002) investigated seasonal variation in body composition variables (i.e., %BF estimated through skinfold measures) during weight-loss programmes (incorporating exercising) in a sample of 177 Japanese females (40-47 years). They found that participants who joined the program during winter obtained more desirable alterations such as increases in FFM and decreases in fat mass compared to participants who joined in summer. They concluded that seasonal changes in environmental factors such as ambient temperature affect body composition variables (e.g., through the impact of shivering and nonshivering thermogenesis in cold temperatures).

Goodwin et al. (2001) (see table 4) assessed body composition (i.e., body mass, BMI and %BF through skinfold measures) and physical activity in a three-year prospective cross-seasonal study in the United Kingdom. They found a significant increase in body mass and BMI in both young and elderly men from summer to winter. However, no

changes in %BF occurred.

Likewise, Plasqui, Kester and Westerterp (2004a) found no seasonal variation in FFM

(assessed with underwater weighing and deuterium dilution method) in 25 healthy

participants (20 -30 years) in a study into seasonal variation in sleeping metabolic rate

in Maastricht (the Netherlands).

In summary, the studies show that it is essential to investigate various components of

body composition to understand seasonal variation in physical activity and body

composition. While some studies demonstrated variation in body weight and %BF

(Shimamoto, Adachi, & Tanaka, 2002; Westerterp, 2001b), others did not show

variation in %BF or FFM (Goodwin et al., 2001; Plasqui et al., 2004a). Age differences

between the samples might account for some of the discrepant findings. While those

studies that found seasonal variation in body composition variables investigated middle-

aged participants, studies which showed no variation investigated younger adults. This

difference might relate to the finding that younger adults are more active than older

adults and may be more likely to maintain their physical activity-levels across the

seasons. The finding that a decrease in physical activity is observed with age (Australian

Bureau of Statistics, 2000) may suggest that older individuals who decrease their

activity-levels are prone to experience seasonal fluctuations in their activity-levels and

an accompanying change in body composition variables.

1.7.3. Studies into seasonality in patients with anorexia nervosa

Prior to the 1990s, research into seasonality in dieting disorders was lacking. Nielsen

(1992) was among the fist to publish reports on seasons of birth in patients with AN and to highlight the importance of studying seasonality in dieting disorders. Since then, studies into seasonality have emerged and they can be subdivided into three categories: a) studies into seasonality and symptoms of seasonal affective disorder in dieting disorders (Brewerton, Krahn, Hardin, Wehr, & Rosenthal, 1993; Lam, Goldner, & Grewal, 1996; Yamatsuji et al., 2003), b) studies into season of birth (Nielsen, 1992; Willoughby et al., 2002), onset and admission (Gotestam, Eriksen, Heggestad, & Nielsen, 1998), and c) studies into the effects of environmental factors on dieting disorder pathology (Penas-Lledo & Waller, 2002b; van Hanswijck de Jonge, Meyer, Smith, & Waller, 2001; Waller, Meyer, & Hanswijck de Jonge, 2001; Willoughby et al., 2002).

Generally, results are still inconsistent as to which patient group appears to be more affected by seasonal variation in environmental variables, patients with AN or BN. For patients with AN, seasonality has been found for time of admission (February-March) and time of birth (i.e., May) in studies in the Northern Hemisphere (Gotestam et al., 1998; Nielsen, 1992). However, no seasonal birth pattern was found in patients from the Southern Hemisphere (Willoughby et al., 2002).

Some studies examining the relationship between ambient temperature at birth and dieting disorder pathology showed a significant correlation for participants with restrictive eating attitudes (Willoughby et al., 2002). Further, temperature at conception has been found to be associated with restrictive dieting disorder pathology (Waller et al., 2001). In addition, residing in warmer climates has been found to increase the risk for dieting disorder pathology (Sloan, 2002) (see also part 1, chapter 4.2.3.).

In conclusion, these studies demonstrate the importance of investigating seasonal variation in AN and the potential impact of environmental factors (e.g., ambient temperature) on behaviours related to the dieting disorder.

1.8. Benefits of the current study

Overactivity (i.e., overexercersing, commitment to exercise and restlessness) has been recognised as fundamental to the pathogenesis of AN (Birmingham & Beumont, 2004; Katz, 1996). However, a definition of 'overactivity' is still lacking and few studies exist that have investigated various components of physical activity in patients with AN. Overexercersing and restlessness have deleterious effects for patients with AN (see also part 3, chapter 1.2.2.) and particularly their relationship with body composition variables is of interest in a disorder where weight gain is essential. An understanding of patterns of physical activity in AN can only be obtained if physical activity is assessed utilising a multidimensional approach. Further, a longitudinal design is required, since physical activity components, particularly leisure-time activities, have been shown to vary considerably over time in the general population. Also, it has been shown that individuals demonstrate differing activity-levels during weekdays and weekends. The concept of seasonality has received attention in the context of dieting disorders since the 1990s and it has been concluded that investigating seasonal patterns and the impact of environmental factors on behaviours is essential for the understanding of AN.

Even though it has been demonstrated that physical activity varies across the seasons and the investigation of seasonality in AN has received some attention, no study has investigated seasonal variation in physical activity in patients with AN.

Thus, this study will provide a comprehensive, multidimensional investigation into physical activity patterns (i.e., duration and body movement) in outpatients with AN and healthy controls across three seasons. Objective monitoring and self-reports will be included in the assessment. The energy expenditure component will not be captured as the focus will be on assessment of the patterns of physical activity rather than obtaining a global measure of energy expenditure. Body composition variables (i.e., %BF, %FFM and FFM) will be assessed using DEXA to investigate the relationship between physical activity and body composition.

1.9. Aims and hypotheses

1.9.1. Aims

The overall aim of this study is to investigate physical activity patterns and body composition in outpatients with AN and healthy controls across three seasons using a multidimensional approach. Specifically, the study aims to:

1. Investigate differences in physical activity components such as duration and body movement, and parameters of body composition between patients and controls.

2. Investigate seasonal variation in physical activity and body composition in patients and controls.

3. Explore the relationship between physical activity components and body composition variables in patients and controls.

The ultimate objective of the study is to provide information on physical activity patterns and body composition and elicit the role of seasonality in physical activity in AN such that the obtained knowledge can be incorporated into treatment approaches for the management of physical activity in patients with AN.

1.9.2. Research questions and hypotheses

1.9.2.1. Physical activity

1. How do physical activity components (i.e., duration and body movement) vary across the seasons in outpatients with AN and healthy controls?

1.1. Do patients with AN and healthy controls differ in physical activity components?

1.2. Do these components vary across the seasons?

1.3. Does the seasonal variation in the physical activity components differ between patients and controls?

1.1. Physical activity pattern

1.1.1. Patients will demonstrate more extrinsic motivation for physical activity (i.e., engaging in physical activities as a means of improving physical appearance) and higher commitment to exercise.

1.1.2. Patients and controls will not differ in the time spent in moderate intensity activities.

1.1.3. Patients with AN will show higher levels of exercise (i.e., time spent in hard and very hard intensity activities).

163

1.1.4. Patients will spend more time in strengthening and flexibility activities compared to controls.

1.1.5. Patients with AN will demonstrate more restlessness (i.e., body movement) compared to controls.

1.2. Activity-levels during weekdays and weekends

1.2.1. Patients and controls will show higher activity-levels (i.e., time spent in moderate, hard and very hard intensity activities and body movement) during weekends compared to weekdays.

1.3. Seasonal variation in physical activity

1.3.1. Time spent in moderate intensity activities will vary across the seasons in patients with AN and healthy controls.

1.3.2. Exercise behaviour (i.e. time spent in very hard intensity activities) will not vary across the seasons.

1.3.3. Body movement will vary across the seasons.

1.4. Differences between patients and controls in seasonal variation

1.4.1. The seasonal variation in physical activity components will differ between the two groups in that patients will show a lower peak to trough difference (i.e., they will maintain a consistent pattern of activity across the seasons).

1.9.2.2. Body composition

2. How do body composition variables (i.e., %BF, %FFM and FFM) vary across the seasons in outpatients with AN and healthy controls?

2.1. Do patients with AN and healthy controls differ in body composition variables?

2.2. Do these variables vary across the seasons?

2.3. Does the seasonal variation in body composition variables differ between patients with AN and healthy controls?

2.1. Body composition

2.1.1. Patients' body weight, BMI, %BF and FFM will be lower compared to controls.

2.1.2. Patients will demonstrate a higher %FFM compared to controls.

2.2. Seasonal variation in body composition

2.2.1. A continuous increase in parameters of body composition will be found in the patient group indicating recovery from the dieting disorder.

2.2.2. The control group will show a seasonal pattern in body composition variables.

1.9.2.3. Physical activity and body composition

3. How do physical activity components and body composition variables correlate in patients with AN and healthy controls?

3.1. Physical activity and body movement

3.1.1. Body movement and FFM will be positively correlated in both groups.

3.1.2. A negative correlation between body movement and body composition variables will emerge in patients with AN but not in healthy controls.

2. Methods

2.1. Design

The present study utilised a repeated case-control design (Zahner, Hsieh, & Fleming, 1995). Physical activity and body composition were assessed repeatedly across three seasons in a female patient group diagnosed with AN/Eating Disorders Not Otherwise Specified (EDNOS (American Psychiatric Association, 1994)) and a healthy control group. Participants started the assessment in autumn (April/May) and were assessed subsequently during winter (July/August) and spring/spring/summer (November/December).

2.2. Participants

2.2.1. Recruitment of participants

Patients with AN/EDNOS who had been diagnosed by experienced psychiatrists were recruited from four specialised dieting disorder services in Sydney, namely the Royal Prince Alfred Hospital, Wesley Private Hospital, Carlingford Day Therapy Centre and Westmead Hospital. Patients who had a current diagnosis of EDNOS had to have had one admission to an inpatient-unit for AN during the past five years or had to be diagnosed as being on the verge of developing a full-diagnosis of AN. The therapeutic team informed the patients about the study and participant information sheets were handed out to them (see Appendix A). If they were interested, they were then given the choice of calling the research coordinator or meeting with her in person to discuss the procedures of the study in detail. If a patient stated that she was not willing to participate, she was not contacted any further. Once a patient agreed to participate, an appointment for the first assessment (autumn) was scheduled. For the subsequent assessments, patients were asked if they were interested in continuing to participate at the end of the first assessment. The research coordinator contacted patients who agreed to ongoing participation after two to three months to schedule the second/third assessment. If patients did not want to continue they were not contacted any further.

Control participants were recruited from the University of Sydney. Advertisements were placed throughout the University in which the study was briefly described and a contact number was provided. Students were also addressed directly during a medical and a dietetics seminar. In winter, the Employment Service of the University advertised the study on their website. If the students expressed interest the research coordinator explained the study over the phone. Once the students agreed to participate an appointment was scheduled for the first assessment. For the second and third assessments, participants were asked at the end of the first assessment if they were interested in continuing to participate. If they agreed, they were contacted two to three months later to schedule the second/third assessment.

Participants were assessed across three seasons. When entering the study and at each follow-up, demographic data was obtained from the participants on their age, occupation, and family background. Due to dropouts and new recruitments, the sample size varied across the seasons. Participants' characteristics are therefore described separately for each season.

2.2.2. Participants in autumn

In autumn, 11 female out- and day-patients diagnosed with AN/EDNOS aged 15-32 years with a mean BMI of 18.8 agreed to participate in the study. All but one patient had been diagnosed with AN in the past five years and had been admitted to an inpatient unit of one of the four specialised units. Their current diagnoses are displayed in table 5. The one patient diagnosed with EDNOS was included in the study as she appeared to be developing the full diagnosis of AN (personal communication with her psychiatrist in March 2002). Only outpatients or patients in day program treatment were asked to participate in the study.

Seventeen female control participants aged 15-35 years with a mean BMI of 22.5 were recruited for the autumn-assessment. They were excluded if they had suffered from a dieting disorder during the past five years as determined through questions during the first contact with the participant. Characteristics of participants in autumn are displayed in table 5.

Table 5: Participants' characteristics in autumn

	Patients (n=11)	Controls (n=17)
Age (years)		
Mean±SD	22± 5.4	24± 5.1
Range	15-32	15-35
BMI		
Mean±SD	18.8± 2.6	22.5± 3.5
Range	15.2-24.3	18.3-31.8
Diagnosis (DSM-IV) N (%)		
AN-R	5 (45.5)	
AN-R/P	2 (18.2)	
EDNOS-R	2 (18.2)	
EDNOS-P	2 (18.2)	
Marital status N (%)		
Single	9 (81.8)	14 (82.4)
Married		2 (11.8)
De Facto	2 (18.2)	1 (5.9)
Currently employed N (%)		
Yes	5 (45.5) [1]	11 (64.7)
No	5 (45.5) [1]	6 (35.3)
Country of birth N (%)		
Australia/NZ	10 (90.9)	12 (70.6)
Europe	1 (9.1)	
Canada		
Asia[2]		4 (23.5)
Kenya		1 (5.9)

AN-R: Anorexia nervosa-restricting subtype
AN-RP: Anorexia nervosa-restricting/purging subtype
EDNOS-R: Eating Disorder Not Otherwise Specified-restricting
EDNOS-P: Eating Disorder Not Otherwise Specified-purging
[1] One participant did not turn up for the interview.
[2] China, Thailand and Malaysia.

2.2.3. Participants in winter

Due to the risk of dropouts (one patient dropped out from autumn to winter), seven more patients – three diagnosed with AN-Restricting type, one with AN-Purging type, two with AN-Restricting and Purging type and one with EDNOS-Restricting type -were recruited from the same Dieting Disorder Services for the winter-assessment. The patient-sample in winter thus consisted of 17 patients aged 15-33 years with a mean BMI of 19.0.

During winter, one control dropped out and five more were recruited through the
Employment Service of the University of Sydney resulting in a sample size of 22
control participants aged 15-35 years with a mean BMI of 22.4. Table 6 provides
information on participants' characteristics during winter.

Table 6: Participants' characteristics in winter

	Patients (n=17)	Controls (n=22)
Age (y)		
Mean±SD	22± 5.4	24± 5.1
Range	15-32	15-35
BMI		
Mean±SD	19.0± 2.5	22.4± 4.2
Range	14.7-25.0	18.0-34.1
Diagnosis (DSM-IV) N (%)		
AN-R	7 (41.2)	
AN-P	1 (5.9)	
AN-R/P	4 (23.5)	
EDNOS-R[1]	3 (17.6)	
EDNOS-P[1]	2 (11.8)	
Marital status N (%)		
Single	16 (94.1)	19 (86.4)
Married		2 (9.1)
De Facto	1 (5.9)	1 (4.5)
Currently employed N (%)		
Yes	8 (47.1)	16 (72.7)
No	9 (52.9)	6 (27.3)
Country of birth N (%)		
Australia/NZ	16 (94.1)	16 (72.7)
Europe	1 (5.9)	
Canada		1 (4.5)
Asia		4 (18.2)
Kenya		1 (4.5)

[1] All but one patient had been diagnosed with AN and had been admitted to an inpatient-unit during the
past 5 years.

2.2.4. Participants in spring/summer

Three patients dropped out from winter to spring/summer. Fourteen patients diagnosed

with AN-R (n=6), AN-RP (n=3), EDNOS-R (n=3) and EDNOS-P (n=2) completed the

spring/summer assessment. Hence, 10 patients completed all three assessments and 14

completed two of the three assessments.

Also, two controls dropped out resulting in 20 control participants aged 15-35 years

with a mean BMI of 22.4 for the spring/summer-assessment. Table 7 summarises

participants' characteristics during spring/summer.

Table 7: Participants' characteristics in spring/summer

	Patients (n=14)	Controls (n=20)
Age (y)		
Mean±SD	22± 5.3	24± 5.3
Range	15-33	15-35
BMI		
Mean±SD	19.7± 2.6	22.4± 4.2
Range	16.1-25.2	18.0-34.1
Diagnosis (DSM-IV) N (%)		
AN-R	6 (33.3)	
AN-R/P	3 (16.7)	
EDNOS-R[1]	3 (16.7)	
EDNOS-P[1]	2 (11.1)	
Marital status N (%)		
Single	13 (92.9)	17 (85.0)
Married		2 (10.0)
De Facto	1 (5.6)	1 (5.0)
Currently employed N (%)		
Yes	10 (71.4)	15 (75.0)
No	4 (28.6)	5 (25.0)
Country of birth N (%)		
Australia/NZ	13 (92.9)	14 (70.0)
Europe	1 (7.1)	
Canada		1 (5.0)
Asia		4 (20.0)
Kenya		1 (5.0)

[1] All but one patient had been diagnosed with AN and had been admitted to an inpatient-unit during the past 5 years.

172

2.2.5. Total sample sizes across the three seasons

In total, 28 participants formed the autumn-sample, 41 the winter-sample and 34 the spring/summer-sample. Of these, 25 participants completed three measurements and 34 completed two. Figure 1 summarises the sample sizes in the different seasons.

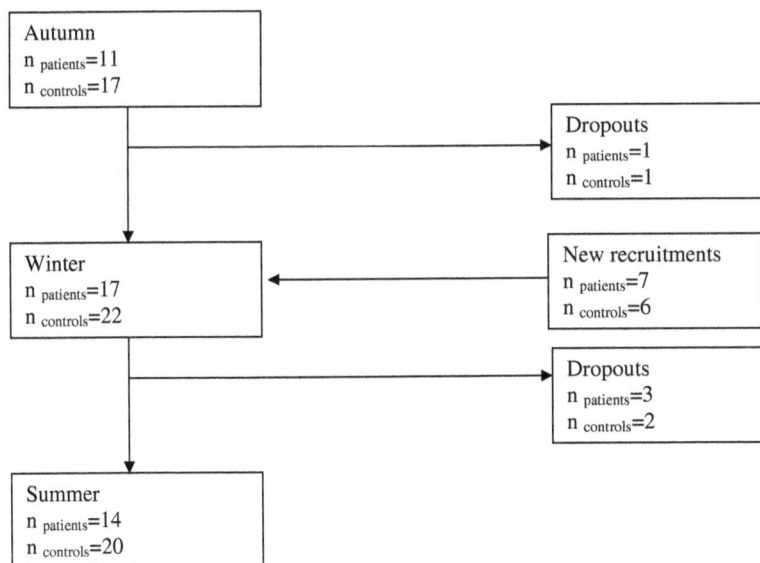

Figure 1: Sample sizes and dropouts for each season

2.2.6. Dropouts

The dropout rates per season were 7.1% (n=2) for autumn and 12.2% (n=5) for winter. All dropouts were Caucasian. Four patients and three controls decided not to participate after having completed one assessment. In autumn, one patient had to be readmitted to an inpatient-unit. Her control participant (a cousin) dropped out with her. In winter, three newly recruited patients dropped out; one stated she was too busy to participate, another one developed severe bulimia (personal communication with her mother in June 2002) and a third one could not be contacted after three attempts. All patients had a diagnosis of AN and presented with a mean BMI of 17.0 (SD=2.6).

One of the controls who decided to discontinue was a friend of a patient that had dropped out. Another control participant became severely ill and could not take part in the study any further (personal communication in August 2002).

Comparisons were made for patients and controls separately, i.e., patients who dropped out were compared with patients who participated (using the autumn and winter data) and dropouts in the control group were compared with control participants. T-test for independent groups were computed.

In the dropout analysis for the patients, dropouts and participants differed significantly in terms of body weight (t $_{(26)}$=-2.2, p=0.04). Dropouts' body weight was significantly lower than that of participants (43.7kg ±2.6 and 53.2kg ±8.3 respectively). No differences emerged in age, body attitudes (total score), eating attitudes (total score), and BMI.

In the dropout analysis for controls, there was no statistically significant difference in age, body attitudes, eating attitudes, body weight, and BMI. Characteristics of the dropouts are presented in table 8.

Table 8: Characteristics of dropouts

	Patients (n=4[1])	Controls (n=3[2])
Age (y)		
Mean/SD	20± 6.4	22± 3.8
Range	15-29	18-25
Body weight (kg)		
Mean/SD	43.7± 2.6	65.0± 8.0
Range	40.6-46.4	55.8-69.6
BMI		
Mean/SD	17.0± 2.6	22.7± 2.1
Range	14.7-19.3	21.5-25.1
Diagnosis (DSM-IV) N (%)		
AN-R	2 (50.0)	
AN-P	1 (25.0)	
AN-R/P	1 (25.0)	
EDNOS-R[3]		
EDNOS-P[3]		

[1] One patient dropped out after the autumn-assessment, 3 patients after the winter-assessment.
[2] One control dropped out after the autumn-assessment, 3 controls after the winter-assessment.
[3] All but one patient had been diagnosed with AN and had been admitted to an inpatient-unit during the past 5 years.

2.3. Ethical considerations

2.3.1. Ethical Approval

The protocol of the study was approved by the Ethics Committees of the University of Sydney, the Central Sydney Area Health Service and the Western Sydney Area Health Service.

2.3.2. Informed consent

All participants gave written informed consent to take part in the study. If they were aged under 16, parents signed the informed consent sheet. They were paid A$25 on arrival for the second and third assessment. Prior to the assessment, participants and/or their parents were provided with participant information sheets (see Appendix A) in which the protocol of the study was described in detail. Any questions were discussed with the research coordinator.

2.3.3. Potential risks

DEXA was used on three occasions in the study to conduct a total body scan. The scans included a minimal exposure of radiation (less than 0.5 milliSieverts (mSv)) which is comparable to the exposure from natural background radiation during one day. The National Health and Medical Research Council (NHMRC) statement (National Health and Medical Research Council, 1995) provided guidelines for the doses of radiation volunteers participating in a research study are exposed to. Accordingly, the effective dose over a year should not exceed 5 mSv. The effective dose participants of this study were exposed to was calculated as 1.5 mSv and thus, did not exceed the recommended radiation exposure.

No potential risks are known from the other measures included in the study.

2.4. Treatment

All patients were or had been treated in one of the four dieting disorder specialised units previously mentioned. Treatment was conducted in either outpatient or daypatient settings. Patients in a day-therapy program were attending a three-day or five-day program. The concept of the programmes has recently been described by Thornton, Beumont and Touyz (2002). The major difference between the two programmes is that patients in the three-day program are in a different stage of readiness to change according to the transtheoretical model of change (Prochaska & DiClemente, 1992). In the three-day program, patients are admitted if they are in the 'action stage' of readiness to change. They are asked to sign a contract and weight gain is set at 500g/week. Further, patients' BMI must be higher than 16. In the five-day program, patients at a lower BMI (<16) are treated. The admission criteria are more flexible and patients' weight gain per week is determined more individually. Therapeutic work focuses on motivation to change.

The outpatients who participated in the study were seen by therapists working at one of the four specialised units. The therapeutic techniques utilised were comparable over the four specialised units (i.e. cognitive behavioural treatment approach). Table 9 provides an overview of patients' treatment status across the three seasons.

Table 9: Treatment status of the patients

	Autumn N (%)
Outpatients	4 (36.4)
Attending 3-day program	2 (18.2)
Attending 5-day program	3 (27.3)
Finished treatment	2 (18.2)
Total	11

177

	Winter N (%)
Outpatients	8 (47.1)
Attending 3-day program	3 (16.7)
Attending 5-day program	3 (16.7)
Finished treatment	3 (16.7)
Total	17
	Spring/summer N (%)
Outpatients	10 (75.0)
Attending 3-day program	
Attending 5-day program	
Finished treatment	4 (25.0)
Total	14

2.5. Setting

Participants were seen at the research office of the Department of Psychological Medicine, University of Sydney. DEXA-scans were taken at the Metabolic Unit of the Royal Prince Alfred Hospital.

2.6. Measures

2.6.1. Questionnaires on dieting disorder pathology

To establish the group-variable (patient and control group) the following questionnaires were administered covering a wide range of symptoms of dieting disorders:

- The Dieting Status Measure (DiSM; (Strong & Huon, 1997)): a stage-based dieting status measure that categorises individuals according to the stage or level of their dieting behaviour. The DiSM was included in this study to show differences in patients' and controls' dieting status, to identify severe dieters in the control group, and to describe the severity of dieting in the patient group.

- The Body Attitude Test (BAT; (Probst, Vandereycken, Van Coppenolle, & Vanderlinden, 1995)): a self-report instrument (20 items) intended to measure the subjective body experience and attitude towards one's body. As body image disturbances are one of the major diagnostic criteria for dieting disorders (American Psychiatric Association (, 1994), the BAT was included in the present study to demonstrate differences between patients and controls, and to determine the degree of body image disturbance in the patient group.

- The Eating Attitude Test (EAT-40; (Garner & Garfinkel, 1979)): a self-report measure of the symptoms of AN (40 items). The EAT was included in the present study to demonstrate differences between patients and controls, and to assess the severity of symptoms in the patient group.

- The Food Choice Questionnaire (FCQ; (Steptoe, Pollard, & Wardle, 1995)): a 36-item questionnaire, developed to assess perceived influences on food selection. Nine distinct factors are assessed (see also part 1, chapter 2.3.). Ideological reasons for food choice – another food choice factor developed by Lindeman and Stark (1999) - was assessed as a tenth factor in this study (see table 10 for item-examples). The FCQ together with the added factor 'ideological reasons' was included in the present study to describe patients' food choices and to show differences between the patient and control group.

Table 10: Items of the factor 'ideological reasons for food choice'

1. Because of my view of the world, there are some foods, which are inappropriate for me.
2. The food I eat tell something about my values and attitudes towards the world.
3. I avoid eating some foods because eating them would conflict with my values.
4. My philosophy of life is manifested in my food choice.

5. My outlook on the world has nothing to do with the food I eat.
6. The food I eat tells something about my spiritual life.
7. I have an ideology or religion, which affects my eating habits.

2.6.1. Assessment of physical activity

Physical activity was assessed utilising a multidimensional approach. The following components of physical activity were included: a) motivation for physical activity and commitment to exercise, and b) quantitative assessment of physical activity (i.e., time spent in various intensities of activities and body movement).

Motivation for physical activities was assessed using the Motives for Physical Activities-Revised Questionnaire (MPAM-R; (Ryan, 1998)). Commitment to Exercise was assessed with the Commitment to Exercise Scale (CES; (Davis et al., 1993a)). The frequency-dimension and duration of physical activities were assessed using the Seven-day Physical Activity Recall (7-PAR, (Sallis, 1997)) and body movement was assessed using a triaxial accelerometer (Tracmor 3; Philips Research, Eindhoven, Netherlands). The energy expenditure of physical activity was not captured in this study. It was not possible to use the doubly labelled water method due to the costs of the method (see chapter 1.3.2.). Even though the physical activity induced energy expenditure can be estimated with the 7-PAR, studies have found varying sizes of correlations when compared to the doubly labelled water method (Sallis & Saelens, 2000; Westerterp, 1999a). Further, Bouten et al (1996) found discrepancies between the output of the Tracmor (counts/min) and physical activity-level in terms of energy expenditure estimated by the doubly labelled water method in an anorexic patient group. The authors explained the discrepancy between movement registration and energy expenditure by changes in energy metabolism in anorexic patients (i.e., a greater than expected reduction in resting metabolic rate (see chapter 1.6.2.)). The current study therefore focused on patterns of physical activity rather than energy expenditure.

2.6.1.1. Motives for Physical Activity

The MPAM-R (Ryan, 1998) is a 30-item questionnaire tapping reasons for engaging in sport or exercise activities. Five general motives are assessed and are displayed in table 11.

Table 11: Motives for Physical Activities-Revised

Motives	Example of items	Number of items
Interest/enjoyment	"Because it's fun."	7 items
Competence	"Because I want to obtain new skills."	7 items
Appearance	"Because I want to improve my body shape."	6 items
Fitness	"Because I want to maintain my physical health and well-being."	5 items
Social motives	"Because I want to be with my friends."	5 items

Items are presented on a 7-point Likert scale in which the participant is required to select a number between 1 ("not at all true for me") and 7 ("very true for me") for each statement. Scores per motive are computed by calculating the mean for the relevant items. Factor analysis of MPAM-R items has been found to yield the expected five-factor solution with items loading on their appropriate factors (Ryan, 1998). Internal consistency scores (Cronbach's alpha) per factor ranged from 0.78 to 0.92. Motives significantly predicting adherence to physical activity were enjoyment, competence and social motives. The questionnaire was included in the present study to assess motives for physical activities in the patient and control groups and to investigate difference in the motive structure.

2.6.1.2. Commitment to Exercise

The CES (Davis et al., 1993a) (see also chapter 1.4.1.2.) is an eight-item questionnaire designed to assess an individual's commitment to the activity of exercising. Davis, Brewer and Ratusny (1993a) found a two-factor structure of the items of the CES, where the first factor describes the obligatory aspect whereby psychological well-being is contingent upon assiduous adherence to a regular and structured exercise regimen. Factor 2 relates to the pathological aspect of exercising in which exercising is continued despite illness.

Participants are given eight statements. Below each statement a horizontal line (128mm) is presented with appropriate bipolar adjectives placed at each end ("not at all important", "very important"), and participants are asked to mark the point which best describes their position on the continuum. The distance from the beginning of the line to the point marked constitutes the score for each item. In this study, the score of each item was converted to a percentage of the total length of the line (e.g., the length of the line was 128mm. A participant marked a point at 100mm. Her value for this item was then computed as 78.1%).

Davis et al. (1993a) demonstrated a sufficiently high internal reliability coefficient of the scale (Cronbach's alpha coefficient for total score= 0.77). In terms of concurrent validity, they found that weight preoccupation was strongly related to CES-scores for both men (R^2=0.31 for Factor 1, and R^2=0.13 for Factor 2) and women (R^2=0.25 for Factor 1, and R^2=0.19 for Factor 2), even when body fat content was held constant. In a further validation study, Davis et al. (1997) showed that patients who were classified as excessive exercisers (n=91) reported more obligatory and pathological attitudes to the activity of exercise than moderately active patients.

The CES was used in the present study to describe participants' attitudes towards the activity of exercising and to analyse differences between patients and controls in terms of the obligatory and pathological attitudes towards exercising. Obligatory attitudes were computed as the mean of items 1, 2, 3, 4, 7 and 8. Pathological attitudes were computed as the means of items 5, 6, 7 and 8 (according to recommendations from Davis, email in March 2002). The items of the CES are presented in table 12.

Table 12: Items of the CES

1.	How important do you think it is to your general well-being not to miss your exercise session?
2.	Does it upset you if, for one reason or another, you are unable to exercise?
3.	If you miss an exercise session, or several sessions, do you try to make them up by putting in more time when you get back?
4.	Do you have a set routine for your exercise sessions, e.g., the same time of the day, the same location, the same number of laps, particular exercises, and so on?
5.	Do you continue to exercise at times when you feel tired or unwell?
6.	Do you continue to exercise even when you have sustained and exercise-related injury?
7.	Do you feel 'guilty' that you have somehow 'let yourself down' when you miss your exercise session?
8.	Are there times when you turn down an invitation to an interesting social event because it interferes with your exercise schedule?

2.6.1.3. Seven-day Physical Activity Recall

The 7-PAR is a semi-structured interview that estimates an individual's time spent in physical activities of three intensities (moderate, hard and very hard) and time spent in strength/flexibility activities for the seven days prior to the interview (Sallis, 1997). A variety of activities are captured ranging from leisure-time activities (such as aerobic exercise, gardening, walking), and work-related activities, (such as carrying heavy objects).

Before the commencement of the interview, the interviewer briefly explains the process to the interviewee. It is stressed that the interview captures the activities of the past week, not a history of usual activities. Definitions of the intensities are given. Moderate intensity activities are defined as similar to how the participant feels when walking at a normal pace (Sallis, 1997). The very hard intensity category is defined as how the participant feels when going for a run and the hard intensity category falls in between the moderate and very hard intensity category. Sleep duration is assessed for each of the past seven days. For easier recalling, the days are subdivided into three parts, morning (the time the interviewee gets up until 12pm), afternoon (12pm to 6pm) and evening (6pm until the interviewee goes to bed). Time spent in different physical activities is recorded for each of the three sections each day. Time spent in strengthening and flexibility activities (such as pushups, pull-ups and Yoga) are assessed after recording activities for each day. The recorded times are rounded according to specified rules (Sallis, 1997):

10-22min	0.25
23-37min	0.50
38-52min	0.75
53min-1.07 hr	1.0
1.08hr – 1.22hr	1.25

Time spent in each intensity category as well as in strength/flexibility activities is computed per day and summed over the seven-day period.

Reliability and validity of the 7-PAR have been frequently analysed (for reviews see (Sallis, 1997; Sallis & Saelens, 2000)). Test-retest reliability scores range from 0.08 (for moderate activity and a 2-week interval; (Sallis, 1997)) to 0.86 (for very hard activities and a 2-week interval; (Rauh, Hovell, Hofstetter, Sallis, & Gleghorn, 1992)). Total and very hard physical activity scores tend to have higher test-retest reliabilities than moderate physical activity scores (Sallis, 1997). Criterion-validity of the 7-PAR was assessed from correlations with self-report logs, direct observation, heart rate monitoring, energy intake, maximal oxygen consumption and accelerometry (for reviews see (Sallis, 1997; Sallis & Saelens, 2000)). Sallis and Saelens (2000) reported validity correlations of the 7-PAR with accelerometers of 0.50 to 0.53 due to the short and specific recall time frame of the 7-PAR.

Shelton and Klesges (1995) summarised the usefulness of the 7-PAR as follows: *The 7-PAR is appropriate in assessing physical activity for individuals, changes in physical activity habits, [and] characterising activity-patterns in a given group* (p.191). Given support for its psychometric properties, the 7-PAR was considered an appropriate tool for the following purposes in the present study: to assess time spent in different intensities of physical activity and strength/flexibility activities in patients with AN and healthy controls, to investigate differences between the two groups and to analyse changes across the three seasons.

2.6.1.4. Objective monitoring with a motion sensor

For objective monitoring of participants' physical activity a portable triaxial accelerometer was used in the present study (Tracmor 3; Philips Research, Eindhoven, the Netherlands; see Appendix B). The Tracmor used in this study was an improved version (Tracmor 3, 7*2*0.8cm; weight: 22g) of the triaxial accelerometer used by Westerterp and Bouten in previous studies (Bouten et al., 1996; Westerterp & Bouten, 1997a). Acceleration signals can be stored in the portable unit for up to three weeks of assessment and are then downloaded onto a computer. In this study, the accelerometer was attached to the lower back of the participants using an elastic belt around the waist.

The accelerometer provides a measure of counts in each of the three planes (i.e., horizontal, vertical, mediolateral; see chapter 1.3.2.2.). The counts per plane are summed to obtain the total counts over the three planes.

Participants wore the accelerometer for six consecutive days during waking hours except while bathing, swimming or showering. They were provided with a sheet to monitor the time they were wearing the Tracmor (see Appendix C). The following variables were analysed: 1) Average counts over active monitoring time divided by 10000 (counts/day, AC-AMT) were computed by summing the counts per day over the six days for the time the participants wore the Tracmor. The mean was computed to obtain the average counts per day over the six-day period. 2) Counts per minute over active monitoring time (CM-AMT) were calculated similarly, but the mean was subdivided by the total time (in minutes) the participant wore the Tracmor. 3) Average time worn (hrs/d) was computed to analyse differences in the length of time the participants wore the Tracmor. 4) Time (in hrs/d) spent in various intensities of body movement. Plasqui et al. (personal communication in March 2002) conducted standard tests in the laboratory to receive intensity categories for the Tracmor-output (counts/min). Twenty-four participants were tested using nine different Tracmors. The participants wore the same Tracmors during the procedure. Participants ran on a treadmill at three different speeds (5km/h, 7km/h and 9km/h) for five minutes at each speed. Between the different speed-trials, they rested for a few minutes so that differences in the Tracmor-output could be identified. Table 13 shows the five categories that emerged. As can be seen in table 13, the Tracmor-data showed a high variability with the maximum for category 3 being higher than the mean of category 4 (maximum for category 3: 7753, Mean category 4=6605). Despite the high variability, the

identified categories provided information to calculate time spent in different intensities
of body movement.

Table 13: Categories for Tracmor-output

	Mean (counts/min/10000)	Minimum	Maximum
Category 1 Walking at 3km/h	1134		
Category 2 Walking at 5km/h	2109	1484	2653
Category 3 Walking/running at 7km/h	3962	2792	7753
Category 4 Walking/running at 9km/h	6605	5737	8444
Category 5 Walking/running more than 9km/h	>6605		

Meijer et al. (1991) investigated the reproducibility of the Tracmor and the inter-
instrument and interindividual variation. They used Tracmor 1 (4*6*8 cm/350g) in their
study. Four healthy participants walked on a treadmill at three different speeds (3, 5 and
7km/h) for five minutes at each speed. Twelve different Tracmors were divided in six
sets (A to F). During all sessions, participants wore one set of two accelerometers. The
sessions with set A were repeated in a second trial one week after the first trial. They
found a test-retest correlation of 0.98 between two trials.

Reliability of the latest Tracmor-version (Tracmor 3) was analysed by Plasqui et al.
(personal communication in March 2002). They asked four participants to run on a
treadmill at three different speeds wearing 10 accelerometers. The same protocol was
repeated on the following day. They also asked participants to wear the 10
accelerometers for two days outside the laboratory during daily life. As a reference the
accelerometer was taken that delivered the median value of all 10 Tracmors and was

given a value of 100%. The other Tracmor values were then expressed as a percentage in relation to this reference. Minima and maxima in relation to this reference are displayed in table 14.

Table 14: Results of a within and between accelerometer reliability-analysis

Comparison for	Minima and maxima in relation to reference (100%)
Within accelerometers (difference between the two laboratory standard treadmill tests two days apart)	81.0-121.0
Between accelerometers for daily life (worn for two days)	76.0-159.0
Between accelerometers for treadmill running	78.0-119.0

As expected the highest variability emerged for the comparison between accelerometers under free-living conditions (minimum: 76.0% and maximum: 159.0%). It has to mentioned, that these values represent extreme values, the majority of the Tracmors were in a 20%-range of the reference value (Plasqui et al., personal communication in January 2004). High intra-individual variation in physical activity has been demonstrated in various studies (Levin et al., 1999; Matthews et al., 2001b). The high variability may result from intra-individual variation in physical activity rather than the low reliability of the Tracmor.

In a validation study of the Tracmor against the doubly labelled water method, Westerterp and Bouten (1997a) found that Tracmor output (counts/min), corrected for the influence of transportation, predicted 64% of the variation in adjusted average daily metabolic rate under free-living conditions. They argued that part of the unexplained variation could be explained by the performance of static exercise or movement against external forces (e.g., pushing, pulling; see also chapter 1.3.2.2.). They concluded that the Tracmor is an objective method that can be used to identify differences in activity patterns between individuals. The Tracmor was utilised in the present study due to several of its advantages, including its high construct validity when correlated with the doubly labelled water method, its acceptability to respondents because of its small size (Westerterp, 1999b), the elimination of subjectivity, and the ability to assess light activities.

2.6.2. Body composition

Similar to physical activity, body composition was assessed following a multidimensional approach (see chapter 1.5.1.). Body composition was assessed at the whole-body level including characteristics such as weight and stature. Further, body composition was assessed at the molecular level where the measured properties involve the attenuation of X-rays by various tissues (DEXA).

2.6.2.1. Body weight

As a measure of weight-stature, the BMI was assessed where stature was measured in metres and weight in kilograms. Measurement of height was taken at each assessment using a stadiometer (Seca; Mod. 220 CE). For weight assessments beam balances (Wedderburn: Tanita BWB-600) were used with accuracy to the nearest of 0.1 kg.

2.6.2.2. Dual-energy X-ray absorptiometry

The same DEXA scanner (Lunar Prodigy 5.60.003; GE Lunar Corporation) was used for the majority of participants to avoid differences in measurements due to different scanners. Two patients were assessed at a different hospital (Westmead Hospital) and hence, a different DEXA-scanner was used from the same brand (Lunar Prodigy 5.60.003; GE Lunar Corporation). Participants were positioned in a supine position with their arms down at their side. The scanner was placed directly above the top of the centre of the head. Scanning of the whole body took up to 10 minutes. Reliability of DEXA is generally excellent (0.97-0.99) and in validity studies, DEXA has been found to compare favourably with fat estimates from neuron activation analysis, underwater weighing, and total body water assessment (see chapter 1.5.1.2.). Accordingly, DEXA-scans were part of the assessment in this study to estimate %BF, %FFM and FFM (in kg, computed as the sum of lean body mass and bone mineral component) in patients and controls, and to analyse changes in body composition variables across the seasons.

2.7. Procedure

On the day of the first assessment, the majority of the participants met with the research coordinator in a research office at the Department of Psychological Medicine at the University of Sydney. Three patients were seen at Westmead Hospital for the assessments. All participants were provided with a participant information sheet (see Appendix A) and were asked to sign a consent form (see Appendix D). They were then provided with the questionnaires. Participants took on average 20 minutes to complete in the questionnaires. At the Metabolic Unit of the Royal Prince Alfred Hospital (for those assessed at the University) height, weight measurement and DEXA-scans took place. Subsequently, the use of the Tracmor was explained to them. A second appointment was scheduled one week later.

During the second appointment, participants returned the Tracmors. The 7-PAR was conducted by the research-coordinator, which took 15 minutes on average. A brief review of the study was conducted and any suggestions for an improvement were discussed with the participants. If they were interested, a time point for the next assessment was scheduled. In terms of feedback, control participants received results of the DEXA-scans after each assessment. In autumn, every patient received direct feedback regarding her body composition results. However, five patients experienced the procedure as overwhelming and distressing. Accordingly, the protocol was changed in that patients' results from their body composition assessment were given to their therapists for further discussion if they desired.

After having finished two assessments, participants were reimbursed for travel expenses (A$25). Figure 2 shows the procedure per season.

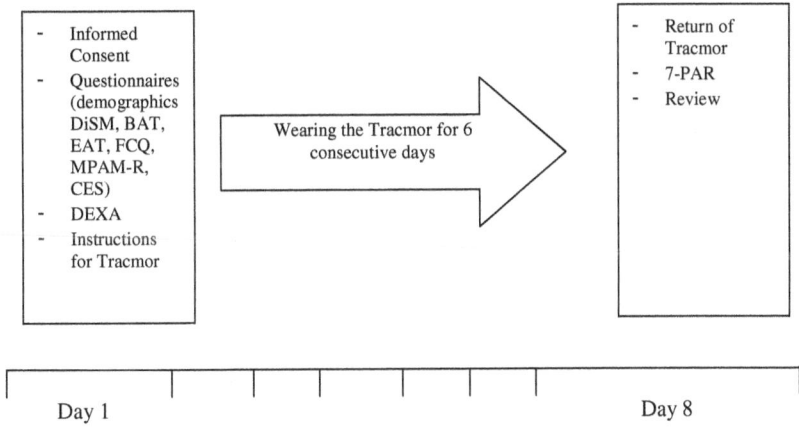

Figure 2: Procedure of the assessment for one season

2.8. Statistics

2.8.1. Data analysis

The computer statistical package SPSS (version 10.0) for Windows was used for the data analysis. Alpha levels of .05 (*) and .01 (**) were used for all statistical tests. Trends for statistical differences were reported when $p \leq 0.10$.

The first step of the analysis was to test if the variables were normally distributed using the Shapiro-Wilks statistic (W), which is appropriate for sample sizes less than 50. If the significance level was $p > 0.01$, it was assumed that the variables did not deviate significantly from the normal distribution. If the assumption of normality was violated, some of the variables were categorised according to suggestions in the literature, frequency-tables were reported and Chi-square and/or Generalised Estimated Equations (GEE) to account for repeated measurements were computed. GEE were computed using SAS (for Windows, version 8.0; SAS Institute Inc., Cary, NC 27513, USA). Other variables that were not normally distributed variables analysed using nonparametric statistics (e.g., Wilcoxon-rank test).

Due to the varying sample sizes over the seasons (see figure 1, chapter 2.2.5.) and thus the presence of missing data, repeated measurements from autumn to spring/summer were tested by formulating mixed models for normally distributed variables, treating season and group as fixed factors and participant as a random factor. With the use of the Sharpened Bonferroni method, alpha-levels were adjusted for multiple comparisons. Pearson correlation coefficients (bivariate) were computed to analyse the relationship between body movement and body composition.

For the seasonal analysis, a general sinusoidal model was used to investigate a within-subjects seasonal variation in physical activity and body composition in the patient and control group (Plasqui et al., 2004a).

$Y = c + A* \text{Sin}[(d - d_0) / 365 * 2\pi]$

Or

$Y = c + A*\cos(2\pi d_0 /365) * \sin(2\pi d/365) - A*\sin(2\pi d_0 /365) * \cos(2\pi d/365)$

$\quad\quad\quad\quad b_1 \quad\quad\quad\quad x_1 \quad\quad\quad\quad\quad b_2 \quad\quad\quad\quad\quad x_2$

c: a constant

A: amplitude

d: day of the year the measurement was done

d_0: phase

Univariate ANOVA was used to determine b_1 and b_2 and an F-test was computed to determine the significance of the sinusoidal model (i.e., to test if the model where b1 and b2 were included gave a better prediction than the model with participants alone). The amplitude (peak to trough distance) and the phase (the point where the sinusoidal curve intersects the mean value) were then calculated as

$A = \sqrt{(b_1^2 b_2^2)}$

$d_0 = 365/2\pi * \text{arcos} (b_1/A)$

The amplitudes for patients and controls in the variables were tested for significant differences with independent t-tests (two-tailed).

2.8.2. Power considerations

A priori power considerations were eliminated by the anticipated difficulty with patient retrieval. Even though access was granted to four therapy centres specialising in dieting disorders in the Sydney metropolitan area the protocol of the study (repeated measurement, monitoring of physical activity and measurement of body composition) limited the number of patients who would agree to participate. The study is one of the first investigating seasonal changes in physical activity and body composition; hence, response rates from other studies can not be quoted. The aim was to obtain 20 patients suffering from AN/EDNOS to participate in the study and 20 healthy controls.

Post-hoc power analyses were performed to determine the power to detect a statistical significant effect for the main hypotheses, thereby using the computer program GPOWER (Faul & Erdfelder, 1992).

3. Results

3.1. Questionnaires on dieting disorder pathology

Results for questionnaires on dieting disorder pathology are presented to demonstrate that a case-control design (patients and controls) was realised with the patient group being characterised by more dieting disorder pathology.

3.1.1. Dieting Status Measure

As expected, patients showed more chronicity in their dieting behaviour with more than 30% classified as 'always dieters' across the seasons compared to less than six percent of controls. Table 15 displays the distribution of the participants over the six DiSM categories across the three seasons.

Table 15: Six categories for DiSM

	Autumn	Winter Patients	Summer	Autumn	Winter Controls	Summer
Dieting status % (N)						
"Never dieted"				41.2 (7)	21.7 (5)	21.7 (5)
"Trier"		5.6 (1)	5.6 (1)	5.9 (1)	21.7 (5)	26.1 (6)
"Ex-dieter"	27.3 (3)	22.2 (4)	16.7 (3)	11.8 (2)	13.0 (3)	8.7 (2)
"Diet sometimes"	18.2 (2)	16.7 (3)	5.6 (1)	29.4 (5)	30.4 (7)	21.7 (5)
"Diet often"	9.1 (1)	5.6 (1)	16.7 (3)	5.9 (1)	8.7 (2)	8.7 (2)
"Always dieting"	45.5 (5)	44.4 (8)	33.3 (6)	5.9 (1)		
	n=11	n=17	n=14	n=17	n=22	n=20

When the six categories were summarised in two categories: 'currently non-dieters' (comprising non-dieters, triers and ex-dieters) and 'currently dieters' (comprising

195

occasional dieters, frequent dieters and severe dieters), a significant group-difference was found (GEE; Chi-square $_{(1, N=101)}$=9.9, p=0.002) with more patients classified as dieters than controls across all three seasons.

3.1.2. Body Attitude Test

Probst et al. (1995) have suggested cut-off points for the BAT-score. They defined a score <36 as non-pathological, whereas a score of >36 indicates a disturbance in body experience. Table 16 summarises the percentage of participants assigned to the two categories across the three seasons.

Table 16: Categories for BAT-score

	Autumn	Winter Patients	Summer	Autumn	Winter Controls	Summer
BAT-categories % (N)						
<36	0	23.5 (4)	21.4 (3)	82.4 (14)	86.4 (19)	80.0 (16)
>36	100.0 (11)	76.5 (13)	78.6 (11)	17.6 (3)	13.6 (3)	20.0 (4)
	n=11	n=17	n=14	n=17	n=22	n=20

As hypothesised, a significant group-difference emerged with more patients than controls assigned to the pathological category of body attitudes across all seasons (GEE; Chi-square $_{(1, N=101)}$=35.1, p<0.001).

3.1.3. Eating Attitude Test

As reported by Rosenvinge and Mouland (1990), outcome can be determined on the basis of results in the EAT: good outcome is thereby defined as an EAT-score <18 and poor outcome as an EAT-score >18. Thus, a cut-off score of 18 was used to distinguish participants with high and low levels of dieting disorder pathology. Table 17 displays

the distribution of the participants across the seasons.

Table 17: Categories for EAT-scores

	Autumn	Winter Patients	Summer	Autumn	Winter Controls	Summer
EAT-categories % (N)						
<18	9.1 (1)	23.5 (4)	14.3 (2)	94.1 (16)	95.5 (21)	95.0 (19)
>18	90.9 (10)	76.5 (13)	85.7 (12)	5.9 (1[1])	4.5 (1[1])	5.0 (1[1])
	n=11	n=17	n=14	n=17	n=22	n=20

[1] One control participant displayed high scores on the EAT and stated to have suffered from a dieting disorder eight years ago. Since her body composition was now in a normal range (i.e., body weight of 64.5kg, BMI=22.1, %BF=34.2), she was included as a control participant.

As expected, a significant group-difference emerged in that patients were more often

assigned to the poor outcome group of the EAT (scores >18) than controls (GEE; Chi-

square $_{(1, N=101)}$=39.4, p<0.01).

3.1.4. Food Choice Questionnaire

The FCQ was administered to participants during winter and spring/summer. As

expected, a significant group differences emerged regarding the factor weight control

($F_{1,37}$=18.6, p<0.01) and familiarity ($F_{1,39}$=28.1, p<0.01). Specifically, patients had

significantly higher scores for weight control across both seasons. Controls considered

familiarity of the food as less important than patients across both seasons. Results for

the following subscales are presented in table 18: weight control, familiarity and

ideological reasons.

Table 18: Results for three food choice factors, weight control, familiarity and ideological reasons

	Winter	Summer	Winter	Summer	F-value	p-value for # group $ within & interaction
		Patients		Controls		
Weight control						
Mean± SD	3.5±0.8	3.4±0.9	2.3±0.8	2.4±0.7	18.6	0.000**
Range	1.3-4.0	1.0-4.0	1.0-4.0	1.3-4.0	0.8	ns
					0.8	ns
Familiarity						
Mean± SD	2.7±0.7	2.9±0.5	1.7±0.6	1.9±0.6	28.1	0.000**
Range	1.3-3.7	2.0-3.3	1.0-3.0	1.0-3.0	2.2	ns
					0.1	ns
Ideological reasons						
Mean± SD	2.1±0.5	1.8±0.6	1.8±0.6	1.7±0.5	1.3	ns
Range	1.0-2.9	1.0-3.0	1.0-3.0	1.0-2.7	4.3	0.046
					2.1	ns
	n=17	n=14	n=22	n=20		

** p<0.01

3.1.5. Summary of questionnaires on dieting disorder pathology

Results from the questionnaires assessing dieting disorder pathology demonstrated that as expected, the patient group showed more dieting disorder pathology than controls across all seasons. Overall, patients were characterised as dieters, displayed pathological body and eating attitudes, and selected their food on the basis of weight concerns and familiarity of the food.

3.2. Physical activity

3.2.1. Motivation for physical activity and commitment to exercise

3.2.1.1. Motivation for physical activity

The MPAM-R was administered during winter and spring/summer. A significant group-difference emerged for the appearance-factor only ($F_{1,37}=10.9$, p=0.002). As predicted, patients considered improvements of their appearance (i.e., extrinsic motivation) due to engagement in physical activity as significantly more important than controls. No differences emerged for the fitness-factor as another extrinsic motive to engage in exercising. Regarding motives of an intrinsic nature (e.g., enjoyment and competence), both groups showed similar scores across the two seasons. They also had similar scores for the social factor (i.e., the motive of engaging in social interactions through exercising). Results are summarised in table 19.

Table 19: Results for motivation for physical activity

MPAM-R motives	Winter	Summer	Winter	Summer	F-value	p-value for # group $ within & interaction
		Patients		Controls		
Interest	5.2±1.3	5.2±1.1	5.1±0.9	4.8±1.4	0.2	ns
	3.3-7.0	2.6-6.9	3.0-7.0	2.4-6.6	2.3	ns
					0.4	ns
Competence	5.3±1.0	5.5±1.2	4.8±0.9	4.8±1.3	2.8	ns
	3.1-6.7	2.6-7.0	2.4-6.1	1.9-7.0	0.1	ns
					0.1	ns
Appearance	5.9±1.1	5.7±1.3	4.6±1.4	4.4±1.2	10.9	0.002**
	3.5-7.0	3.2-7.0	1.8-6.7	2.2-6.3	1.4	ns
					0.2	ns
Fitness	5.9±0.9	5.9±0.8	5.9±0.9	5.8±0.8	0.03	ns
	3.8-7.0	4.8-7.0	3.0-7.0	4.0-7.0	0.04	ns
					0.02	ns
Social	3.3±1.4	3.3±1.6	3.4±1.3	3.0±1.5	0.03	ns
	1.0-5.4	1.0-5.8	1.0-5.2	1.0-5.4	0.3	ns
					0.3	ns
	N=17	N=22	N=14	N=20		

** p<0.01

3.2.1.2. Commitment to exercise

Consistent with the hypothesis, patients scored significantly higher on both the obligatory aspect (CES-1; $F_{1,40}=17.3$, p<0.01) and pathological aspect (CES-2; $F_{1,40}=27.6$, p<0.01) of commitment to exercise across all seasons when compared to controls. For the obligatory aspect, a significant seasonal difference emerged with patients' scores increasing from autumn to winter and decreasing during spring/summer, and controls' scores constantly decreasing across the three seasons ($F_{2,56}=4.6$, p=0.02). Regarding the pathological aspect of exercising, patients' and controls' scores decreased across the seasons ($F_{2,56}=8.0$, p<0.01). Results are presented in table 20.

Table 20: Results for commitment to exercise

	Autumn	Winter	Summer	Autumn	Winter	Summer	F-value	p-value for # group $ within & interaction
		Patients			Controls			
Obligatory attitudes								
	61.0±	63.1±	58.9±	37.1±	31.2±	27.6±	17.3	0.000**
	27.8	26.7	22.4	22.3	20.9	19.9	4.6	0.015*
	153.5-93.4	1.8-97.8	9.3-86.5	4.7-74.6	5.8-70.7	3.8-66.2	0.2	ns
Pathological attitudes								
	57.0±	56.1±	49.0±	23.6±	18.1±	14.6±	27.6	0.000**
	24.9	27.7	25.7	24.3	17.4	14.4	8.0	0.001**
	6.8-94.0	4.3-95.5	8.6-88.1	0-74.6	0-68.0	0-47.3	1.4	ns
	N=11	N=17	N=14	N=17	N=22	N=20		

* $p<0.05$
** $p<0.01$
Values for the items were converted as a percentage of the total length of the line for each item. Items for obligatory and pathological values were then summed up and mean values for each scale were computed (Davis et al., 1993a).

3.2.1.3. Summary of motivation for physical activity and commitment to exercise

As hypothesised, patients showed more extrinsic motivation in terms of improving their physical appearance through physical activity compared to controls. Patients' motivation to improve their physical appearance remained significantly higher than controls across each of the seasons. Further, patients demonstrated higher obligatory and pathological attitudes towards exercising than controls in all seasons. Patients' obligatory increased during winter and decreased during spring/summer, and pathological attitudes decreased across the seasons.

3.2.2. Duration and frequency of physical activity

Results from the 7-PAR will be presented in sequence of the hypotheses:

1. Results on differences between patients and controls in the 7-PAR variables, that
   is a) time in moderate intensity activities, b) time in hard intensity activities, c)
   time in very hard intensity activities, d) strengthening and flexibility activities.

2. Results on seasonal variation in the 7-PAR variables in patients and controls.

3. Results on differences in the seasonal variation in the 7-PAR variables between
   patients and controls.

Three control participants were identified as outliers and therefore excluded from the
analysis as their time spent in very hard intensity activities, strength and/or flexibility
was more than one standard deviation higher than the means for controls. One of the
three participants attempted to lose weight during winter and spring/summer, one was
training for a triathlon and the third one for a rugby competition. The sample size for
control participants for the 7-PAR was 14 for autumn, 19 for winter and 17 for
spring/summer.

3.2.2.1. 7-PAR variables across the seasons

3.2.2.1.1. Time in moderate intensity activity

Patients and controls reported an increase in their daily time spent in moderate intensity
activities from autumn to spring/summer (season: $F_{2,49}=8.1$, p<0.01). No significant
group-difference or interaction emerged. Table 21 displays the reported time spent in
moderate intensity activities across the seasons.

Table 21: Reported daily time spent in moderate intensity activities across the seasons

	Autumn	Winter	Summer	Autumn	Winter	Summer	F-value	p-value for # group $ within & interaction
		Patients			Controls			
Mean ambient temperature (°C)	21.2	14.0	21.5	21.2	14.0	21.5		
Reported daily time spent in moderate intensity activities (hrs/d)	0.57± 0.27 0.17- 1.25	0.54± 0.41 0.0-2.58	1.36± 0.47 0.21- 3.21	1.21± 2.0 0.0-8.08	1.02± 0.38 0.13- 2.25	1.34± 1.30 0.08- 5.39	2.73 8.1 0.2	ns 0.001** ns
	N=10[1]	N=17	N=14	N=14	N=19	N=17		

[1] One patient did not show up for the interview.
** p<0.01
Mean ambient temperature from the Bureau of Meteorology (Observatory Hill, Sydney).

3.2.2.1.2. Time in hard intensity activity

As predicted, a significant group-difference for time spent in hard-intensity activities emerged (F $_{1,45}$=6.1, p=0.017). Patients reported spending more time in hard intensity activities than controls across all seasons. No differences emerged across the seasons and the interaction failed to reach statistical significance (see table 22).

Due to a significant deviation from the normal distribution (Shapiro Wilks statistic W=0.835, p=0.01), the variable was also categorised into two categories (engagement in hard-intensity activities: yes/no). The categorisation showed that all patients (100.0%) reported engaging in hard intensity across all seasons, whereas 78.6% (n=11) of the controls in autumn, 78.9% (n=15) in winter and 70.6% (n=12) reported engaging in hard intensity activities.

Table 22: Reported daily time spent in hard intensity activities across the seasons

	Autumn	Winter	Summer	Autumn	Winter	Summer	F-value	p-value for # group $ within & interaction
		Patients			Controls			
Mean ambient temperature (°C)								
	21.2	14.0	21.5	21.2	14.0	21.5		
Reported daily time spent in hard intensity activities (hrs/d)								
	0.41±	0.43±0.34	0.55±	0.18±	0.21±	0.36±	6.1	0.017*
	0.34	0.04-1.54	0.34	0.19	0.22	0.33	2.3	ns
	0.08-1.36		0.04-1.38	0-1.08	0-1.07	0-1.33	0.2	ns
	N=10[1]	N=17	N=14	N=14	N=19	N=17		

[1] One patient did not show up for the interview.
** p<0.01

3.2.2.1.3. Time in very hard intensity activity

In accordance with the hypothesis, a significant group difference emerged for time spent in very hard intensity activities ($F_{1,43}$=4.6, p=0.04). Patients reported spending significantly more time in very hard intensity activities compared to controls across all seasons. Further, there was a significant seasonal effect ($F_{2,49}$=4.4, p=0.02). In both groups, time spent in very hard activities increased significantly during spring/summer. The distribution of the variable was significantly different from the normal-distribution (Shapiro Wilks statistic W=0.760, p=0.01), hence the variable was categorised into two categories (very hard-intensity activity: yes/no). Table 23 displays the distribution of the participants. No significant differences emerged in the number of patients and controls engaging in very hard intensity activities across the seasons when Chi-squares tests were computed for each group separately (Chi-square $_{patients\ df=1N=41}$=2.81, p=0.25; Chi-square $_{controls\ df=1N=50}$=2.26, p=0.32).

A significant group-difference emerged for spring/summer (Chi-square $_{(df=1,\ N=24)}$=3.77, p=0.05), with a higher percentage of patients indicating engagement in very hard activities (64.3%, n=9) compared to 29.4% (n=5) of controls. No significant group-differences emerged for the other two seasons (Chi-square $_{autumn\ (df=1,\ N=24)}$=0.24, p=0.63; Chi-square $_{winter\ (df=1,\ N=36)}$=0.34, p=0.56), thus offering only partial support for the hypothesis that patients would spend more time engaging in very hard activities.

Table 23: Engagement in very hard-intensity activities (yes/no)

	Autumn	Winter Patients	Summer	Autumn	Winter Controls	Summer
Mean ambient temperature (°C)						
	21.2 14.0		21.5	21.2 14.0		21.5
Engagement in very hard-intensity activities % (n)						
Yes	36.4 (4)	35.3 (6)	64.3 (9)	50.0 (7)	26.3 (5)	29.4 (5)
No	54.5 (6)	64.7 (11)	35.7 (5)	50.0 (7)	73.7 (14)	70.6 (12)
	n=10[1]	n=17	n=14	n=14	n=19	n=17

[1] One patient did not show up for the interview.

Computing GEE showed no significant results for changes in the amount of patients or controls engaging in very hard intensity activities across the seasons (Chi-square $_{patients\ (2,\ N=97)}$=2.9, p=0.23; Chi-square $_{controls\ (2,\ N=97)}$=2.20, p=0.14). No group-differences emerged (Chi-square $_{(2,\ N=97)}$=1.43, p=0.23) when computed across the seasons. Hence, contrary to the hypothesis, a similar amount of patients and controls engaged in very hard intensity activities across the seasons. Finally, the interaction between group and season failed to reach statistical significance (Chi-square $_{(2,\ N=97)}$=2.81, p=0.09).

3.2.2.1.4. Strengthening and flexibility activities

Due to a deviation from the normal distribution the variables were categorised into two categories (engagement in strengthening/flexibility activities: yes or no). Table 24 displays the distribution of the participants across the seasons.

205

Table 24: Categories for strengthening and flexibility activities

	Autumn	Winter Patients	Summer	Autumn	Winter Controls	Summer
Mean ambient temperature (°C)	21.2 14.0	21.5	21.2	14.0 21.5		
Strength % (n)						
yes	36.4 (4)	44.4 (8)	33.3 (6)	7.1 (1)	36.8 (7)	11.8 (2)
no	54.5 (6)	50.0 (9)	44.4 (8)	92.9 (13)	63.2 (12)	88.2 (15)
Flexibility % (n)						
yes	63.6 (7)	66.7 (12)	61.1 (11)	28.6 (4)	42.1 (8)	29.4 (5)
no	27.3 (3)	27.8 (5)	16.7 (3)	71.4 (10)	57.9 (11)	70.6 (12)
	N=10[1]	N=17	N=14	N=14	N=19	N=17

[1] One patient did not show up for the interview during autumn.

As predicted, a significant group-difference emerged, with more patients engaging in strengthening activities across the seasons when computing GEE (Chi-square $_{(2, N=97)}$=5.81, p=0.02). A significant within-group difference emerged for the control group (Chi-square $_{(2, N=97)}$=5.52, p=0.02), with more controls engaging in strengthening activities during winter than any other season. No seasonal difference emerged for the patients (Chi-square $_{(2, N=97)}$=0.14, p=0.70). The interaction between group and season was not significant (Chi-square $_{(2, N=97)}$=2.32, p=0.31).

Likewise, the GEE-analysis showed a significant group-difference for flexibility activities, with more patients than controls reporting engaging in flexibility activities across all seasons (Chi-square $_{(2, N=97)}$=13.0, p<0.01). No changes in the amount of patients and controls engaging in flexibility activities emerged across the seasons (Chi-square $_{patients (2, N=97)}$=0.33, p=0.85; Chi-square $_{controls (2, N=97)}$=0.89, p=0.64). Also, the interaction between group and season failed to reach statistical significance (Chi-square $_{(2, N=97)}$=0.82, p=0.66).

3.2.2.1.5. Summary of differences between patients and controls in the 7-PAR variables

As expected, patients and controls did not differ in the reported time spent in moderate intensity activity across the seasons. Reported time spent in moderate intensity activities increased from autumn to spring/summer in both groups.

As hypothesised, patients reported spending more time in hard intensity activities compared to controls across all seasons. Reported time spent in hard intensity activities did not differ across the seasons in both groups. Consistent with the hypothesis, reported time spent in very hard intensity activities was significantly higher in patients than in controls, particularly during spring/summer. Contrary to the hypothesis, the number of patients and controls indicating engagement in very hard intensity activities did not differ in autumn and winter, while a trend for a difference emerged in spring/summer (i.e., more patients than controls indicated engagement in very hard intensity activities). As expected, more patients than controls indicated engaging in strengthening and flexibility activities. Reported engagement in strengthening activities changed across the seasons in the control group but not in the patient group (i.e., more control participants reported engagement in strengthening activities in winter). Reported engagement in flexibility activities did not vary across the seasons for both groups.

3.2.2.2. 7-PAR variables for weekdays and weekend days

Time (hours per day) spent in moderate, hard and very hard-intensity activities was calculated for weekdays and weekend days. Due to the distribution of the variables (i.e., a significant deviation from the normal distribution and a floor-effect) nonparametric statistics (Wilcoxon's rank test) were computed to analyse differences between time spent in the different intensity activities for weekdays and weekend days across the

207

seasons. The analyses were run separately for each group for each of the three seasons. Sharpened Bonferroni tests were computed to account for multiple comparisons.

After Sharpened Bonferroni corrections, no significant differences emerged. There was however, a trend for a difference in reported time spent in moderate intensity activity between weekdays and weekend days in winter in the patient group (Wilcoxon-test, Z=-1.95, p=0.05, p-value need according to Sharpened Bonferroni=0.006). Specifically, patients reported spending more time in moderate intensity activity during the weekend rather than during weekdays. No differences emerged for autumn and spring/summer. Also, reported time spent in hard and very hard intensity activities did not differ between weekdays and weekend days.

In the control group, contrary to the hypothesis, no differences emerged in the reported time spent in moderate, hard and very hard intensity activities during weekdays and weekends across all three seasons.

3.2.2.2.1. Summary of 7-PAR variables for weekdays and weekend days

Contrary to the hypothesis, across two seasons, patients demonstrated a similar activity pattern for weekdays and weekend days for moderate, hard and very hard intensity activities. In winter, a trend for increases in patients' reported time spent in moderate intensity activities emerged during the weekend.

Activity-levels in controls did not differ during weekdays and weekend days in autumn, winter and spring/summer.

3.2.2.3. Seasonal variation in the 7-PAR variables in patients and controls

Seasonal analyses were computed for the following 7-PAR variables:

- Time (hrs/d) in moderate intensity activities

- Time (hrs/d) in hard intensity activities

- Time (hrs/d) in very hard intensity activities.

In the patient group, reported time spent in moderate intensity activities showed a seasonal variation with a minimum during winter and a maximum during spring/summer (p=0.01). Patients reported on average 1:36 hours/day during spring/summer compared to 0:57 hours/day and 0:54 hrs/d for autumn and winter, respectively. The mean time spent in moderate intensity activities over the year was 1:09 hours/day and the amplitude (peak to trough distance) was 0:42 ± 0:12. The phase (date where the curve intersects the mean value) was the 7th of September.

Likewise, a trend for a seasonal variation emerged in the control group (p=0.10). Controls reported spending most time in moderate intensity activities during spring/summer (Mean=1:34 hours/day) and least during winter (Mean=1:02 hours/day). The amplitude was 0:39 ± 0:16. The phase was the 12th of October. Figure 3 shows the seasonal curve for both groups.

Seasonal variation in moderate intensity activities

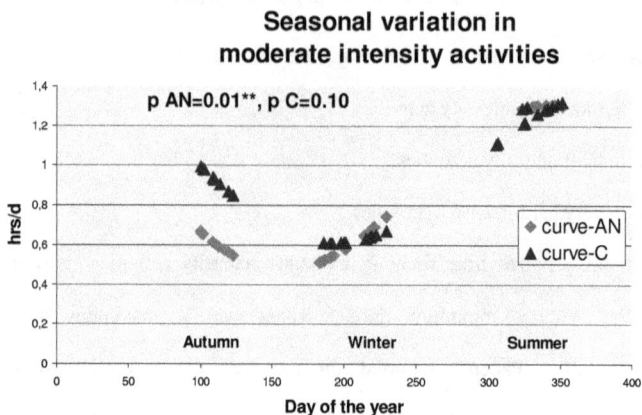

Figure 3: Seasonal variation in moderate intensity activities

No group difference in the amplitudes (peak to trough distance) emerged between patients and controls (t $_{(1)}$=0.15, p=0.90) indicating that patients and controls showed a similar seasonal pattern in terms of the reported time spent in moderate intensity activities.

No seasonal variation emerged for time spent in hard and very hard intensity activities, neither in the patient nor in the control group.

3.2.2.3.1. Summary of seasonal variation in 7-PAR variables in patients and controls

As hypothesised, reported time spent in moderate intensity activities varied across the seasons in both groups. Patients and controls increased the amount of time they spent in moderate activities during spring/summer. Further, in contrast to the hypothesis, variation in moderate intensity activities did not differ between patients and controls as hypothesised. Instead, both groups showed a similar seasonal pattern.

As expected, patients' exercise behaviour (i.e., time spent in very hard intensity activities) did not vary across the seasons. Likewise, controls reported spending a similar amount of time in very hard intensity activities across the seasons.

3.2.3. Body movement

3.2.3.1. Counts per day and counts per minute

The following variables were analysed: 1) Average counts over active monitoring time (counts/day, AC-AMT), 2) counts per minute over active monitoring time (CM-AMT), 3) average time the Tracmor was worn (hours per day) and 4) time (hours per day) spent in intensity categories of body movement.

Two outliers (control participants) were identified with AC-AMT of more than one standard deviation above the mean for controls. The two outliers were the same as for the 7-PAR variables (i.e., one participant was training for a triathlon while another participant was attempting to lose weight). Due to problems in analysing the Tracmor-data, dropouts and new recruitments, varying sample sizes across the seasons emerged resulting in 28 Tracmor-sets for autumn, 35 for winter and 33 for spring/summer. Figure 4 displays examples of Tracmor-outputs per day for a patient and a control.

Tracmor-output for a patient over one day

sum of counts/10000

06:00 07:00 09:00 11:00 13:00 15:00 17:00 19:00 21:00 23:00 01:00 03:00

Tracmor-output for a control over one day

sum of counts/10000

06:00 07:00 09:00 11:00 13:00 15:00 17:00 19:00 21:00 23:00 01:00 03:00

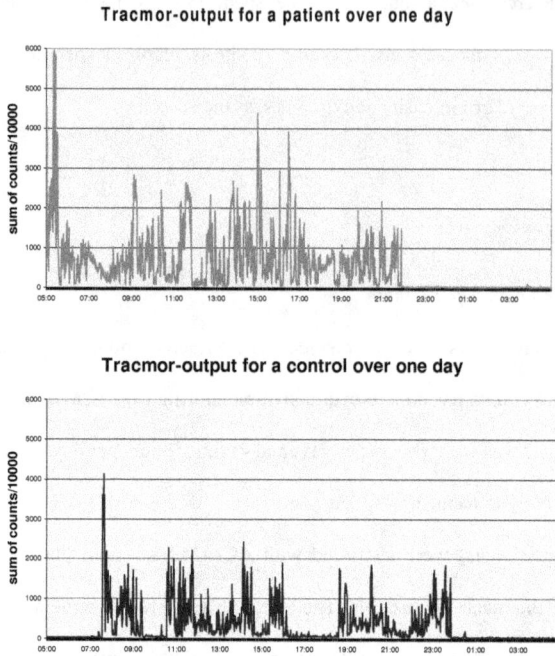

Figure 4: Tracmor-output for a patient and a control over one day

There was a significant group difference in AC-AMT with patients showing higher counts across all seasons ($F_{1,39}$=6.1, p=0.018). After Sharpened Bonferroni corrections however, the difference just failed to reach statistical significance (p-value needed according to Sharpened Bonferroni=0.016). Further, patients tended to show higher CM-AMT across all seasons ($F_{1,41}$=6.1, p=0.017; p-value needed according to Sharpened Bonferroni=0.016). The seasonal comparison and the interaction failed to reach statistical significance. In addition, patients and controls did not differ in the time they wore the Tracmor and the time did not differ across the seasons. Results are presented in table 25.

Table 25: Body movement across the seasons

	Autumn	Winter	Summer	Autumn	Winter	Summer	F-value	p-value for # group $ within & interaction
		Patients			Controls			
Mean ambient temperature (°C)								
	21.2	14.0	21.5	21.2	14.0	21.5		
AC-AMT (Mean ± SD; Range)								
	753011±	694848±	777940±	649802±	552759±	553686±	6.1	0.018*[1]
	282762	291998	226182	159826	171656	137823	1.3	ns
	277658-	330473-	549294-	410736-	188112-	342858-	1.8	ns
	1212671	1472072	1340844	996875	832400	798799		
CM-AMT (Mean ± SD; Range)								
	864±	811±	881±	779±	662±	647±	6.1	0.017*[1]
	277	289	214	193	218	155	1.2	ns
	475-1223	434-1576	646-1396	579-1223	236-1151	401-964	1.8	ns
Average time worn per day (hrs/d)								
	14:16±	14:03±	14:36±	13:56±	13:57±	14:14±	0.4	ns
	1:50	1:08	1:07	1:14	0:54	1:03	0.4	ns
	9:44-	12:34-	13:12-	10:45-	12:03-	11:36-	0.1	ns
	16:31	15:39	17:07	16:11	15:25	15:55		
	N=11	N=14	N=13	N=15	N=19	N=18		

AC-AMT: Average counts over active monitoring time
CM-AMT: Counts per minute over active monitoring time
* p<0.05
[1] p-value needed according to Sharpened Bonferroni=0.016.

3.2.3.2. Time in intensity categories of body movement

Participants' time spent in five categories of body movement (see table 13, chapter 2.6.1.4.) was computed. A trend for a group difference emerged for the time spent in category 2 (walking at 5km/h; $F_{1,40}$=5.5, p=0.024; p-value from Sharpened Bonferroni=0.0125). Patients spent more time in this activity-category across all seasons. Further, patients spent significantly more time in category 4 (activities similar to walking/running at 9km/h; $F_{1,39}$=5.8, p=0.021; p-value needed according to Sharpened Bonferroni=0.025). There were no differences either between groups or across the seasons for the other categories. Results are presented in table 26.

Table 26: Results for time in two intensity categories of body movement

	Autumn	Winter Patients	Summer	Autumn	Winter Controls	Summer	F-value	p-value for # group $ within & interaction
Mean ambient temperature (°C)	21.2	14.0	21.5	21.2	14.0	21.5		
Time in Category 2 (Walking at 5km/h) (hrs/d)								
	2:04±	2:10±	2:32±	1:55±	1:44±	1:54±	5.5	0.024*[1]
	0:26	0:46	0:43	0:35	0:30	0:35	1.7	ns
	1:20-	1:10-	1:29-	1:00-	0:56-	1:01-	1.0	ns
	2:38	4:17	3:37	3:03	2:31	3:26		
Time in Category 4 (Walking/running at 9km/h) (hrs/d)								
	0:23±	0:22±	0:24±	0:13±	0:10±	0:08±	5.8	0.021*[2]
	0:20	0:29	0:21	0:14	0:11	0:10	0.1	ns
	0:01-	0:01-	0:03-	0:00-	0:00-	0:00-	1.0	ns
	0:55	1:59	1:19	0:48	0:35	0:32		
	N=11	N=14	N=13	N=15	N=19	N=18		

* $p<0.05$.
[1] p-value needed according to Sharpened Bonferroni=0.0125.
[2] p-value needed according to Sharpened Bonferroni=0.025.

3.2.3.3. Summary for differences in body movement

As hypothesised, patients tended to show significantly more body movement (i.e., counts/day and average counts/min) than controls across all three seasons. Specifically, patients spent more time in moderate levels of body movement (i.e., movement as in walking 5 km/hr) and more time in very hard levels of body movement (e.g., running at a speed of nine km/hour) across all seasons.

3.2.3.4. Body movement for weekdays and weekend days

AC-AMT (counts per day) were calculated separately for weekdays and weekend days. Two-way ANOVAs with repeated measures for group and AC-AMT for day of the week were computed for each season separately.

In autumn, patients and controls demonstrated less body movement for weekends than for weekdays ($F_{1,24}$=7.6, p=0.011; p-value needed according to Sharpened Bonferroni=0.016).

In winter, a trend for a group difference emerged ($F_{1,31}$=3.9, p=0.056; p-value needed according to Sharpened Bonferroni=0.025), with patients showing more body movement during weekdays and weekends. Further, a significant interaction between day of the week and group was found ($F_{1,31}$=6.2, p=0.018; p-value needed according to Sharpened Bonferroni=0.05). While patients increased their body movement during the weekend, controls decreased their body movement.

For spring/summer, a significant group difference emerged ($F_{1,29}$=11.4, p=0.002; p-value needed according to Sharpened Bonferroni=0.05), with patients showing significantly more body movement during both weekdays and weekends. Further, a significant effect for day of the week emerged, with patients and controls showing more body movement during weekdays ($F_{1,29}$=5.7, p=0.02; p-value needed according to Sharpened Bonferroni=0.05). Table 27 displays the results.

Table 27: Body movement for weekdays and weekend days

	Weekdays	Weekend days	F-value	p-value # group $ within & interaction
		AC-AMT (counts/day) Mean±SD		
Autumn				
Patients (n=11)	781160± 283793	696713± 320867	1.2	ns
Controls (n=15)	727876± 234013	574238/ 119761	7.6	0.011*[1]
			0.6	ns
Winter				
Patients (n=14)	681518± 292572	719492± 337020	3.9	0.056
Controls (n=19)	585352± 174520	489478± 182788	1.2	ns
			6.2	0.018*[2]
Summer				
Patients (n=13)	811105± 227215	716562± 249297	11.4	0.002**[3]
Controls (n=18)	570331± 165858	522895± 145376	5.7	0.023*[3]
			0.6	ns

*p<0.05
**p<0.01
AC-AMT: Average counts over active monitoring time.

3.2.3.4.1. Summary of body movement for weekdays and weekends

Contrary to the hypothesis, patients displayed less body movement during weekends in autumn and spring/summer. Likewise, controls demonstrated less body movement during these seasons. In winter, as expected, patients increased their body movement during the weekend, while controls demonstrated a decrease in body movement.

3.2.3.5. Seasonal variation in body movement in patients and controls

Seasonal analyses were computed for the following Tracmor-variables:

- Counts per minute (CM-AMT)

- Time (minutes per week) in five intensity categories of body movement.

No seasonal variation emerged in CM-AMT in either the patient or the control group. There were no significant differences in the time (minutes/week) spent in the five Tracmor-categories across the three seasons, neither for patients nor for controls.

Patients and controls tended to keep their body movement at a similar level across the seasons. Neither controls nor patients changed the amount of time spent in various intensity categories of body movement across the seasons.

3.3. Body composition

Body composition variables included the following: a) body weight (in kg), b) BMI, c) %BF; %FFM and FFM (in kg). Results will be presented in the sequence of the hypotheses.

3.3.1. Body weight and body mass index

There was a significant group difference for body weight ($F_{1,39}$=16.7, p<0.01) and a significant interaction for group and season ($F_{2,56}$=3.4, p=0.04; p-value needed according to Sharpened Bonferroni=0.04). From winter to spring/summer, patients' body weight increased an average of 2.7 kg. In contrast, controls' body weight increased an average of 0.6 kg from autumn to winter, and decreased an average of 0.5 kg during spring/summer.

The BMI followed a similar pattern in that patients' BMI was significantly lower than that of controls and increased gradually across the seasons. Controls' BMI remained stable across the seasons with a small decrease from autumn to winter (this is related to an increase in participants' height, i.e., mean for height in autumn=1.67m ±4.6 and mean for height in winter=1.68m ±6.9. Recruitment of new control participants caused the increase in height. Hence, the mean for height for controls in autumn was 1.67m ± 4.7 and the

217

mean for height for 'newly recruited' controls was 1.71m ±10.8). Results are presented

in table 28.

Table 28: Results for body weight and body mass index

	Autumn	Winter Patients	Summer	Autumn	Winter Controls	Summer	F-value	p-value for # group $ within & interaction
Mean ambient temperature (°C)	21.2	14.0	21.5	21.2	14.0	21.5		
Body weight (kg)	51.8±8.8	51.8±8.4	54.5±8.4	62.4±10	63.0±9.9	62.5±9.5	16.7	0.000**
	37.1-70.9	39.7-73.7	39.9-74.4	52.9-85.9	51.9-87.3	52.6-89.6	1.0	ns
							3.4	0.04
BMI	18.8±2.6	19.0±2.5	19.7±2.6	22.5±3.5	22.4±4.0	22.4±4.2	11.9	0.001**
	15.2-24.3	14.7-25.0	16.1-25.2	18.3-31.8	18.4-32.6	18.0-34.1	0.7	ns
							2.8	ns
	N=11	N=17	N=14	N=17	N=22	N=20		

** p<0.01

3.3.2. Percentage body fat, %FFM and FFM

Percentage BF was significantly lower in the patient group ($F_{1,39}$=17.7, p<0.01). While

patients' %BF decreased slightly during winter (-0.2%), it increased during

spring/summer (+3.5%). Controls' %BF increased during winter (+0.9%) and decreased

during spring/summer (-2.0%). The different results are reflected in a trend for a

significant interaction ($F_{2,56}$=3.9, p=0.027; p-value needed according to Sharpened

Bonferroni=0.025).

For %FFM, a significant group difference ($F_{1,39}$=17.7, p<0.01) and a trend for a

significant interaction between group and season emerged ($F_{2,54}$=3.9, p=0.027; p-value

needed according to Sharpened Bonferroni=0.025). Patients' %FFM was significantly

higher compared to controls across all seasons. While patients' %FFM increased in

218

winter (+0.2%) and decreased in spring/summer (-3.5%), controls' %FFM decreased in winter (-0.9%) and increased in spring/summer (+2.0%).

A trend for a group difference in FFM (in kg) emerged (F $_{1,39}$=3.9, p=0.056; p-value needed according to Sharpened Bonferroni=0.05). Controls tended to have higher FFM compared to patients across all seasons. FFM further changed across the seasons (F $_{2,54}$=3.9, p=0.025; p-value needed according to Sharpened Bonferroni=0.025). FFM increased continuously in the patient group. In the control group, FFM decreased during winter (-0.3kg) and increased during spring/summer (+0.9kg). Results are presented in table 29.

Table 29: Results for %BF and percentage FFM

	Autumn	Winter Patients	Summer	Autumn	Winter Controls	Summer	F-value	p-value for # group $ within & interaction
Mean ambient temperature (°C)	21.2	14.0	21.5	21.2	14.0	21.5		
%BF								
	22.2±11	22.0±11	25.5±8.7	31.9±6.0	32.8±7.7	30.8±8.6	17.7	0.000**
	7.7-41.7	4.8-42.0	12.7-43.1	21.9-49.2	19.2-51.3	20.2-51.8	2.4	ns
							3.9	0.027*
%FFM								
	77.8±11	78.0±11	74.5±8.7	68.1±6.0	67.2±7.7	69.2±8.6	18.1	0.000**
	58.3-92.3	58.0-95.2	56.9-87.3	50.8-78.1	48.7-80.8	48.2-79.8	4.9	0.01*
							3.8	0.03*
FFM (kg)								
	39.5±3.2	39.9±3.1	40.3±3.8	42.1±4.9	41.8±4.9	42.7±5.0	3.89	0.056
	33.8-44.7	34.5-47.8	34.5-47.8	37.7-52.2	35.8-51.4	34.9-53.3	3.93	0.025*
							1.93	ns
	N=11	N=16 [1]	N=13 [2]	N=17	N=22	N=20		

*p<0.05
**p<0.01
[1] n=16; one patient did not have a DEXA-scan.
[2] n=13; one patient did not have a DEXA-scan.

3.3.3. Seasonal variation in body composition variables

Seasonal analyses were computed for the following body composition variables:

- Body weight (in kg)

- BMI

- % BF

- % FFM

- FFM (in kg)

No seasonal variation emerged for body weight, BMI, %BF, %FFM and FFM (in kg) in patients. In controls, body weight and BMI showed no seasonal variation, while a trend for a seasonal variation emerged for %BF and %FFM (p=0.10). Controls' %BF increased during winter (+0.9%) and decreased during spring/summer (-2.0%).

Consequently, their %FFM decreased during winter (-0.9%) and increased during spring/summer (+2.0%)

In addition, FFM varied across the seasons in the control group (p=0.01). FFM decreased during winter (-0.3kg) and increased during spring/summer (+0.9 kg). The amplitude was 0.59kg (±0.17). The phase was the 5th of November. Figure 5 displays the seasonal variation in FFM in controls.

Seasonal variation in FFM in controls

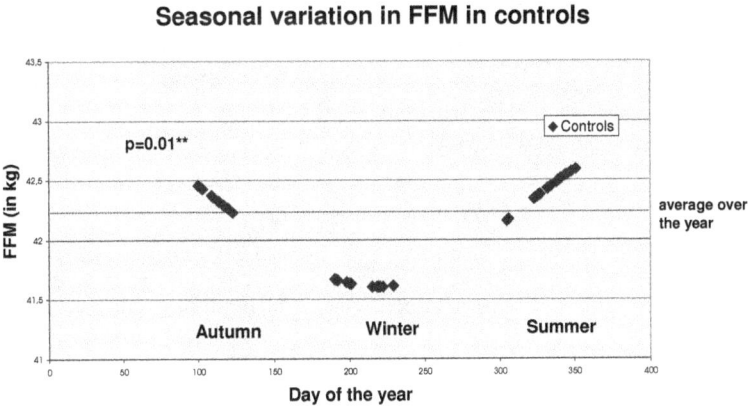

Figure 5: Seasonal variation in FFM (in kg) in controls

3.4. Physical activity and body composition

3.4.1. Time in intensity categories of body movement and body composition

Pearson correlation coefficients (bivariate) were computed for both groups, thereby computing correlations across all seasons to increase statistical power. The Sharpened

Bonferroni method was used to account for multiple correlations. Correlations were computed for the following variables:

- Time (minutes per week) spent in category 1 (walking at 3 km/hr) with %BF, %FFM and FFM (in kg)

- Time (minutes per week) spent in category 2 (walking at 5km/hr) with %BF, %FFM and FFM (in kg)

- Time (minutes per week) spent in category 3 (walking at 7km/hr) with %BF, %FFM and FFM (in kg)

- Time (minutes per week) spent in category 4 (running at 9 km/hr) with %BF, %FFM and FFM (in kg)

- Time (minutes per week) spent in category 5 (running faster than 9 km/hr) with %BF, %FFM and FFM (in kg).

Of the body composition variables, only FFM correlated significantly with time in various intensity body movement in both groups. In the patient group, FFM was positively correlated with time spent in category 2, 3, 4 and 5. Specifically, the higher the patients' FFM, the higher the time spent in the four categories. A trend emerged for a negative correlation between %BF and the time spent in category 5 (i.e., very hard intensity) (r=-.29, p=0.08).

In the control group, FFM (in kg) was positively correlated with the time spent in category 4 and 5; indicating that the more time controls' spent in higher intensities of body movement, the higher their FFM. Table 30 displays the results.

Table 30: Correlations between time in intensity categories of body movement and %BF and FFM

Time (minutes per week) in	%BF	FFM (in kg)
	Patients	
Category 2 Walking at 5km/h		.49 0.002** n=36
Category 3 Walking/running at 7km/h		.50 0.002** n=36
Category 4 Walking/running at 9km/h		.51 0.002** n=36
Category 5 Walking/running more than 9km/h	-.29 p=0.08 n=36	.58 0.000** n=36

	%BF	FFM (in kg)
	Controls	
Category 4 Walking/running at 9km/h		.41 0.001** n=58
Category 5 Walking/running more than 9km/h		.34 0.009** n=58

** p<0.01

223

4. Discussion

The overall aim of the present study was to investigate physical activity patterns in outpatients with AN and healthy controls across three seasons using a multidimensional approach. Specifically, the study aimed to assess seasonal variation in physical activity and body composition, and to explore the relationship between physical activity and body composition variables in the two groups.

4.1. Summary of major findings on physical activity

In this study, outpatients with AN were characterised by higher extrinsic motivation for physical activity (i.e., improvement of their physical appearance) and higher commitment to exercise than controls across autumn, winter and spring/summer.

Further, while patients reported spending a similar amount of time in moderate intensity activities and demonstrated a similar seasonal variation for moderate intensity activities (i.e., with increases in spring/summer) as controls, they showed higher levels of exercise (i.e., time spent in hard and very hard intensity activities) than controls. In terms of seasonal variation for hard and very hard intensity activities for the patients, no seasonal variation emerged. However, time spent in very hard intensity activities increased in both groups in spring/summer and the number of patients reporting engagement in very hard intensity activities was higher compared to controls during spring/summer. In addition, more patients than controls indicated engaging in strengthening and flexibility activities across all three seasons.

Across two seasons (i.e., autumn and spring/summer), patients demonstrated similar activity-levels (i.e. moderate, hard and very hard intensity activities) during weekdays and weekends. In winter, however, a trend emerged for patients to report increases in the time spent in moderate intensity activities during the weekend. In contrast, activity-levels in controls did not differ during weekdays and weekend days in autumn, winter and spring/summer.

With regard to body movement, patients showed more body movement (i.e., counts/day and counts/min) than controls across all three seasons. Patients decreased their body movement during weekends in autumn and spring/summer. In winter, however, patients tended to increase their body movement during the weekend and were thus different from controls. Specifically, controls decreased their body movement during the weekends in all three seasons.

Patients and controls tended to keep their body movement at a similar level across the seasons.

4.1.1. Discussion of findings on motivation for physical activity and commitment to exercise

As expected, patients with AN demonstrated more extrinsic motivation for physical activity and higher commitment to exercise across the seasons. This finding is consistent with previous studies on the relationship between motives for exercise, commitment to exercise and dieting disorder pathology (Davis et al., 1995; Davis & Fox, 1993b; McLaren et al., 2001; Mond et al., 2004). In combination, these results support the notion that a comprehensive understanding of overactivity in AN necessitates attention to both the quantitative and the qualitative aspects of exercise

225

behaviour. Indeed, Strober et al. (1997) demonstrated in their outcome study that compulsion to exercise – a qualitative component – was a significant predictor of relapse. Windauer et al. (1993) also assessed the qualitative dimension in their follow-up study with 16 weight-recovered anorexic patients in which it was found that six patients (37.5%) were exercising heavily or vigorously with the intention of controlling their body weight and shape.

Similarly, patients in this study were recovering from the dieting disorder (in terms of their body weight and %BF) but still demonstrated obligatory and pathological attitudes towards exercise.

Seasonality was found for obligatory attitudes towards exercise (defined as psychological well-being being contingent upon assiduous adherence to a regular and structured exercise regimen). In the present study, patients' obligatory attitudes worsened during winter and improved during spring/summer. A worsening of individuals' mood states during the winter-season has been consistently shown in the literature (for reviews see (Kasper, Wehr, Bartko, Gaist, & Rosenthal, 1989; Magnusson, 2000); see also part 1, chapter 1.2.). Moreover, Penas-Lledo, Vaz Leal and Waller (2002a) suggested that exercise in patients with AN is used as a compensating mechanism to cope with emotional distress. Thus, increases in obligatory attitudes towards exercise during winter might result from peaks in depressive mood during this season and the attempt to decrease depressive mood states by focussing on the activity of exercise.

Also, environmental factors during winter (i.e., decrease in the hours of daylight) may decrease activity-levels in patients. Patients may be aware of this decrease, as demonstrated in a study in healthy participants in the Netherlands (Plasqui &

Westerterp, 2004b) and may therefore become more obsessed with maintaining their exercise level during this season. As a conclusion, challenging patients' attitudes becomes crucial during the winter season.

In terms of patients' motives for exercise, as shown by Frederick (1994), exercise for body-related motives is associated with anxiety and depression. Likewise, Mond et al. (2004) demonstrated positive associations between exercising for weight loss, attractiveness and body toning with a reduced quality of life. These results emphasise the need to challenge patients' motives and commitment to exercise during treatment. Seasonal variation in patients' attitudes (i.e., more obsessive attitudes during winter) need to be integrated into the treatment process.

4.1.2. Discussion of findings on duration and frequency of physical activity

Patients and controls did not differ in the time they spent in moderate intensity activities and a group similarity in seasonal variation (with decreases in winter) emerged. While this is the first study to have investigated seasonal variation in physical activity among patients with AN, the obtained results are in accordance with studies in the general population (Matthews et al., 2001a; Plasqui & Westerterp, 2004b) that demonstrated seasonal variation, particularly in moderate intensity activities. Moderate intensity activities comprise activities such as walking, carrying light objects and household activities. It can be assumed that the amount of walking in particular, varies with seasonal changes in environmental factors (such as decreased hours of daylight during the winter season).

It is of interest that patients in this study tended to increase the time they spent in moderate intensity activities during the weekends in winter only. Awareness of decreased activity-levels during the week in winter may have caused this increase during the weekend. Hence, patients may try to compensate for their decreased activity-levels by being more active on the weekend. Despite this attempted compensation, they do not manage to increase the time spent in moderate activities to their summer levels. Compensation of decreased activity-levels in winter has been discussed by Plasqui and Westerterp (2004b) who found a seasonal variation in the PAL particularly in those participants who were highly active. They argued that active people may try to compensate for a reduction in moderate intensity activities during winter by engaging in sports activities. Patients in the present study, however, did not increase sport activities during weekends in winter but rather increased moderate intensity activities. It remains to be clarified if these increases in moderate intensity activities during weekends in winter reflect restlessness and the inability to relax on the weekend or whether patients allow themselves 'time off exercise' during weekends but compensate with increases in moderate intensity activities.

The finding that patients and controls differed particularly in exercise behaviours (i.e., hard and very hard intensity activities, strengthening and flexibility activities) is consistent with studies demonstrating overexercising in patients with AN (Beumont, Booth, Abraham, Griffiths, & Turner, 1983; Davis et al., 1994; Kron et al., 1978; Penas-Lledo, Vaz Leal, & Waller, 2002a; Sharp, Clark, Dunan, Blackwood, & Shapiro, 1994). The activity pattern of patients in this study further confirms clinical accounts (Beumont et al., 1994; Katz, 1996) that documented the solitary exercise routine of patients. Here, only one patient reported engaging in a team sport (i.e., soccer). The majority of patients selected individual and fitness-related sports (such as gym classes and Yoga). As discussed previously, they further demonstrated extrinsic exercise motivation and increased commitment to exercise. Fitness-related activities may reinforce the motive-structure (i.e., exercising to lose weight and become more physically attractive) and commitment to exercise. Further, patients in this study were recovering from AN as demonstrated by increases in body composition variables (i.e., body weight and %BF). Hence, engagement in solitary fitness-related activities was still found to be present in recovering outpatients with AN and thus confirms previous findings that demonstrated increased exercise levels in patients despite weight-recovery (Windauer et al., 1993). As already suggested by Beumont et al. (1994), treatment strategies should therefore aim to initiate engagement in team sports in patients with AN to increase intrinsic motivation (i.e., enjoyment) and the psychologically beneficial outcomes of engagement in sports and exercise (Frederick, 1994).

These strategies may become particularly important when treating patients during spring/summer since this season constitutes a 'high-risk season' for increased engagement in physical activity in patients with AN. Accordingly, the findings of the current study revealed that patients' time in moderate intensity activities increased during spring/summer and the number of patients reporting exercise tended to increase in this season (from 35.3% in winter to 64.3% in spring/summer). It is of importance to investigate if patients' body composition is affected by this increase in activity. Hence, a further descriptive analysis into changes in body composition variables dependent on the engagement in very hard intensity activities across the seasons was conducted. Only those patients who completed all three assessments were integrated to compare body composition changes across three seasons (i.e., n=11 for autumn, n=9 for winter and n=10 for spring/summer; see also figure 1). The descriptive analysis showed that patients engaging in very hard intensity in spring/summer activities differed from those who did not in their changes in body composition. Specifically, patients who exercised during spring/summer (n=5) lost an average of 2.2kg of body weight from winter to spring/summer. This decrease in body weight constituted of a loss in FFM (-1.1kg) and a loss in BF (-1.1.kg). In contrast, patients' body weight who did not exercise in spring/summer (n=5) remained stable from winter to spring/summer. These results need to be replicated in larger sample sizes. However the findings suggest that spring/summer represents a high risk for patients who exercise. Specifically, they tend to increase their exercise with negative effects on their body composition.

Two explanations for the increase in patients' physical activity during spring/summer can be put forward. First, it can be speculated that sociocultural pressures to be fit and toned for summer may have caused the increase in patients who exercise in spring/summer as already discussed by Huon and Lim (2000) As Griffiths et al. (1999) demonstrated in a study with female anorexic, bulimic, EDNOS patients and healthy controls, patients internalised sociocultural attitudes towards their appearance to a greater extent than healthy controls (see also part 1, chapter 1.3.3.). Thus, it is likely that these pressures cause increased exercise levels in spring/summer as well as increased obligatory attitudes that may already emerge during the winter season as previously discussed.

Second, patients' body composition changed from autumn to spring/summer in the current study. Analysing those patients that completed three assessments, those who reported exercising in spring/summer showed an increase in body weight from autumn to spring/summer of 4.0kg and their BMI changed from 17.8 in autumn to 19.2 in spring/summer. Bouten et al. (1996) demonstrated that those patients at higher BMI (>17.5) showed higher levels of physical activity and were characterised as overactive when compared to controls. Bouten's findings confirm findings into increases in physical activity in patients with AN during weight gain (Falk et al., 1985; Kaye, Gwirtsman, George, Ebert, & Petersen, 1986). The increase in patients reporting to exercise during spring/summer found in the current study may therefore be related to increases in patients' BMI. In the current study however, BMI of those patients who reported exercising was already 19.2 during winter, and no increase in the number of patients reporting exercise occurred (only 3 out of 9 patients reported exercising). Hence, the first explanations seems more likely to account for increases in exercise in spring/summer.

Seasonal variation in admission to hospitals has recently been found in a study in Norway. Gotestam, Eriksen, Heggestadt and Nielsen (1998) applied data of 837 eating disorder admissions between 1990 and 1994 to Norwegian general hospitals as a database. They found seasonal variation in admission rates with peaks in February/March (i.e., spring season). It remains to be clarified if increases in physical activity during spring/summer potentially triggered by obligatory attitudes towards exercise during the winter-season might be related to the increase in admission rates during spring-season.

Altogether, the results for duration and frequency of physical activities confirmed the importance of studying seasonal variation in physical activities in patients with AN. The present study demonstrated that the considerable seasonal variation in physical activity (Uitenbroek, 1993), particularly in moderate intensity activities, is also evident in an anorexic patient group residing in Sydney, Australia. It is possible that patients are not as obsessive with regards to engagement in moderate activities as they are with regards to exercise. Thus, they do not maintain a similar pattern of moderate intensity activities across the seasons. However, it was also speculated from findings in the present study that any environmental factor (e.g., hours of daylight) that reduces the time patients spend in physical activities during winter may result in an attempt to compensate for the decrease. Patients therefore tended to increase the time spent in moderate intensity activities on weekends in winter. This activity-pattern during weekends may worsen patients' inability to relax and needs to be addressed during treatment.

The current investigation further demonstrated increases in patients' physical activity (moderate intensity activity and exercise) in spring/summer. Clinicians needs to focus on this increase during the treatment process as it is hypothesised that perceived sociocultural pressures to be fit for summer may trigger the rise in exercise.

4.1.3. Discussion of findings on body movement

Results obtained from the objective monitoring of body movement offered partial support for the results from the interview. Again, patients differed from controls in that they spent more time in hard intensity body movement (i.e., body movement similar to running at 9 km/hr) across the three seasons. This is in accordance with the interview data, where patients reported spending more time in hard and very hard intensity activities. Further, patients tended to increase their body movement during the weekend in winter and were thus different from controls. A similar pattern emerged for reported time in moderate intensity activities during weekends in winter. Implications of these findings (i.e., the assumption that overexercising continues to be present in outpatients with AN and the possibility that patients compensate for decreased activity-levels in winter by increasing moderate intensity activities on weekends) have been discussed previously.

Thus for hard intensity activities, it can be concluded that the interview and the Tracmor show agreement in their assessment of activities. Agreement rates were not computed in this study and a comparison with the gold-standard (i.e., the doubly labelled water method) was not feasible. However, studies into the criterion-validity of the 7-PAR (Sallis, 1997; Sallis & Saelens, 2000) found high correlations between accelerometry and reported time spent in very hard intensity activities, probably reflecting the fact that exercise behaviour is more salient to the memory than moderate or light intensity activities and is therefore recalled more accurately (Baranowski, 1988). Future studies should compute agreement rates - preferably using the doubly labelled water method as the gold standard - to demonstrate the usefulness and validity of interviews and accelerometry for physical activity assessment in an anorexic patient population. Ensuring the validity of self-report measures of physical activity in the context of AN is particularly important given the notorious denial of symptomatology known to characterise the disorder (Vitousek, Daly, & Heiser, 1991) (see also part 3, chapter 4.5.2.1.). While still lacking, it is thus imperative that validated assessment tools for the assessment of physical activity in patients with AN are developed.

In terms of the differences in body movement between patients and controls, it is of interest that patients showed higher body movement (counts/min and counts/day) than controls across the three seasons. While consistent with the current hypotheses, these results contrast with the findings from Bouten et al (1996) who found no differences in the Tracmor-output between patients and controls. However, the current study differed from Bouten's study (1996) in that patients with AN were not as severely ill compared to Bouten's patients. Specifically, in Bouten's study, BMI ranged between 12.5 and 18.3, while BMI ranged between 15.2 and 25.2 in the current study.

An additional difference between the two studies is the fact that different versions of the Tracmor were utilised in the two studies (i.e., Tracmor 1 (Bouten et al., 1996) and Tracmor 3 in the current study). The two versions are equally sensitive to assess body movement and the frequency ranges are similar (0.11-20Hz and 0.1-7.5Hz for Tracmor 1 and 3, respectively). They do, however, differ in size (i.e., the Tracmor 1 weighs 250 g and has a size of 11*7*3,5 cm compared to Tracmor 3 that weighs 22g and has a size of 7*2*0.8cm). Patients may have been more aware of the Tracmor in Bouten's study and may thus have deliberately decreased their activity-level. In the present study, several patients mentioned that they adapted to wearing the Tracmor and ceased to notice wearing it after some time (personal comments of participants in final review in spring/summer 2002). Hence, results from the current study suggest that outpatients with AN demonstrate more body movement than healthy controls.

Ekelund et al (2002) argued that the low body movement in obese participants is due to the increasing costs of moving large body mass. Therefore, anorexic patients' high body movement might result from the easiness with which they can move their light body as their body composition is still significantly different from that of healthy controls (i.e., decreased body weight and %BF). Likewise, Casper (1998) commented on behavioural activation in patients with AN. She identified behavioural arousal/activation as one symptom specific for AN triggered by starvation. Accordingly, caloric deprivation severe enough to result in significant weight loss provokes in individuals, with a vulnerability to develop AN, sensations of behavioural arousal and activation. This activation is often experiences as mentally and physically energizing.

Contrary to interview-results for moderate intensity activities, body movement did not vary across the seasons in patients with AN. It is of interest that patients' body movement did not vary across the seasons. This finding contradicts Matthews' findings. At least two explanations can be proposed to account for this result: a) The high standard deviations (see table 25) might account for the lack of a significant result. Since the standard deviation is a measure of how well the mean represents the data (Field, 2000), it can be concluded from the data of the current study that the data points were distant to the mean (e.g., the range for counts/min in autumn was 584-991 counts/min).

b) Patients may override the seasonality in body movement through increased restlessness during winter. In the activity-based anorexia (ABA) paradigm (for detail see part 3, chapter 1.4.3.), rats on a restricted feeding schedule increase their level of activity (i.e., wheel-running) resulting in a further decrease in body weight. Recently, the role of ambient temperature in the paradigm has been investigated. Lambert (1992) mentions the role of thermogenesis to account for the increased activity in emaciated rats, suggesting an inverse relationship between body temperature and running. Morrow et al. (1997) showed in their study that rats increased their activity before their body temperature dropped, resulting in the assumption that the initial increase in activity relates to factors other than temperature regulation. As weight loss progresses, thermal needs would then become prominent (Gutierrez, Vazquez, & Boakes, 2001a). The hypothesis that hyperactivity is linked to hypothermia, predicts that activity will be higher at lower ambient temperatures. Morrow et al. (1997) studied the impact of various ambient temperatures on rats' survival using the ABA-paradigm and found that

235

warming animals with a heat lamp (increasing the ambient temperature from 21°C to 37°C) significantly increased the likelihood and length of survival.

Extrapolated to humans with AN, restless hyperactivity and fidgeting may play a similar thermoregulatory role to that of running in ABA rats as recently investigated (Bergh, Brodin, Lindberg, & Soedersten, 2002; Birmingham, Gutierrez, Jonat, & Beumont, 2004; Gutierrez & Vazquez, 2001b) (see also part 3, chapter 1.4.3.). In the context of the current study, it can be speculated that decreases in ambient temperature in winter may trigger patients' activity so as to cope with thermal needs. This increase in body movement may override the seasonality usually observed in physical activity. It remains to be clarified if this pattern holds true for outpatients with AN who are recovering in terms of their body composition. If restlessness still occurs in outpatients and shows increases during winter, treatment strategies such as rewarming may need to be implemented (see part 3, chapter 1.4.3.).

In conclusion, results from the objective monitoring offered partial agreement with results from the interview (i.e., patients showed more hard intensity body movement and increased their body movement during weekends in winter). Further, the Tracmor-data of the current study suggest that patients with AN show higher body movement than controls which may be contributed to by the ease with which they can move their lean body. This elevated activity does not change across the seasons. It can be speculated that increased restlessness during winter potentially caused through a decrease in the ambient temperature may result in the lack of seasonal variation in body movement in patients. In contrast, controls demonstrate a seasonal variation in their body movement with decreases in winter.

4.2. Summary of major findings on body composition

As hypothesised, patients' had lower body weight, BMI and %BF compared to controls across the three seasons. Further, patients had a higher %FFM than controls while FFM (in kg) tended to be higher in controls. Patients' body composition changed from autumn to spring/summer with increases in body weight, BMI, %BF and FFM particularly during spring/summer. Percentage FFM decreased during spring/summer. Controls demonstrated a seasonal pattern in their body composition variables. In winter, controls' body weight and %BF increased, while %FFM and FFM decreased. In spring/summer, body weight and %BF decreased and %FFM and FFM increased. These results are in accordance with the hypotheses.

4.2.1. Discussion of findings on body composition

In the current study, patients' body composition differed from that of controls as predicted. Patients had significantly lower body weight, %BF and FFM across the three seasons. Further, they had a higher %FFM. Across the seasons, patients' body weight, %BF and FFM increased while %FFM decreased during spring/summer.

In agreement with studies into changes in body composition variables (Orphanidou et al., 1997; Polito et al., 1998; Probst et al., 2001), patients in this study demonstrated increases in body weight and %BF. While FFM increased continuously across the seasons, the %FFM (of body weight) decreased. Hence, in this study, patients' gain in body weight constituted of gains in fat mass and FFM, where the increase in fat mass was larger than the increase in FFM. Specifically, the composition of the weight gain was 73.3% BF and 26.7% FFM. This finding is in line with previous studies, which found that body fat increased most significantly when patients gain weight (Orphanidou et al., 1997; Probst et al., 2001). In comparison to Orphanidou et al (1997) who found in their study with 26 patients with AN that weight gain constituted of 78% fat, 21% lean body mass and 1% bone mineral, the increase in BF was slightly lower in the current study. Orphanidou et al. suggested that the low rate of regained lean body mass found in their study can be partly explained by the variability in the amount and type of physical activity. Accordingly, patients were more constrained in terms of their activity-levels and they were encouraged to be more physically active only as their medical and nutritional statuses improved.

In contrast, Probst, Goris, Vandereycken and Van Coppenolle (2001) found a composition of weight gain in their patients (N=130) of 55.4% fat and 44.5% FFM. They hypothesised that a fitness training program (20 sessions, 2 times/week), supervised by a therapist could increase FFM regained. However, the possible influence of an adapted fitness training program on body composition has not been assessed in detail.

In the current study, outpatients and patients attending day programmes were assessed and thus, their physical activity was not constrained. In addition, patients demonstrated higher activity-levels (i.e., in moderate intensity activity and exercise) during spring/summer. Also, FFM correlated significantly with patients' time spent in moderate and strenuous body movement. It can therefore be concluded that the larger gain in patients' FFM in the current study compared to Orphanidou's results were due to increased levels of physical activity. Yet, FFM gains were lower than results from Probst et al and this suggests that an inclusion of a fitness training program might enhance gains in FFM during weight gain.

The issue of weight gain, particularly gains in BF, is a very sensitive issue in the treatment of AN. Mayer (2002) has reviewed studies into body composition changes and critically discussed the role of abnormal fat distribution in patients with AN (i.e., BF was deposited preferentially to the trunk and away from the periphery). He also discussed the difficulty for patients to accept that weight gain might predominantly occur as gains in BF given that their worst fears ("It's all going to my stomach") might be realised.

Increases in FFM during weight gain may therefore be desirable to make patients' weight gain easier and minimise loss of muscle mass (Polito et al., 1998). As suggested by Probst et al. (2001), fitness training programmes or graded exercise programmes during the refeeding process could increase FFM and aim to achieve desirable weight gains (i.e., constituting of BF and FFM) in patients with AN. First attempts have already been made in developing graded structured exercise programmes with the particular aim to increase muscle mass and prevent decreases in bone mass (Beumont et al., 1994; Thien et al., 2000; Ziemer & Ross, 1970) (see also part 3, chapter 1.4.1.) and future research into these exercise programmes is warranted.

Concerning the control group, body composition variables were found to demonstrate a seasonal pattern. While only a trend emerged for seasonal changes in %BF and %FFM (p=0.10), the seasonal change in FFM was statistically significant (p=0.01). Controls' FFM decreased during winter and increased during spring/summer. This finding contrasts with studies which investigated seasonal changes in body composition variables in the general population. Plasqui et al. (2004a) found no seasonal variation in FFM (assessed with underwater weighing and deuterium dilution method) in 25 healthy participants (10 males and 15 females, 20 -30 years) in Maastricht (the Netherlands).

Plasqui's study and the current study are very similar in that both assessed students and university staff in a similar age range across the seasons. Yet, while Plasqui's students were mainly recruited from the Department of Human Biology (specialising in human body movement), participants from the current study were recruited from a variety of settings (i.e., for the autumn assessment, three were (17.6%) dietetic students, four were (23.5%) medical students, three (17.6%) were studying other subjects, four (23.5%) were working at the university hospital (n=4, 23.5%) and three (17.6%) were employed in other jobs). It can be speculated that Plasqui's participants may have been more interested in body movement and physical activity reflected in their higher PAL-values (average PAL was 1.82 which is higher than the population average of 1.77) and stable fitness-levels across the seasons. It may be that active people are less likely to demonstrate seasonal changes in their FFM. Consistent with this suggestion, Plasqui and Westerterp (2004b) hypothesised in a study into seasonal variation in physical activity energy expenditure that those participants who were highly active tried to compensate for decreases in moderate intensity activities in winter by engaging in sports activities. While these participants were unable to maintain their PAL, they may have been successful in maintaining their FFM.

In contrast, participants in the current study demonstrated decreases in FFM during winter and increases during spring/summer. They did not attempt to maintain their physical activity-levels across the seasons, which is demonstrated in seasonal changes in physical activities (i.e., in moderate intensity activities, very hard intensity activities and body movement). It remains to be clarified if people who are not highly active across the year are more prone to changes in FFM. To what extent changes in physical activity may cause these changes in FFM needs to be investigated. In the current study, FFM was significantly correlated with time spent in strenuous body movement in the control group. While controls' time spent in strenuous body movement did not follow a seasonal pattern, time in very hard intensity activities (assessed with the interview) increased during spring/summer. These inconsistent findings (from objective and subjective data) leave the question unanswered as to the role of seasonal changes in activity-levels and their potential impact on seasonal changes in FFM. Future studies should investigate seasonality in FFM in highly active and moderately active participants. In conclusion, results from control participants (but not from the patients) demonstrated a seasonal pattern in body composition variables, particularly in FFM.

4.3. Summary of findings on physical activity and body composition

As hypothesised, patients' body movement (i.e., moderate to high intensity body movement) correlated positively with FFM. Thus, the more time patients spent in moderate to strenuous intensity body movement, the higher their FFM. Patients' %BF tended to correlate negatively with time spent in strenuous intensity of body movement. For controls, a similar result emerged for FFM, but only time spent in very hard and strenuous intensity body movement (i.e., body movement similar to running at or more than 9 km/hr) were positively correlated with controls' FFM. As expected, no significant correlation emerged for % BF.

4.3.1. Discussion of findings on physical activity and body composition

It is of interest that FFM correlated positively with time spent in moderate intensity body movement in the patient but not in the control group. Patients with higher FFM were thus characterised by a higher activity-levels that comprised activities in the moderate to strenuous range. While controls with high FFM may spend short periods of time in high intensity activities and may reduce their activity outside training sessions to light intensity activities as suggested by Kempen, Saris and Westerterp (1995) and Westerterp (2001a), patients with high FFM may keep a moderate activity-level even outside high-intensity activity periods. It is possible that this is related to their heightened restlessness and their engagement in contrived activities (i.e., activities of daily life designed to increase energy expenditure such as walking instead of catching the bus (Beumont et al., 1994); see also part 3, chapter 1.2.).

Achieving weight gains that constitutes of BF and FFM during the treatment process has been discussed previously and positive effects of graded exercise programmes have been presented. In this context, it is essentially important to differentiate between the different aspects of physical activity. Generally, physical activity can have beneficial consequences for patients with AN (e.g., van Marken Lichtenbelt, Heidendal and Westerterp (1997) recently demonstrated a positive relationship between bone mineral density and PAL in patients with AN (see also part 3, chapter 1.2.1.)).

However, it remains to be specified in future studies which physical activities should be maintained and integrated (i.e., in the form of an exercise program) into treatment in which patient group. From the current results it can be proposed that in patients with a high FFM who are engaging in moderate and strenuous activities, time spent in moderate intensity activities may need to be monitored and potentially discouraged. It can be assumed that patients who are active in moderate and strenuous activities will engage in both contrived activities with the aim of increasing their energy expenditure during activities of daily life, and exercising. Since treatment aims to build up a normal life-style, these contrived activities should be challenged as they may be closely linked to pathological attitudes and motives for engagement in physical activity and may also impact on patients' energy expenditure. Further, monitoring and challenging engagement in moderate intensity activities (e.g., contrived activities) might be less difficult for patients who exercise excessively and might thus enhance compliance to treatment. Challenging their excessive exercise could be introduced subsequently, with the chances of success enhanced through such a graded program.

It was hypothesised to find a negative correlation between %BF and time spent in strenuous activities in the patient group. Here, patients' %BF tended to correlate negatively with body movement. Specifically, the more time patients spent in strenuous intensity body movement, the lower their %BF. While the correlation did not reach statistical significance (p=0.08), the nonsignificant finding is probably related to the small sample size of the current study. The trend of a negative correlation is however, noteworthy and given the importance of the finding, this trend will be tentatively discussed here.

The finding that patients at lower %BF tended to spend more time in strenuous body movement contradicts the results from Falk et al. (1985) who found a positive relationship between percentage of target weight and average wrist activity (r=.81, p<0.01) and between percentage target weight and average ankle activity (r=.76,

243

p<0.01). Falks' study and the current study differed in several aspects. First, Falk et al (1985) assessed hospitalised patients and hence, their activity was restricted due to the more structured setting. Secondly, Falk et al used actometers, in contrast to the triaxial accelerometers (that have been validated against the doubly labelled water method) implemented in the current study. Third, Falk et al focussed on percentage target weight, while the present study assessed %BF, %FFM and FFM using DEXA.

Further, results from the current study differ from findings from Bouten et al (1996). They found high intensity activity-levels in patients at BMIs above 17.5 only. Patients at lower BMIs engaged more often in sedentary activities. Hence, physical activity was related to BMI in their study. In the present study, the relationship between time spent in various intensities of body movement and BMI or body weight failed to reach statistical significance. Numerous problems have been listed regarding body weight assessments in patients with AN (Birmingham, Muller, & Goldner, 1998) (see also chapter 1.5.1.1.). Among others, body weight might be confounded due to fluid loading, constipation, heavy clothing or fluid shifts secondary to vomiting, diuretic and laxative abuse. As a consequence, BMI may not be a predictor of relative body fatness (Probst et al., 1996). Exercising patients can thus gain FFM and lose fat mass and still show no body weight variation (Trocki & Shepherd, 2000). If that is the case, patients' body weight may not be related to physical activity while %BF might - as is indeed suggested by the findings of the current study.

Compared to the two previous studies which investigated the relationship between physical activity and body composition in AN, the present study had several advantages: physical activity was assessed objectively with validated tools, body composition was assessed using DEXA (thus obtaining estimates of %BF and FFM), and finally, patients were assessed under free-living conditions rather than in a hospital setting. These advantages provide some evidence for suggesting that there is indication for a negative correlation between %BF and time spent in strenuous activities in patients with AN. While the correlation needs to be replicated, a potential negative relationship between %BF and strenuous activities in AN and the finding that patients with AN demonstrated higher body movement compared to controls calls for an explanation. Hitherto, it remains unclear as to why patients with AN at low %BF engage in higher activity-levels, particularly strenuous activities or excessive exercise.

The paradigm of activity-based anorexia (ABA, chapter 1.6.2.) has received some attention as an animal model for hyperactivity in human AN. In studies with rodents, it has been shown that rats on a restricted feeding schedule are able to maintain energy balance and survive when access to food is restricted to 1-1.5 hours during the night but show a progressive loss of body mass and die within days when given access to a running wheel. Hebebrand et al. (2003) reviewed suggested explanations for the paradoxical hyperactivity in animals. Among the explanation were the following: a) increased activity may be interpreted as increased foraging behaviour (i.e., running in response to food shortage may increase the odds for survival). b) Hyperactivity may serve a thermoregulatory role (see also part 3, chapter 1.4.3.) in that wheel running causes an increase in body temperature. c) Body fat mass may impact on locomotor activity as suggested by the study of genetically obese mouse and rat strains. The spontaneous activity of obese rats is lower and the treatment of obese mice with leptin not only decreases food intake but increases spontaneous activity.

Regarding hyperactivity in patients with AN, the role of leptin has been recently discussed by Hebebrand et al (2003) (see chapter 1.4.2.). In addition, it has been suggested that the serotonin system may influence affect and activity in AN. Favaro, Lorenza, Alberto and Paolo (2000) conducted a study with 16 patients with AN and investigated the ratio between tryptophan and other large neutral amino acids (TRP/LNAA) in excessive exercisers (exercising one hour/day) and nonexercisers. Tryptophan and the other LNAA compete for transport across the blood brain barrier. Since tryptophan is the precursor for the synthesis of serotonin in the central nervous system, the TRP/LNAA ratio determines serotonin synthesis. Favaro et al. (2000) demonstrated that the excessive exercisers had significantly higher TRP/LNAA ratios than the nonexercisers. They concluded that in the presence of low body fat and insufficient energy intake, energy may be provided by the release of amino acids from skeletal muscle. This release may be enhanced in patients who exercise excessively since exercising further increases energy requirements. They further suggest a self-medication mechanism where patients may counteract low levels of tryptophan resulting from their undernutrition by physical activity and by lowering energy intake. Casper (1998) comes to a similar conclusion in her review on behavioural activation and the lack of concern in patients with AN. She argues that caloric deprivation severe enough to result in significant weight loss may provoke behavioural activation. This activation is experienced as energising by the patients and is channelled into exercise. Casper (1998) concludes that the 'cheerfulness' and paradoxical liveliness seen in patients are offsprings of a starvation-induced energising sensation.

In conclusion, the relationship between patients' body composition variables and hyperactivity needs to be further investigated and understood to develop adequate treatment strategies.

4.4. Methodological concerns

The present study had several limitations regarding the assessment, selected sample and design. Three assessment-related problems emerged:

First, agreement rates between the interview and the Tracmor-output in terms of energy expenditure were not calculated in this study. Since the aim was to investigate the patterns of physical activity rather than obtain a global measure of energy expenditure, energy expenditure was not part of the assessment. However, physical activity is also defined through its energy costs apart from its duration and frequency. Particularly in the context of AN, where weight restoration is the essential aim of treatment, physical activity related energy expenditure and its variation across the seasons should be explored in future studies. Ideally, assessment of patterns of physical activity (through interviews and objective monitoring) should be combined with the assessment of energy expenditure (through the double labelled water method).

Second, even though the Tracmor has been validated against the doubly labelled water method (Westerterp & Bouten, 1997a), researchers in the Netherlands are still optimising its design and psychometric characteristics (Plasqui in November 2003, personal communication). The Tracmor has several advantages compared to uniaxial accelerometers or wristwatches, particularly regarding its practicality. Its small size renders it convenient for participants to wear. This is particularly important in the context of AN, since patients may tend to decrease their activity-levels because of feeling observed. In a final interview, where patients were asked which of the procedures (i.e., the assessment of physical activity or body composition) were most uncomfortable, only one patient (7.1%) mentioned the Tracmor. It can therefore be concluded that the Tracmor provides a useful tool in the assessment and self-monitoring of physical activity in patients with AN.

Third, categories for intensity of body movement have to be reanalysed and replicated. As can be seen from table 25, the range in counts/min within the categories was high (e.g., for category 3: minimum: 2792, maximum: 7753). The maximum in category 3 was higher than the mean of category 4. Validation of the Tracmor categories are currently underway in Maastricht (Plasqui in November 2003, personal communication) and once published, different intensities of body movement can be objectively assessed in patients with AN.

In terms of the selected sample, three problems emerged:

First, the present study involved patients at different stages of treatment and recovery, with these differences reflected in their body composition. Both cross-sectional and longitudinal studies would be useful in terms of providing insight into how physical activity-levels change over the course of the dieting disorder, how seasonal variation may be present and how body composition is affected.

Also, controls with a wide range in body composition variables (e.g., range for %BF in autumn: 21.9-49.2%) participated in the study. Since the intention was to compare patients with AN with healthy controls with a range in body composition variables, control participants at high body weight or %BF were not excluded from the current study. However, as previously discussed, it is more difficult to move the body for participants at higher body mass. Thus, to determine differences between patients and controls more precisely in terms of body movement, control participants may be subdivided into different groups depending on their body composition in future studies.

In addition, the sample size of the current study was small, resulting in diminished statistical power. Unfortunately, research on AN is frequently limited to small sample sizes arsing from the unique problems encountered when conducting research with this population (e.g., the relative rarity of the condition and patients' resistance to the medical world) (Orimoto & Vitousek, 1992; Shaw & Garfinkel, 1990). Due to the small sample size, the present findings are preliminary and reported trends for statistical differences (with p-values ≤ 0.10) need to be replicated.

A limitation of the current design was the fact that participants were only assessed across three seasons (i.e., autumn, winter and spring/summer). Future studies should aim to assess participants across four seasons, preferably over a period of two years to enable conclusions with regards to seasonal changes over the year. Since this study was the first to investigate physical activity and body composition across the seasons, it nevertheless provides an important preliminary investigation into the seasonality of these components in AN.

4.5. Conclusions and future directions

The present study investigated physical activity patterns in outpatients with AN and healthy controls across three seasons. In terms of physical activity patterns, outpatients demonstrated higher commitment to exercise and extrinsic motivation for exercise, and higher exercise levels and body movement across the three seasons when compared to controls. Patients at lower %BF tended to show higher exercise levels. Seasonal variation in time spent in moderate intensity activities was found in both groups. In spring/summer, more patients than controls engaged in exercise and the number of patients reporting engagement in exercise increased.

These results highlight the importance of physical activity in AN. The fact that exercising and commitment to exercise is still present in an outpatient sample and remains high across the seasons, and the fact that patients' body movement is increased across all seasons and tended to negatively correlate with patients' %BF demonstrate the need to integrate physical activity as a standard component into the treatment of AN. Challenging patients' motives and counteracting their excessive exercising and restlessness appear to be important components of the treatment. Seasonality of physical activity (i.e., in obligatory attitudes towards exercise, moderate intensity activities and exercise) also requires greater recognition and integration into treatment. That is, clinicians need to be aware of increases in patients' activity-levels particularly during spring/summer, probably triggered by increased obligatory attitudes towards exercise during winter. Energy costs of this increase in activity need to be determined to investigate impacts on body composition variables and if necessary, adapt energy requirements in this season.

5. Reference list

American Psychiatric Association ((1994). *Diagnostic and statistical manual of mental disorders.* (4 ed.) Washington, DC: American Psychiatric Association.

Australian Bureau of Statistics (2000). *Participation in sport and physical activities.* Canberra: Australian Bureau of Statistics.

Ballor, D. L. & Poehlman, E. T. (1994). Exercise-training enhances fat-free mass preservation during diet-induced weight loss: A meta-analytical finding. *International Journal of Obesity, 18,* 35-40.

Baranowski, T. (1988). Validity and reliability of self report measures of physical activity: An information-processing perspective. *Research Quarterly, 59,* 314-327.

Bassett, D. R. (2000). Validity and reliability issues in objective monitoring of physical activity. *Research Quarterly for Exercise & Sport, 71,* 30-36.

Bergh, C., Brodin, U., Lindberg, G., & Soedersten, P. (2002). Randomized controlled trial of a treatment for anorexia and bulimia nervosa. *Proc Natl Acad Sci (PNAS), 99,* 9486-9491.

Beumont, P. J. V., Booth, A. L., Abraham, S., Griffiths, D. A., & Turner, T. R. (1983). A temporal sequence of symptoms in patients with anorexia nervosa: A preliminary report. In P.L.Darby, P. E. Garfinkel, D. M. Garner, & D. V. Coscina (Eds.), *Anorexia nervosa: Recent devlopments in research* (pp. 129-136). New York: Liss.

Beumont, P. J. (1984). A clinician looks at animal models of anorexia nervosa. In N.W.Bond (Ed.), *Animal models in psychopathology* (pp. 177-206). Sydney: Academic Press.

Beumont, P. J. V., Russell, J. D., & Touyz, S. W. (1993). Treatment of anorexia nervosa. *Lancet, 341,* 1635-1640.

Beumont, P. J., Arthur, B., Russell, J. D., & Touyz, S. W. (1994). Excessive physical activity in dieting disorder patients: Proposals for a supervised exercise program. [Review] [48 refs]. *International Journal of Eating Disorders, 15,* 21-36.

Birmingham, C. L., Jones, P. J. H., Orphanidou, C. I., Bakan, R., Cleator, I. G. M., Goldner, E. M. et al. (1996). The reliability of bioelectrical impedance analysis for measuring changes in the body composition of patients with anorexia nervosa. *International Journal of Eating Disorders, 19,* 311-315.

Birmingham, C. L., Muller, J. L., & Goldner, E. M. (1998). Randomized trial of measures of body fat versus body weight in the treatment of anorexia nervosa. *Eating & Weight Disorders, 3,* 84-89.

Birmingham, C. L. & Beumont, P. (2004). *The medical management of eating disorders: A textbook with manuals for health care professionals.* Cambridge.

Birmingham, C. L., Gutierrez, E., Jonat, L., & Beumont, P. Randomized controlled trial of warming in anorexia nervosa. *International Journal of Eating Disorders,* (in press).

Blair, S. N. (1995). Measurement of physical activity. In K.D.Brownell & C. G. Fairburn (Eds.), *Eating disorders and obesity. A comprehensive handbook* (pp. 111-116). New York: The Guilford Press.

Booth, M., Owen, N., Baumann, A., & Gore, C. J. (1995). *Active and inactive Australians. Assessing and understanding levels of physical activity.* Canberra: Department of the Environment, Sport and Territories.

Booth, M. (2000). Assessment of physical activity: An international perspective. *Research Quarterly for Exercise & Sport, 71,* 114-120.

Bouten, C. V., van Marken Lichtenbelt, W. D., & Westerterp, K. R. (1996). Body mass index and daily physical activity in anorexia nervosa. *Medicine and Science in Sports and Exercise, 28,* 967-973.

Brewerton, T. D., Krahn, D. D., Hardin, T. A., Wehr, T. A., & Rosenthal, N. E. (1993). Findings from the Seasonal Pattern Assessment Questionnaire in patients with eating disorders and control subjects: Effects of diagnosis and location. *Psychiatry Research, 52,* 71-84.

Casper, R. (1998). Behavioral activation and lack of concern, core symptoms of anorexia nervosa? *International Journal of Eating Disorders, 24,* 381-393.

Caspersen, C. J., Powell, K. E., & Christenson, G. M. (1985). Physical activity, exercise, and physical fitness: Definitions and distinctions for health-related research. *Public Health Reports, 100,* 126-131.

Dannenberg, A. L., Keller, J. B., Wilson, P. W., & Castelli, W. P. (1989). Leisure time physical activity in the Framingham Offspring Study. Description, seasonal variation, and risk factor correlates. *American Journal of Epidemiology, 129,* 76-88.

Davis, C., Fox, J., Cowles, M., Hastings, P., & Schwass, K. (1990). The functional role of exercise in the development of weight and diet concerns in women. *Journal of Psychosomatic Research, 34,* 563-574.

Davis, C., Brewer, H., & Ratusny, D. (1993a). Behavioral frequency and psychological commitment: Necessary concepts in the study of excessive exercising. *Journal of Behavioral Medicine, 16,* 611-628.

Davis, C. & Fox, J. (1993b). Excessive exercise and weight preoccupation in women. *Addictive Behaviors, 18,* 201-211.

Davis, C., Kennedy, S. H., Ravelski, E., & Dionne, M. (1994). The role of physical activity in the development and maintenance of eating disorders. *Psychological Medicine, 24,* 957-967.

Davis, C., Kennedy, S. H., Ralevski, E., Dionne, M., Brewer, H., Neitzert, C. et al. (1995). Obsessive compulsiveness and physical activity in anorexia nervosa and high-level exercising. *Journal of Psychosomatic Research, 39,* 967-976.

Davis, C., Katzman, D. K., Kaptein, S., Kirsh, C., Brewer, H., Kalmbach, K. et al. (1997). The prevalence of high-level exercise in the eating disorders: etiological implications. *Comprehensive Psychiatry, 38,* 321-326.

Davis, C., Katzman, D. K., & Kirsh, C. (1999). Compulsive physical activity in adolescents with anorexia nervosa: a psychobehavioral spiral of pathology. *Journal of Nervous & Mental Disease, 187,* 336-342.

De Coverley Veale, D. M. W. (1987). Exercise dependence. *British Journal of Addiction, 82,* 735-740.

Ekelund, U., Poortvliet, E., Nilsson, A., Yngve, A., Holmberg, A., & Sjostrom, M. (2001). Physical activity in relation to aerobic fitness and body fat in 14- to 15-year-old boys and girls. *European Journal of Applied Physiology, 85,* 195-201.

Ekelund, U., Aman, J., Yngve, A., Renman, C., Westerterp, K. R., & Sjostrom, M. (2002). Physical activity but not energy expenditure is reduced in obese adolescents: A case-control study. *American Journal of Clinical Nutrition, 76,* 935-941.

Ellis, K. J. (2000). Human body composition: In vivo methods. *Physiological Reviews, 80,* 649-671.

Epling, W. F., Pierce, W. D., & Stefan, L. (1983). A theory of activity based anorexia. *International Journal of Eating Disorders, 3,* 7-46.

Epling, W. F. & Pierce, W. D. (1996). An overview of activity anorexia. In W.F.Epling & W. D. Pierce (Eds.), *Activity anorexia. Theory, research, and treatment* (pp. 3-12). Mahwah, N.J.: Lawrence Erlbaum Associates.

Exner, C., Hebebrand, J., Remschmidt, H., Wewetzer, C., Ziegler, A., & Herpertz, S. (2000). Leptin suppresses semi-starvation induced hyperactivity in rats: Implications for anorexia nervosa. *Molecular Psychiatry, 5,* 476-481.

Falk, J. R., Halmi, K. A., & Tryon, W. W. (1985). Activity measures in anorexia nervosa. *Archives of General Psychiatry, 42,* 811-814.

Faul, F. & Erdfelder, E. (1992). GPOWER: A priori, post-hoc and compromise power analyses for MS-DOS (computer program) (Version 2) [Computer software]. Bonn: Bonn FRG: Bonn University, Department of Psychology.

Favaro, A., Caregaro, L., Burlina, A., & Santonastaso, P. (2000). Tryptophan levels, excessive exercise, and nutritional status in anorexia nervosa. *Psychosomatic Medicine, 62,* 535-538.

Field, A. (2000). *Discovering statistics using SPSS for Windows.* London: Sage Publications.

Frederick, C. M. (1994). Differences in motivation for sport and exercise and their relations with participation and mental health. *Journal of Sport Behavior, Vol 16,* 124-146.

Freedson, P. S. & Miller, K. (2000). Objective monitoring of physical activity using motion sensors and heart rate. *Research Quarterly for Exercise and Sport, 71,* 21-29.

Frey, J., Hebebrand, J., Muller, B., Ziegler, A., Blum, W. F., Remschmidt, H. et al. (2000). Reduced body fat in long-term followed-up female patients with anorexia nervosa. *Journal of Psychiatric Research, 34,* 83-88.

Garner, D. M. & Garfinkel, P. E. (1979). The Eating Attitude Test: An index of the symptoms of anorexia nervosa. *Psychological Medicine, 9,* 279.

Garrow, J. S. & Summerbell, C. D. (1995). Meta-analysis: Effect of exercise, with or without dieting, on the body composition of overweight subjects. *European Journal of Clinical Nutrition, 49,* 1-10.

Goodwin, J., Pearce, V. R., Taylor, R. S., Read, K. L. Q., & Powers, S. J. (2001). Seasonal cold and circadian changes in blood pressure and physical activity in young and elderly people. *Age and Ageing, 30,* 311-317.

Gotestam, K. G., Eriksen, L., Heggestad, T., & Nielsen, S. (1998). Prevalence of eating disorders in Norwegian general hospitals 1990-1994: admissions per year and seasonality. *International Journal of Eating Disorders, 23,* 57-644.

Griffiths, R. A., Russell, J., Schotte, D., Thornton, C., Touyz, S., & Varano, P. (1999). Sociocultural attitudes toward appearance in dieting disordered and nondieting disordered subjects. *European Eating Disorders Review, Vol 7,* 193-203.

Gull, W. W. (1874). Anorexia nervosa (apepsia hysterica, anorexia hysterica). *Transactions of the Clinical Society of London, 7,* 22-28.

Gutierrez, E., Vazquez, R., & Boakes, R. A. (2001a). Ambient temperature: a neglected factor in Activity-based Anorexia.
Ref Type: Unpublished Work

Gutierrez, E. & Vazquez, R. (2001b). Heat in the treatment of patients with anorexia nervosa. *Eating and Weight Disorders, 6,* 49-52.

Hebebrand, J., Exner, C., Hebebrand, K., Holtkamp, C., Casper, R. C., Remschmidt, H. et al. (2003). Hyperactivity in patients with anorexia nervosa and in semistarved rats: Evidence for a pivotal role of hypoleptinemia. *International Journal of Eating Disorders, 79,* 25-37.

Herrin, M. (2003). Exercise management. In M.Herrin (Ed.), *Nutrition counseling in the treatment of eating disorders* (pp. 181-188). New York: Brunner-Routledge.

Heymsfield, S. B., Allison, D. B., Heshka, S., & Pierson, R. N. (1995). Assessment of human body composition. In D.B.Allison (Ed.), *Handbook of assessment methods for eating behaviors and weight-related problems* (pp. 515-560). Thousand Oaks: Sage Publications.

Huon, G. & Lim, J. (2000). The emergence of dieting among female adolescents: Age, body mass index, and seasonal effects. *International Journal of Eating Disorders, 28,* 221-225.

Kasper, S., Wehr, T. A., Bartko, J. J., Gaist, P. A., & Rosenthal, N. E. (1989). Epidemiological findings of seasonal changes in mood and behavior. *Archives of General Psychiatry, 46,* 823-833.

Katz, J. L. (1996). Clinical observations on the physical activity of anorexia nervosa. In W.F.Epling & W. D. Pierce (Eds.), *Activity anorexia: Theory, research and treatment* (pp. 199-207). Mahwah N.J.: Lawrence Erlbaum Associates.

Kaye, W. H., Gwirtsman, H. E., George, T., Ebert, M. H., & Petersen, R. (1986). Caloric consumption and activity levels after weight recovery in anorexia nervosa: A prolonged delay in normalization. *International Journal of Eating Disorders, 5,* 489-502.

Kempen, K. P. G., Saris, W. H. M., & Westerterp, K. R. (1995). Energy balance during 8-week energy-restricted diet with and without exercise in obese women. *American Journal of Clinical Nutrition, 62*, 722-729.

Kron, L., Katz, J. L., Gorzynski, G., & Weiner, H. (1978). Hyperactivity in anorexia nervosa: a fundamental clinical feature. *Comprehensive Psychiatry, 19*, 433-440.

Lam, R. W., Goldner, E. M., & Grewal, A. (1996). Seasonality of symptoms in anorexia and bulimia nervosa. *International Journal of Eating Disorders, 19*, 35-444.

Lambert, K. G. (1992). The activity-stress paradigm: Possible mechanisms and applications. *The Journal of General Psychology, 120*, 21-32.

Lasègue, C. H. (1964). De l'anorexia hysterique. In M.Kaufman & M. Heiman (Eds.), *Evolution of a psychosomatic concept: Anorexia nervosa* (pp. 141-155). New York: International Universities Press.

Leenders, N. Y., Sherman, W. M., Nagaraja, H. N., & Kien, C. L. (2001). Evaluation of methods to assess physical activity in free-living conditions. *Medicine & Science in Sports & Exercise, 33*, 1233-1240.

Levin, S., Jacobs, D. R. Jr., Ainsworth, B. E., Richardson, M. T., & Leon, A. S. (1999). Intra-individual variation and estimates of usual physical activity. *Annals of Epidemiology, 9*, 481-488.

Levine, J. A., Eberhardt, N. L., & Jensen, M. D. (1999). Role of nonexercise activity thermogenesis in resistance to fat gain in humans. *Science, 283*, 212-214.

Lindeman, M. & Stark, K. (1999). Pleasure, pursuit of health or negotiation of identity? Personality correlates of food choice motives among young and middle-aged women. *Appetite, 33,* 141-161.

Magnusson, A. (2000). An overview of epidemiological studies in seasonal affective disorder. *Acta Psychiatrica Scandinavica, 101,* 176-184.

Matthews, C. E., Freedson, P. S., Herbert, J. R., Stanek, E. J., Merriam, P. A., Rosal, M. C. et al. (2001a). Seasonal variation in household, occupational, and leisure time physical activity: Longitudinal analyses from the Seasonal Variation of Blood Cholesterol Study. *American Journal of Epidemiology, 153,* 172-183.

Matthews, C. E., Hebert, J. R., Freedson, P. S., Stanek, E. J., Merriam, P. A., Ebbeling, C. B. et al. (2001b). Sources of variance in daily physical activity levels in the Seasonal Variation of Blood Cholesterol Study. *American Journal of Epidemiology, 153,* 987-995.

Mayer, L. (2002). Body composition changes in anorexia nervosa: A review. *Eating Disorders Review, 13,* 1-3.

McLaren, L., Gauvin, L., & White, D. (2001). The role of perfectionism and excessive commitment ot exercise in explaining dietary restraint: Replication and extension. *International Journal of Eating Disorders, 29,* 307-313.

Meijer, G. A., Westerterp, K. R., Verhoeven, F. M., Koper, H. B., & ten Hoor, F. (1991). Methods to assess physical activity with special reference to motion sensors and accelerometers. *IEEE Transactions on Biomedical Engineering, 38,* 221-229.

Mond, J. M., Hay, P. J., Rodgers, B., Owen, C., & Beumont, P. J. V. Relationships between exercise behaviour, eating-disordered behaviour and quality of life in a community sample of women: When is exercise 'excessive'? *European Eating Disorders Review*, (in press).

Montoye, H. J., Kemper, H. C., Saris, W. H. M., & Washburn, R. A. (1996). *Measuring physical activity and energy expenditure*. Champaign, IL: Human Kinetics.

Montoye, H. J. (2000). Introduction: Evaluation of some measurements of physical activity and energy expenditure. *Medicine & Science in Sports & Exercise, 32*, S439-S442.

Morrow, N. S., Schall, M., Grijalva, C. V., Geiselman, P. J., Garrick, T., Nuccion, S. et al. (1997). Body temperature and wheel running predict survival times in rats exposed to activity-stress. *Physiology and Behavior, 62*, 815-825.

National Health and Medical Research Council (1995). Recommendations for limiting exposure to ionizing radiation. *NHMRC Radiation Health Series, 39*.

Nielsen, S. (1992). Seasonal variation in anorexia nervosa? Some preliminary findings from a neglected area of research. *International Journal of Eating Disorders, 11*, 25-36.

Orimoto, L. & Vitousek, K. B. (1992). Anorexia nervosa and bulimia nervosa. In P.H.Wilson (Ed.), *Principles and practice of relapse prevention* (pp. 85-127). New York: Guilford Press.

Orphanidou, C. I., McCargar, L. J., Birmingham, C. L., & Belzberg, A. S. (1997). Changes in body composition and fat distribution after short-term weight gain in patients with anorexia nervosa. *American Journal of Clinical Nutrition, 65,* 1034-1041.

Penas-Lledo, E., Vaz Leal, F. J., & Waller, G. (2002a). Excessive exercise in anorexia nervosa and bulimia nervosa: Relation to eating characteristics and general psychopathology. *International Journal of Eating Disorders, 31,* 370-375.

Penas-Lledo, E. & Waller, G. (2002b). Pattern of birth and eating attitudes in young adults: Failure to replicate in a warmer climate. *International Journal of Eating Disorders, 32,* 367-371.

Pirke, K. M., Trimborn, P., Platte, P., & Fichter, M. (1991). Average total energy expenditure in anorexia nervosa, bulimia nervosa, and healthy young women. *Biological Psychiatry, 30,* 711-718.

Plasqui, G., Kester, A. D. M., & Westerterp, K. R. Seasonal variation in sleeping metabolic rate, thyroid activity and leptin. *American Journal of Physiology,* (in press).

Plasqui, G. & Westerterp, K. R. Seasonal variation in total energy expenditure, physical activity and physical fitness in Dutch young adults. *Obesity Research,* (in press).

Platte, P., Pirke, K. M., Trimborn, P., Pietsch, K., Krieg, J. C., & Fichter, M. (1994). Resting metabolic rate and total energy expenditure in acute and weight recovered patients with anorexia nervosa and in healthy young women. *International Journal of Eating Disorders, 16,* 45-52.

Polito, A., Cuzzolaro, M., Raguzzini, A., Censi, L., & Ferro-Luzzi, A. (1998). Body composition changes in anorexia nervosa. *European Journal of Clinical Nutrition, 52*, 655-662.

Probst, M., Vandereycken, W., Van Coppenolle, H., & Vanderlinden, J. (1995). The Body Attitude Test for patients with an eating disorder: Psychometric characteristics of a new questionnaire. *Eating Disorders: The Journal of Treatment and Prevention, 3*, 133-145.

Probst, M., Goris, M., Vandereycken, W., & Van Coppenolle, H. (1996). Body composition in female anorexia nervosa patients. *British Journal of Nutrition, 76*, 639-647.

Probst, M., Goris, M., Vandereycken, W., & Van Coppenolle, H. (2001). Body composition of anorexia nervosa patients assessed by underwater weighing and skinfold-thickness measurements before and after weight gain. *American Journal of Clinical Nutrition, 73*, 190-197.

Prochaska, J. J., Sallis, J. F., Sarkin, J. A., & Calfas, K. J. (2000). Examination of the factor structure of physical activity behaviors. *Journal of Clinical Epidemiology, 53*, 866-874.

Prochaska, J. O. & DiClemente, C. C. (1992). Stages of change in the motivation of problem behaviors. In M.Herson, R. M. Eisler, & P. M. Miller (Eds.), *Progress in Behavior Modification* (pp. 184-214). Sycamore, IL: Sycamore Press.

Rauh, M. J. D., Hovell, M. F., Hofstetter, C. R., Sallis, J. F., & Gleghorn, A. (1992). Reliability and validity of self-reported physical activity in Latinos. *International Journal of Epidemiology, 21,* 966-971.

Rosenvinge, J. H. & Mouland, S. O. (1990). Outcome and prognosis of anorexia nervosa. A retrospective study of 41 subjects. *British Journal of Psychiatry, 156,* 92-97.

Routtenberg, A. & Kuznesof, A. (1967). Self-starvation of rats living in activity wheels on a restricted feeding schedule. *Journal of Comparative and Physiological Psychology, 64,* 414-421.

Ryan, R. M. (1998). Intrinsic motivation and exercise adherence. *International Journal of Sport Psychology, Vol 28,* 335-354.

Sallis, J. F. (1997). Seven-day physical activity recall. *Medicine & Science in Sports & Exercise, 29 Supplement,* 89-103.

Sallis, J. F. & Saelens, B. E. (2000). Assessment of physical activity by self-report: Status, limitations, and future directions. *Research Querterly for Exercise and Sport, 71,* 1-14.

Sharp, C. W., Clark, S. A., Dunan, J. R., Blackwood, D. H. R., & Shapiro, C. M. (1994). Clinical presentation of anorexia nervosa in males: 24 new cases. *International Journal of Eating Disorders, 15,* 125-134.

Shaw, B. F. & Garfinkel, P. E. (1990). Research problems in the eating disorders. *International Journal of Eating Disorders, 9,* 545-555.

Shelton, M. L. & Klesges, R. C. (1995). Measures of physical activity and exercise. In D.B.Allison (Ed.), *Handbook of assessment methods for eating behaviors and weight-related problems. Measures, theroy, and research* (pp. 185-201). Thousand Oaks: Sage Publications.

Sherwin, C. M. (1998). Voluntary wheel running: A review and novel interpretation. *Animal Behaviour, 56,* 11-27.

Shimamoto, H., Adachi, Y., & Tanaka, K. (2002). Seasonal variation of alterations in exercise-induced body composition in obese Japanese women. *European Journal of Applied Physiology, 86,* 382-387.

Sloan, D. M. (2002). Does warm weather climate affect eating disorder pathology? *International Journal of Eating Disorders, 32,* 240-244.

Steptoe, A., Pollard, T. M., & Wardle, J. (1995). Development of a measure of the motives underlying the selection of food: The Food Choice Questionnaire. *Appetite, 25,* 267-284.

Strober, M., Freeman, R., & Morrell, W. (1997). The long-term course of severe anorexia nervosa in adolescents: Survival analysis of recovery, relapse and outcome predictors over 10-15 years in a prospective study. *International Journal of Eating Disorders, 22,* 339-360.

Strong, K. G. & Huon, G. (1997). The development and evaluation of a staged-based Dieting Status Measure (DiSM). *Eating Disorders: The Journal of Treatment and Prevention, 5,* 97-104.

Thien, V., Thomas, A., Markin, D., & Birmingham, C. L. (2000). Pilot study of a graded exercise program for the treatment of anorexia nervosa. *International Journal of Eating Disorders, 28,* 101-106.

Thornton, C., Beumont, P., & Touyz, S. (2002). The Australian experience of day programs for patients with eating disorders. *International Journal of Eating Disorders, 32,* 1-10.

Touyz, S., Beumont, P. J., & Hook, S. (1987). Exercise anorexia: A new dimension in anorexia nervosa? In P.J.Beumont, G. D. Burrows, & R. C. Casper (Eds.), *Handbook of eating disorders. Part 1: Anorexia and bulimia nervosa* (pp. 143-157). Amsterdam: Elsevier.

Touyz, S. & Beumont, P. J. (1999). Anorexia nervosa: New approaches to management. *Modern Medicine of Australia, June,* 95-110.

Tremblay, A., Doucet, E., & Imbeault, P. (1999). Physical activity and weight maintenance. *International Journal of Obesity, 23,* S50-S54.

Trocki, O. & Shepherd, R. W. (2000). Change in body mass index does not predict change in body composition in adolescent girls with anorexia nervosa. *Journal of the American Dietetic Association, 100,* 457-460.

U.S.Department of Health and Human Services (1997). Monthly estimates of leisure-time physical inactivity- United States 1994. *Morbidity and Mortality Weekly Reports, 46,* 393-397.

266

Uitenbroek, D. G. (1993). Seasonal variation in leisure time physical activity. *Medicine and Science in Sports and Exercise, 25,* 755-760.

van Hanswijck de Jonge, L., Meyer, C., Smith, K., & Waller, G. (2001). Environmental temperature during pregnancy and eating attitudes during teenage years: A replication and extension study. *International Journal of Eating Disorders, 30,* 413-420.

van Marken Lichtenbelt, W. D., Heidendal, G. A., & Westerterp, K. R. (1997). Energy expenditure and physical activity in relation to bone mineral density in women with anorexia nervosa. *European Journal of Clinical Nutrition, 51,* 826-830.

Van Staveren, W. A., Deurenberg, P., Burema, J., de Groot, L. C. P. G., & Hautvast, J. G. A. J. (1986). Seasonal variation in food intake, pattern of physical activity and change in body weight in a group of young adult Dutch women consuming self-selected diets. *American Journal of Clinical Nutrition, 10,* 133-145.

Vitousek, K. B., Daly, J., & Heiser, C. (1991). Reconstructing the internal world of the eating disordered individual: Overcoming denial and distortion in self-report. *International Journal of Eating Disorders, 10,* 647-666.

Waller, G., Meyer, C., & Hanswijck de Jonge, L. (2001). Early environmental influences on restrictive eating pathology among nonclinical females: The role of temperature at birth. *International Journal of Eating Disorders, 30,* 204-208.

Westerterp, K. R. & Bouten, C. V. C. (1997a). Physical activity assessment: comparison between movement registration and doubly labeled water method. *Zeitschrift fuer Ernaehrungswissenschaften, 36,* 263-267.

Westerterp, K. R. & Goran, M. I. (1997b). Relationship between physical activity related energy expenditure and body composition: A gender difference. *International Journal of Obesity, 21,* 184-188.

Westerterp, K. R. (1999a). Assessment of physical activity level in relation to obesity: current evidence and research issues. *Medicine & Science in Sports & Exercise, 31,* S522-S525.

Westerterp, K. R. (1999b). Physical activity assessment with accelerometers. *International Journal of Obesity, 23,* S45-S49.

Westerterp, K. R. (2001a). Pattern and intensity of physical activity. *Nature, 410,* 539.

Westerterp, K. R. (2001b). Seasonal variation in body weight: An experimental case study. *Journal of Thermal Biology, 26,* 525-527.

Willoughby, K., Watkins, B., Beumont, P., Maguire, S., Lask, B., & Waller, G. (2002). Pattern of birth in anorexia nervosa II: A comparison of early-onset cases in the southern and northern hemispheres. *International Journal of Eating Disorders, 32,* 18-23.

Wilmore, J. H. (1995). Body composition. In K.D.Brownell & C. G. Fairburn (Eds.), *Eating disorders and obesitiy. A comprehensive handbook* (pp. 42-45). New York: The Guilford Press.

Windauer, U., Lennerts, W., Talbot, P., Touyz, S., & Beumont, P. (1993). How well are 'cured' anorexia nervosa patients? An investigation of 16 weight-recovered anorexic patients. *British Journal of Psychiatry, 163,* 195-200.

World Health Organisation Collaborating Centre for Mental Health and Substance Abuse (1997). Dieting Disorders. In World Health Organisation Collaborating Centre for Mental Health and Substance Abuse (Ed.), *Management of Mental Disorders. Treatment Practice Protocols* (pp. 464-525). Darlinghurst NSW: World Health Organisation Collaborating Centre for Mental Health and Substance Abuse.

Yamatsuji, M., Yamashita, T., Arii, I., Taga, C., Tatara, N., & Fukui, K. (2003). Seasonal variations in eating disorder subtypes in Japan. *International Journal of Eating Disorders, 33,* 71-77.

Yates, A., Leehey, K., & Shisslak, C. M. (1983). Running- an analogue of anorexia? *New England Journal of Medicine, 308,* 251-255.

Zahner, G. E. P., Hsieh, C. C., & Fleming, J. A. (1995). Introduction to epidemiologic research methods. In M.T.Tsuang, M. Tohen, & G. E. P. Zahner (Eds.), *Textbook in psychiatric epidemiology* (pp. 23-53). New York: Wiley-Liss.

Zahorska-Markiewicz, B. & Markiewicz, A. (1984). Circannual rhythm of exercise metabolic rate in humans. *European Journal of Applied Physiology & Occupational Physiology, 52,* 328-330.

Ziemer, R. R. & Ross, J. L. (1970). Anorexia nervosa: A new approach. *American Corrective Therapy Journal, 24,* 34-42.

6. Appendices

6.1. Appendix A: Participant information sheet (Western Sydney Area Health Service)

WESTERN SYDNEY AREA HEALTH SERVICE
WESTMEAD, NSW 2145

PARTICIPANT INFORMATION

Research study into variation of physical activity in patients with anorexia nervosa throughout the year

Chief investigator: Professor Pierre Beumont
Western Sydney Investigators: Dr M Kohn, Dr B Lampropoulos

Subject Information Sheet A

Purpose of the study

You are invited to take part in a research study into variation of physical activity in patients with anorexia nervosa throughout the year. The object is to investigate seasonal patterns of physical activity throughout the year. Patients with anorexia nervosa often engage in very hard exercising. Programmes have been developed to help patients to overcome the urge to exercise. However, physical activity does not only consist of exercise. We can be active in different intensities (eg light, moderate, hard) and we can be active in different contexts (eg vacuuming in the household, carrying light objects at work). Physical activity in persons without an eating disorder follows a seasonal pattern with peaks in springtime and troughs during winter. The seasonal pattern of activity in patients with anorexia nervosa has never been investigated in Australia. If we knew the variation in seasonal activity, treatment could be modified accordingly. The study is being conducted by Tanja Hechler (research coordinator, PhD-student, Department of Psychological Medicine), Prof. Peter Beumont (University Professor, Academic Head of Psychiatry at Royal Prince Alfred Hospital), Prof. Stephen Touyz (University Professor, Department of Psychology), Dr. Michael Kohen (staff specialist, Department of Adolescent Medicine, Children's Hospital at Westmead and Westmead Hospital), Dr. Basiliki Lampropoulos (staff specialist, Department of Adolescent Medicine, Westmead Hospital), Dr. Margaret Sheridan (Consultant Psychiatrist at Wesley Private Hospital) and Dr. Vincent Leow (Consultant Psychiatrist at Wesley Private Hospital).

What will happen in the study?

If you agree to take part in the study you will be asked to complete the following measurements and procedures during one week in the following two seasons of year 2002/2003. This means you will have to come and see us on 4 occasions throughout the whole year:
At the beginning of the study short questionnaires, assessing your demographics, history of your eating/dieting problems, eating attitudes (the Eating Attitude Test), commitment to exercise (the Commitment to Exercise Scale), dieting status (Dieting Status Measure), attitudes towards your body (Body Attitude Test), motives for food choice (Food Choice Questionnaire) and motives for physical activities (Motives for Physical Activities-Revised) will be handed out to you. It will take you about 15 to 20 min to answer them.

At each of the four assessments we will assess the following variables:
* Body weight
* Height
* Skinfold measurements at 4 sites on your body; triceps, biceps, at your back and above your hip using a special instrument (caliper). The procedure takes 15min and does not cause any pain.
* On the second and fourth occasions we will assess your physical activity by asking you to report it with the help of an interview: conducted at the end of the assessment-week. The interview will take about 15 to 20min.
* Physical activity by monitoring your body movements with a portable device of half the size of a cigarette package (called "Tracmor"); you will wear it for one week around your waist while you are 1awake, except while showering or swimming. Along with the Tracmor you will be given an activity diary, where you briefly write down your activities.
* On 2 occasions (the first and third time you will come in) we will measure your body composition using a technique, called DEXA. The DEXA-scans will be conducted at the Department of Nuclear Medicine (New **Children's** Hospital). In the laboratory you will lie on a bed and your body will be scanned with a special machine. You will be requested to wear a hospital gown (with your underwear kept on) and will be asked to take off any jewelry. This procedure gives us a picture of your body and its composition, in particular. It takes about 10min and includes a minimal amount of radiation exposure, **which is comparable to the natural 'background' radiation everyone is exposed to each day (less than 5 microsieverts).**

To summarise, there will be two time points where we would like to assess you throughout the year

One week in winter 2002 (July) and one week in summer 2002 (November, December).

All aspects of the study, including results, will be strictly confidential and only the investigators named above will have access to information on participants. A report of the study may be submitted for publication, but individual participants will not be identifiable in such a report.

While we intend that this research study furthers medical knowledge and may improve treatment of anorexia nervosa in the future, it may not be of direct benefit to you.

Participation in this study is entirely voluntary: you are in no way obliged to participate and - if you do participate - you can withdraw at any time. Whatever your decision, please be assured that it will not affect your medical or psychological treatment or your relationship with medical staff.

Complaints

If you have any concerns about the conduct of the study, you may contact the Westmead Hospital Patient Representative, Ms Jillian Gwynne Lewis, Telephone No 9845 7014 or email jillian_lewis@wsahs.nsw.gov.au.

Contact information

When you have read this information, Tanja Hechler (02-9515-5844) will discuss it with you further and answer any question you may have. If you would like to know more at any stage, please feel free to contact Prof. P. Beumont (02-9515-6040). **After hours, you can contact Tanja Hechler on her mobile on 0402-644791**. This information sheet is for you to keep.

Participant's Name:_____ Signature:

Date:

6.2. Appendix B: Photo of the Tracmor

6.3. Appendix C: Tracmor sheet

USE OF THE TRACMOR

Dear participant,

Thanks again for your time and interest in our research study. This information refers to the use of the Tracmor and shall make its use as easy as possible to you. We ask you to wear the Tracmor for 6 days during waking hours, starting the morning after your first assessment. Just put the Tracmor, which is attached to a belt, around your waist so that it is placed at your back under your clothes. We would like to ask you to write down the time, when you get up in the morning, and the time, when you start wearing the Tracmor. Also, could you please write down briefly the activities you engage in during the days? Please, do not wear the Tracmor while showering, bathing or swimming, as this would ruin the instrument. In the evening, you can take off the Tracmor and we ask you to write down the time, you take it off, as well as the time, when you go to bed.

In case, any problems might occur or you might have questions, please contact Tanja on (02) 9515 5844.

Thank your very much.

6.4. Appendix D: Consent form

WESTERN SYDNEY AREA HEALTH SERVICE
WESTMEAD NSW 2145

CONSENT TO PARTICIPATE IN RESEARCH

Title of Research Project: Variation of physical activity in patients with anorexia nervosa and healthy controls throughout the year

Name of Researcher: Prof. Pierre Beumont; Dr M Kohn, Dr B Lampropoulos and Tanja Hechler

1. I understand that the researcher will conduct this study in a manner conforming with ethical and scientific principles set out by the National Health and Medical Research Council of Australia and the Good Clinical Research Practice Guidelines of the Therapeutic Goods Administration.

2. I acknowledge that I have read the Participant Information Sheet relating to this study. I acknowledge that I understand the Participant Information Sheet. I acknowledge that the general purposes, methods, demands and possible risks and inconveniences which may occur to me during the study have been explained to me by _____ ("the researcher") and I, being over the age of 16 years acknowledge that I understand the general purposes, methods, demands and possible risks and inconveniences which may occur during the study.

3. I acknowledge that I have been given time to consider the information and to seek other advice.

4. I acknowledge that refusal to take part in this study will not affect the usual treatment of my condition.

5. I acknowledge that I am volunteering to take part in this study and I may withdraw at any time.

6. I acknowledge that this research has been approved by the Western Sydney Area Health Service Human Research Ethics Committee.

7. I acknowledge that I have received a copy of this form and the Participant Information Sheet, which I have signed.

Before signing, please read 'IMPORTANT NOTE' following.

Name of participant _____Date of Birth

_____

Address of participant

_____

Name of parent or guardian (where applicable)

_____

Address of parent or guardian (where applicable)

_____

Signature of participant _____Date:

_____

Signature of parent or guardian (where applicable) _____Date:

_____

Signature of researcher _____Date:

_____

Independent Witness:
I, _____ (name of independent witness)
Of _____ hereby certify as follows:

1. I was present when _____ ('the participant') appeared to read or had read to her a document entitled Participant Information Sheet; or I was told by _____ ('the participant') that she had read a document entitled Participant Information Sheet.
2. I was present when _____ ('the researcher') explained the general purposes, methods, demands and the possible risks and inconveniences of participating in the study to the participant. I asked the participant whether she had understood the Participant Information Sheet and understood what she had been told and she told me she did understand.

3. I observed the participant sign the consent to participate in research and she appeared to me to be signing the document freely and without duress.
4. The participant showed me a form of identification, which satisfied me as to her identity.
5. I am not involved in any way as a researcher in this project.

Name of independent witness _____

Address _____

Signature of independent witness _____

Relationship to participant of independent witness _____

Part 3:

How do clinical specialists understand the role of physical activity in dieting disorders?

Table of contents

List of tables

List of figures

Publication

How do clinical specialists understand the role of physical activity in eating disorders?

Tanja Hechler, Pierre Beumont, Peta Marks, Stephen Touyz.

Article to be submitted to the European Eating Disorder Review.

Abstract

Objective: To assess clinical specialists' understanding of the link between physical activity and eating disorder with special focus on anorexia nervosa (AN), and describe their assessment and management strategies for physical activity.

Method: A semi-structured questionnaire was administered to 33 clinical specialists from four different country-groups (USA/Canada, Europe, Japan/China, Australia/NZ).

Results: The majority of respondents (84,8%) perceived physical activity as an important component in the pathogenesis and maintenance of eating disorders. Those respondents who considered physical activity to be less important were all from Japan and/or China. The majority (>75,0%) incorporated a comprehensive assessment. Psychoeducation, challenging patients' beliefs and self-monitoring were the most frequently used treatment strategies.

Conclusion: Even though the clinical specialists acknowledged the importance of physical activity, comprehensive assessment tools and published exercise programmes were rarely used, indicating the need to extend treatment guidelines to include physical activity. In addition, when examining clinical presentations of eating disorders, cross-cultural differences in the experience of physical activity should be considered as a potential differing factor, particularly between Asian and Caucasian patients.

Keywords: eating disorder, clinical specialists, survey, physical activity, treatment

1. Overview

This part of the thesis has two objectives: first, to review the literature on the understanding of physical activity and management strategies for physical activity in patients with anorexia nervosa (AN); secondly, to assess clinicians' understanding of the role of physical activity in the context of AN and describe their assessment and management strategies. This analysis provides insight into the degree to which clinical specialists incorporate strategies from the published programmes in their treatment of patients with dieting disorders[1] with special focus on AN.

A detailed review on different perspectives on the role of physical activity in patients with dieting disorders is provided (chapter 1.1). Various components of physical activity in patients with dieting disorders are described (chapter 1.2.). These are excessive exercising, restless hyperactivity, and compulsive attitudes towards exercising. Negative effects of each of the components have been investigated and studies are summarised. In addition, assessment tools for physical activity (chapter 1.3.) and five strategies for management of physical activity in patients with dieting disorders are presented (chapter 1.4.). These are response prevention, physical activity as an incentive for weight gain, exercise programmes, body-orientated strategies (BOT, Feldenkrais and Yoga) and the use of heat treatment. Guidelines for the treatment of dieting disorders from various countries are examined in terms of the degree to which they incorporate assessment and management of physical activity in dieting disorders (chapter 1.5.). Subsequently, methods and results (chapters 2. and 3.) of the survey

---

[1] Since anorexia nervosa and bulimia nervosa represent consequences of weight losing behaviour of which dieting is the principal component, the term 'dieting disorder' rather than 'eating disorder' will be used throughout this dissertation (Touyz & Beumont, 1999).

conducted to assess international clinicians' understanding and management of physical

activity in AN are presented and critically discussed (chapter 4).

1.1. The role of physical activity in patients with dieting disorders[2]

Clinical observations of excessive exercise and hyperactivity in patients with AN have raised the question as to the role of physical activity in the development and maintenance of AN. Is physical activity an important symptom for the pathogenesis and maintenance of AN? Historically, Gull (1874) and Lasègue (1964) commented on high levels of physical activity of patients with AN as early as 1874. Until the 1980s however, research into physical activity and AN was lacking and the attitude prevailed that physical activity was an interesting but seemingly unimportant symptom in AN (Epling, Pierce, & Stefan, 1983). Long and Hollin (1995) explained this lack of research by the following reasons: a high level of activity was not necessarily an obstacle to weight gain and it has been assumed that the hyperactivity seen in AN patients is self-correcting. However, for a number of patients excessive exercising has been preceding the dieting disorder (Davis, Fox, Cowles, Hastings, & Schwass, 1990; Davis, Kennedy, Ravelski, & Dionne, 1994; Kron, Katz, Gorzynski, & Weiner, 1978) and recovered patients have been found to still exercise to excess (Windauer, Lennerts, Talbot, Touyz, & Beumont, 1993). Accordingly, overactivity has recently been recognised as fundamental to the pathogenesis of AN (Beumont, Arthur, Russell, & Touyz, 1994; Davis, Katzman, & Kirsh, 1999; Katz, 1996; Thien, Thomas, Markin, & Birmingham, 2000). Most anorexic patients present with overactivity and it is almost as characteristic as the dietary restriction and is just as difficult to modify (Birmingham & Beumont, 2004a).

---

[2] In the present study, the focus lies on patients with anorexia nervosa (AN). The term 'patients with dieting disorders' will thus only be used, if patients with other dieting disorders than AN are referred to.

If physical activity is an important symptom in the pathogenesis and maintenance of AN, what is the link between the two phenomena? Since 1990, researchers have investigated potential links and come up with various models to explain the connection. Throughout the course of research until now however, a clear definition of physical activity in AN is lacking (Katz, 1996). Terms typically used are excessive exercise, overactivity, hyperactivity, restlessness and commitment to exercise. Accordingly, the proposed models focus on the link between AN and the defined component of physical activity used in the model, rather than establishing a relationship between AN and physical activity comprising various components of physical activity, such as excessive exercise, restless hyperactivity and commitment to exercise.

Regarding excessive exercising in AN, Eisler and LeGrange (1990) presented four different models for the link between excessive exercise, illustrating different approaches for the understanding of the role of physical activity in AN. Model 1 states that AN and excessive exercisers are distinct diagnostic groups and the similarities between them are only superficial. Even though they might share a high level of physical activity, the underlying motives are different. While the AN patient is physically active to lose weight, the athlete intends to improve her performance and will diet to achieve a leaner body mass.

Model 2 states that AN and excessive exercise are overlapping groups and excessive exercise can lead to the development of AN. Excessive exercise is hereby seen as a syndrome that develops from normal engagement in healthy exercise. There are two ways, how this could happen: a) through the addiction to starvation, when athletes diet to increase their performance, resulting in a starvation dependence, which may

288

eventually lead to AN; b) physical activity may lead to reduction in food intake (Blundell & King, 1999).

Model 3 claims that AN and excessive exercise are related to some other underlying disorder. Eisler and LeGrange (1990) present two versions for the model. The strong version states that both disorders are manifestations of a third disorder, for example of affective disorders. The model has been severely criticised and it is now recognised that neither AN nor excessive exercise are simply a variant of affective disorders. The weaker version states that another illness might predispose to the development of AN and excessive exercise.

Model 4 claims that etiological factors (such as genetic, personality, familial or social factors) that might normally lead to the development of AN can lead in some cases to a disorder that is superficially different but is in effect the same disorder with different manifestations.

Recent research into AN and physical activity (e.g., by Casper (1998) or Davis et al. (1997; 1999; 1994)) support model 2 assuming that AN and excessive exercise are overlapping groups and that excessive exercise can lead to a development of AN. However, questions still remain unanswered as to the sequence of the two disorders. Does a reduction in food intake and weight loss result in behavioural activation (Casper, 1998) and starvation-induced hyperactivity (Epling & Pierce, 1996)? Or does engagement in sports and exercise during childhood and a family background characterised by interest in sports combined with obsessive and addictive personality traits predispose to be physically active and concerned about weight (Davis et al., 1994; Touyz, Beumont, & Hook, 1987)? Obsessive and pathological attitudes towards exercise resulting from the personality traits will then foster an increase in exercise and motivation to lose weight (Davis et al., 1999).

While understanding the role of physical activity in AN would seem to be essential for its treatment, and perhaps even for preventing the development of AN, clinical specialists' understanding of the role of physical activity in AN and their perception of its involvement in the pathogenesis and maintenance of AN have not previously been explored. It is assumed, that where clinicians consider physical activity an important symptom of AN and thus agree with recent publications, they will include the issue of physical activity in their treatment approaches.

1.2. Components of physical activity in dieting disorders with special focus on AN

Research into physical activity and AN has now progressed from focussing solely on overexercising to analysing impact on energy expenditure of non-exercise activities such as fidgeting or restlessness (Platte et al., 1994). Recently, Birmingham and Beumont (2004a) described two different components of physical activity in patients: deliberate exercise to burn calories (strenuous exercising, burning calories during daily activities or walking) and restlessness with sleep disturbance (see also part 2, chapter 1.2.). Davis, Brewer and Ratusny (1993a) added obessionality to these components, investigating the pathological and obligatory aspects of patients' attitude towards exercise when, for example, exercising continues despite exhaustion. Beumont, Arthur, Russell and Touyz (1994) suggested the following subdivision of physical activity components: 1) excessive exercising, 2) restless hyperactivity and 3) contrived activity (to maximise energy expenditure during daily activities). In part 2 (chapter 1.3.), the various components of physical activity have been presented. In this study, physical activity will be analysed according to the following three categories: excessive exercise, restless hyperactivity and commitment to exercise.

1.2.1. Excessive exercising in patients with AN

Although the phenomenon of excessive exercise in patients with AN has been recognised as early as 1874, and criteria for exercise dependence have been published (De Coverley Veale, 1987) (for details see part 2, chapter 1.4.1.), clinical consensus as to how to define excessive exercising is still lacking (Davis, Brewer, & Ratusny, 1993a; Herrin, 2003; Katz, 1996). In 1978, Kron, Katz, Gorzynski, and Weiner defined 'hyperactivity' as a day-to-day level of physical activity in patients that was greater than most of the peers. The definition required that the patients engaged in some form of strenuous daily exertion, for example jogging, swimming, biking or skating (p.434). Recent definitions have followed the approach in specifying the amount, duration and type of exercise. Davis and Fox (1993b) for example, defined excessive exercising as exercising at least six times a week for at least one hour per session in one of the following activities: swimming, bicycling, running, skating, home exercises, dance classes, aerobic or weight training. In this paper, excessive exercising will be defined accordingly.

1.2.1.1. Effects of excessive exercise

Beumont et al. (1994) have listed deleterious effects of excessive exercise and studies examining negative effects are summarised.

Effects of excessive exercise have been investigated in terms of the impact on patients' energy expenditure. Alterations in energy metabolism result from energy restriction (Polito et al., 2000) and alterations in energy metabolism have been shown in patients with AN relative to the degree of weight loss (Vaisman et al., 1991). Total energy expenditure (TEE) is usually subdivided into three components: 1) basal metabolic rate (BMR; defined as the energy expended by a person who is fasting and at rest in the morning under comfortable ambient conditions), 2) thermic effect of food (TEF or diet-induced thermogenesis (DIT); defined as the increase in BMR in response to food intake) and 3) energy expenditure through physical activities (PAEE; considered the most variable component of energy expenditure) (Ravussin, 1995).

In AN, reduced BMR has been consistently reported (Casper, Schoeller, Kushner, Hnilicka, & Gold, 1991; Krahn, Rock, Dechert, Nairn, & Hasse, 1993; Melchior, Rigaud, Rozen, Malon, & Apfelbaum, 1989; Platte et al., 1994; Polito et al., 2000; Schebendach et al., 1995; van Marken Lichtenbelt, Heidendal, & Westerterp, 1997). Alterations in energy expenditure have to be taken into account when developing optimal dietary interventions to promote weight gain. Studies into TEE and AN have demonstrated the importance of PAEE when estimating energy expenditure in AN. These studies found no differences between TEE in patients and controls (Casper et al., 1991; Pirke, Trimborn, Platte, & Fichter, 1991). The finding was explained by increased physical activity levels that impacted on the TEE (Pirke et al., 1991). Along the same lines, van Marken Lichtenbelt, Heidendal and Westerterp (1997) found significantly lower levels of average daily metabolic rate (assessed through doubly labelled water method) but demonstrated that patients with AN either showed very low activity or very high activity levels compared to moderate intensity activity levels for controls.

Wakefield et al. (2004) therefore suggest that patients' with excessive exercising require higher energy intake during the refeeding process. In summary, excessive exercise in patients with AN affects the already altered energy metabolism in that increases in PAEE may lead to unexpectedly high TEE, and hence, might increase energy requirements during the refeeding process.

Excessive exercise has been shown to decrease food intake in the general population, as recently reviewed by Blundell and King (1999). Thus, the greater the individual's physical activity, the more difficult it becomes to raise the energy intake above the expended energy. Also, appetite tends to be suppressed under periods of extremely intense physical activity (Blundell & King, 1999). It could therefore be hypothesised that weight loss will be accelerated in patients engaging in high levels of exercise in addition to decreased food intake and a loss of appetite.

Excessive exercise plays an important albeit controversial role in the development of osteopenia. In the general population, physical activity is necessary for bone mineral acquisition and maintenance throughout adult life and high impact exercise such as running stimulates the accrual of bone mineral content in the skeleton (Mehler, 2003). However, physical activity has both a protective and a harmful effect on bone density in patients with AN. Osteopenia has been described as a serious and possibly irreversible medical complication of AN (Rock, 1999). Almost 50% of patients have bone mineral density (BMD) measurements more than two standard deviations below that of age- and gender-matched controls (Grinspoon, Herzog, & Klibanski, 1997; Rock, 1999). The current literature suggests that rather than being a predictor of low BMD, excessive exercising might have a mediating effect on BMD through its impact on weight loss (Goebel, Schweiger, Kruger, & Fichter, 1999; Grinspoon et al., 1997; Mehler, 2003).

Excessive exercise in patients with AN contributes to further weight loss with the overall net result being detrimental to bone density (Mehler, 2003). On the other hand, van Marken Lichtenbelt et al. (1997) recently demonstrated a positive relationship between BMD and physical activity (determined through doubly labelled water method) in patients with AN. Sixty-nine percent of the variation in BMD could be explained through physical activity energy expenditure. Van Marken Lichtenbelt et al. (1997) suggest that despite negative impacts of excessive exercising, potential benefits of engaging in normal exercise-patterns for patients with AN have to be recognised.

Abnormal circulatory responses to exercise and a decreased working capacity (maximal work performed expressed in watts per kilogram) have been demonstrated in patients with AN (Biadi et al., 2001; Nudel, Gootman, Nussbaum, & Shenker, 1984). Nudel et al (1984) recommended that patients who develop ECG abnormalities during exercise be identified because they might be at higher risk for cardiac complications during intense exercise, and such exercise might have to be discouraged.

Excessive exercise has found to be associated with more unhealthy general and bulimic eating attitudes (assessed through the EAT-40 and the Bulimic Investigatory Test) and with higher somatisation and anxiety in patients with AN (Penas-Lledo, Vaz Leal, & Waller, 2002). It is hypothesised by Penas-Lledo et al. (2002) that exercise is used as a compensating mechanism to cope with emotional distress.

Because it impacts on patients' weight loss, food intake, appetite, BMD and cardiac function, excessive exercise should be considered a serious symptom of AN. It is also associated with higher psychopathology in terms of anxiety and somatisation. Management of excessive exercise in patients therefore not only seems justified but extremely important from a physical and psychological health point of view. However, positive impacts of a healthy exercise-pattern need to be recognised. According to Beumont et al. (1994), because exercise is part of a healthy lifestyle, patients should be taught to integrate a healthy amount of exercise in their daily life rather than insisting on complete abstinence from all exercise.

1.2.2. Restless hyperactivity in patients with AN

The phenomenon of restless hyperactivity in patients with AN is considered the most striking form of physical activity (Beumont et al., 1994) (see part 2, chapter 1.4.2.). Beumont et al. (1994) described it as follows: *the patient finds it difficult to keep still even for a short period, and becomes noticeably distressed if constrained to do so* (p.27). Even when weight decreases to the extent that exercising cannot be continued, restless hyperactivity is still present. Katz (1996) described the phenomenon similarly adding that the diffuse restlessness is almost invariably associated with progressive insomnia.

1.2.2.1. Negative effects of restless hyperactivity

Negative effects of the restless hyperactivity have not been investigated systematically. However, it can be hypothesised that besides patients' sleep their energy expenditure would be negatively affected. In terms of energy expenditure, restless hyperactivity can be classified as nonexercise activity energy expenditure (Levine, Eberhardt, & Jensen, 1999). Nonexercise activity energy expenditure or thermogenesis (NEAT) is defined as energy expenditure resulting from activities not considered as exercise such as sitting, standing and fidgeting. The role of NEAT on TEE as a second component of physical activity energy expenditure has been systematically investigated by Levine et al. (1999).

They found that NEAT proved to be the principal mediator of resistance to fat gain in normal weight participants. While these results have recently been mentioned in the context of physical activity and AN (de Zwaan, Aslam, & Mitchell, 2002; Pirke et al., 1991; Platte, Lebenstedt, Rueddel, & Pirke, 2000) so far there has been no study investigating NEAT in AN patients. It is therefore still unclear, how many calories patients with AN expend on NEAT and whether NEAT might be an important factor in resisting weight gain hence, demonstrating negative effects of restless hyperactivity.

Even though research into negative effects of restless hyperactivity is still in its early stages, a potential impact on patients' energy expenditure has been speculated. If restless hyperactivity through NEAT prevents patients from gaining weight, strategies to manage and counteract the restlessness will become necessary.

1.2.3. Commitment to exercise in patients with dieting disorders

Davis et al. (1993a) defined commitment to exercise as the degree to which feelings of well-being are influenced by exercising, the degree to which adherence to exercise is maintained in the face of various adverse conditions and the extent to which one's exercise regime interferes with social commitments (see part 2, chapter 1.4.1.2.). Patients describe feeling an increasingly strong compulsion to be physically active even when they no longer enjoy it – indeed even when the process becomes painful and exhausting (Davis et al., 1999). All pleasurable and recreational activities are sacrificed to maintain the exercise regime.

1.2.3.1. Negative effects of the commitment to exercise

In a long-term study into course of recovery and relapse in AN, Strober, Freeman and Morrell (1997) identified compulsive drive to exercise at time of discharge as a predictor of early relapse (see also part 2, chapter 1.4.1.2.). These results demonstrate the importance of addressing the commitment towards exercise during treatment to increase patients' psychological well being, counteract potential relapses and the progressing isolation of the patients.

1.2.4. Summary of negative effects of the components of physical activity

It is clear that there are a number of negative consequences resulting from excessive exercise, restless hyperactivity and obsessive-compulsive attitudes towards exercising. The positive impacts of exercise for example on BMD indicate that prevention of all exercise might not be an appropriate treatment strategy. However, physical activity components need to be addressed in treatment. The following section gives an overview of suggested assessment and treatment strategies for management of physical activity in patients with dieting disorders.

1.3. Assessment of physical activity in patients with dieting disorders

Assessment tools for physical activity in healthy participants are presented in part 2 (chapter 1.3.2.). In dieting disorder research, Shelton and Klesges (1995) pointed out that the need for assessing physical activity in the area of AN and bulimia nervosa (BN) is much less clear compared to obesity. Physical activity is thus often only assessed initially using interview-techniques. Interestingly, hardly any study has been published recommending guidelines for the assessment of the various components of physical activity in patients with dieting disorders. An exception are the guidelines of the World Health Organisation (1997) where eight questions on exercise behaviour are included in the Eating Behaviour Assessment Interview, comprising the frequency of exercise, motivation for exercise and the type of exercise.

Assessment of restless hyperactivity in patients with AN is difficult. The doubly labelled water method would be the gold-standard to assess the energy costs of restlessness, but the cost of ^{18}O is considerable (Montoye, Kemper, Saris, & Washburn, 1996) and therefore this method is not feasible in a clinical context. Bouten, van Marken Lichtenbelt and Westerterp (1996) used objective monitoring with triaxial accelerometers to assess patients' restless hyperactivity. In the clinical setting, objective monitoring may be promising to include as a form of self-monitoring (see also part 2, chapter 1.3.2.2.). Exner et al. (2000) used self-reports and clinicians' estimates of patients' restless hyperactivity. These two methods (objective monitoring and patients' and clinicians' reports) appear to be promising tools to assess restless hyperactivity in patients. Assessing the commitment to exercise is easier and several questionnaires have been designed, for example the Commitment to Exercise Scale (CES) (Davis et al., 1993a) (see part 2, chapter 2.6.1.2.).

In summary, guidelines for a comprehensive assessment of various components of physical activity in patients with dieting disorders do not exist. Exercise is usually assessed in terms of its frequency through interviews and in terms of the commitment to exercise by the use of questionnaires. Restless hyperactivity is difficult to assess in clinical settings, but self-monitoring with accelerometers and clinician's observations may be promising.

1.4. Treatment strategies for management of physical activity

Treatment strategies to manage physical activity and its various components in patients with dieting disorders were first described in the 1970s. At that time, response prevention was the method of choice; for example, patients were required to spend an hour of supervised bedrest after their meals to prevent them from compulsive overexercising (Touyz et al., 1987). In a case study (two patients with AN), Mavissakalian (1982) investigated the effects of flooding and response prevention (i.e., patients were prevented from engaging in any activity after food intake). Continuous weight gain in both patients could be demonstrated. Blinder (1970) suggested using physical activity as a reinforcer for weight gain. In his case-studies (three patients with AN) patients were allowed to engage in physical activity depending on their weight gain. All patients showed favourable changes in their mood and interpersonal relations within a short time of initiation of the treatment.

Recent suggestions for managing physical activity in patients with dieting disorders include the use of specific exercise programmes, where exercise is subsequently integrated into treatment and therapeutic techniques are centred around psychoeducation, motives for engaging in sports and management of commitment to exercise. Another line of research, focussed on negative body experience in patients with dieting disorders (Probst, Van Coppenolle, & Vandereycken, 1995) and aimed to re-establish positive body experience through the use of body-orientated strategies and movement groups such as Yoga or Feldenkrais (Laumer, Bauer, Fichter, & Milz, 1997). Finally, recent research into the impact of heat treatment suggests that warming patients counteracts restless hyperactivity (Birmingham, Gutierrez, Jonat, & Beumont, 2004b; Gutierrez & Vazquez, 2001a). The following chapter summarises the different treatment strategies and reports on evaluation where conducted.

1.4.1. Exercise programmes

Ziemer and Ross (1970) were the first to demonstrate that a graduated exercise program for patients with AN did not endanger well-being or overall psychiatric treatment. It was not until 20 years later, that further programmes for exercise and physical activity management were published (Beumont et al., 1994; Carraro, Cognolato, & Bernardis, 1998; Long & Hollin, 1995; Thien et al., 2000). Since then, exercise programmes were suggested by researchers from USA, U.K., Italy, Australia and Canada. These programmes differ in the patient group they are aimed at (in- versus outpatients; patients with AN only or patients with dieting disorders), in the specified criteria for attendance, objectives and conducted evaluation. Three research groups conducted a follow-up study of their suggested programmes (one of them did a randomised-control trial; (Thien et al., 2000)). The programmes are summarised in table 1 in terms of the patient group, criteria for attendance, components, objectives and evaluation.

Table 1: Exercise programmes

	Ziemer and Ross (1970) USA
Patient group	Inpatients with AN
Criteria for attendance	Evidence of sustained and progressive weight gain Arbitrary weight of 100 pounds (45.5kg) was chosen if sustained for at least one week Patient's psychological readiness to accept a structured exercise program
Components	Six phases: Phase I: Observation, no control, weight loss; one week, focusing on observation Phase II: Exercise restriction and sustained weight gain; control of patient's dietary intake and energy expenditure; restricting patient's movements Phase III: Limited exercise and continued weight gain; one month, exercise daily under supervision Phase IV: Expanding exercise, mobilisation and weight stabilisation; activities including swimming, walking, dancing, greater responsibility to the patient Phase V: "Blending" with continued weight stabilisation; (4 weeks), daily running and exercise for all parts of the body Phase VI: Figure control and consistent weight stabilisation; relaxation of controls; participating in all exercises
Objectives	Sustain progressive weight gain Avoid unnecessary energy expenditure Increase and sustain muscle tone Provide an outlet – in a controlled way- for the patient's psychological need for excessive exercise Increase the patient's appetite through physiological means Provide an activity focused around a one-to-one relationship with another person who may serve as an identification model Increase in a gradual way, the patient's awareness of 'realistic' exercise tolerance Counter the patient's tendency to overexercise secretly and 'cheat'. When it was recognised that these patients would probably continue to exercise secretly, they were provided with a routine that would endanger their weight gain markedly if they continued secretly on their own.
Evaluation	Case-study with one patient Description of changes in the following variables: - Body weight increased from 45.5kg to 54.6kg - Improvement in mood and compliance with prescribed exercise and eating - Body image; increased interest in feminine appearance, figure and posture

	Beumont et al. (1994)
	Australia
Patient group	Inpatients with AN and BN; specification in terms of exercise for both patient groups)
Criteria for attendance	Entirely voluntary Activity coordinator to prepare an exercise profile and assess the therapeutic value of the program for the patient Patient has attained a nutritional status that will provide adequate physical and psychological function; minimal BMI of 14 Participation contingent upon reasonable compliance with refeeding and steady rate of weight gain
Components	Stretching and flexibility (for 30 minutes) Posture improvement: education on physical, psychological and social significance of posture and the role of body language, exercises Weight training Social sports Aerobic style exercises: walking, swimming, low impact aerobics Preparation for discharge: discharge plan in terms of activities
Objectives	Promote healthy exercise Encourage body awareness and healthy body image Improve efficiency of movement and introduce posture awareness and its relationship to self-esteem Increase in weight gained as lean mass Reduce irrational feelings of fatness by increasing body tone and fitness Incentive for patients on an operant conditioning program Social sports Stress reduction through recreational sport Correct irrational beliefs regarding exercise
Evaluation	Touyz, Lennerts, Arthur and Beumont (1993) N=39 inpatients with AN (consecutive admissions) Assigned to two treatment programmes: 1) Lenient, flexible, behavioural program (n=20) 2) Lenient, flexible, behavioural program and three hours per week of structured anaerobic exercise program (n=19) Outcome Amount of weight gain (in kg) after 4 and 6 weeks Results Age difference between group 1 and 2 (1>2) No significant differences in the rate of weight gain over 4 and 6-week period Discussion The inclusion of an exercise program appears to have improved patient compliance and staff satisfaction but has not adversely affected the ability of patients to regain weight.

	Long and Hollin (1995) UK
Patient group	Outpatients with AN
Criteria for attendance	Weight normalised (90% of normal range of body weight) Suffering from 'negative' addiction to exercise

Components	Two-phase approach:
	Phase 1: since many patients are in the contemplation stage of change, work at the
	     motivational level
	Techniques
	- feed-back
	- discussion of questionnaire data
	- self-monitoring of exercise behaviour and compulsion to exercise
	- exercise education
	- motivational interviewing
	- decisional balance sheet to summarise clients' perceived positive and negative
	     effects of exercise change
	Phase 2
	self-targeted reduction in activity and the use of weekly monitoring sheets
	stimulus control strategies
	cognitive restructuring to modify exercise related cognition (that may include fantasies
	of body deterioration, bloating and motivational loss if exercise is not carried out); in that
	patients develop and rehearse a list of coping self-statements in order to handle
	temptation or urges to exercise to excess
	exposure and response prevention

Objectives	Absence of compulsion to exercise Reduction in the amount of exercise Engagement in exercise for reasons of enjoyment and self-fulfilment
Evaluation	Six patients with a diagnosis of AN Measures Morgan-Russell Scales EDI Body Shape Questionnaire Brief Symptom Inventory Anorectic Observation Scale Commitment to Exercise Questionnaire Questionnaire to assess exercise, behaviour and cognitions Results 4 'good' outcome 2 'poor' outcome Two patients with 'poor' outcome continued to be 'negatively' addicted to exercise. Four patients with 'good' outcome saw exercise as less vitally important

303

	Carraro, Cognolato and Bernardis (1998)
	Italy
Patient group	Outpatients with AN, BN and Eating Disorders Not Otherwise Specified (EDNOS)
Criteria for attendance	Not specified
Components	Adapted Physical Activity (APA)
	Multi-dimensional approach
	Assessment including psychometric tests (EDI, EAT, SCL90, Body Attitude Questionnaire)
	Groups of 10 patients
	Meeting subdivided into:
	- Introductory stage: explnataion of APA
	- Psychophysical activation stage
	- Development of the set theme
	- Speaking to each other about experience
	- Exercises, games and activities
Objectives	identity: to explore lesser known areas of one's identity and roles other than that of 'patient suffering from a dieting disorder
	somatic: to improve physical condition and posture
	social relations: to improve communication skills, including the use of codes other than speech
	educational: to encourage patients to build a healthy image of movement and their bodies as they move and to discourage hyperactivity
Evaluation	No evaluation conducted
	Suggestions for evaluation tools:
	Discussion among patients
	Individual clinical talks and group psychotherapy
	Discussions among staff
	Louvain Observation Scale for Objectives in Psychomotor Therapy
	Video recordings
	Thien Thomas, Markin and Birmingham (2000)
	Canada
Patient group	Outpatients with AN
Criteria for attendance	Level 1: <75% of ideal body weight (IBW) or <19% body fat (BF)
Components	Graded exercise program with a clear exercise prescription
	Level of activity dependent on % IBW and % BF
	Activities:
	Stretching
	Isometric exercise
	Low impact cardiovascular exercise
	Resistive strengthening
Objectives	Prevent decrease in bone mass
	Prevent the risk for developing atherosclerosis
	Increase compliance

Evaluation	Randomised-control trial
	Exercise-group (n=5)
	Control group (n=7)
	Measures
	Quality of Life (SF-36)
	BMI
	%BF
	Primary outcomes: change in 3 subscales of SF-36:
	role functioning
	social functioning
	energy and fatigue
	Secondary outcomes: change in
	Total score of SF-36
	BMI
	BF
	Results
	No difference between groups in % BF, BMI
	Improvement in questionnaire but not statistically significant

As can be seen in table 1, evaluations of the various exercise programmes are rare and if conducted, the number of patients was small. Thus, conclusions about the effectiveness of the various programmes have to be drawn carefully. Further, because the programmes vary in their objectives, the studies are difficult to compare in terms of outcome-variables (variables range from changes in body composition (Beumont et al., 1994; Long & Hollin, 1995; Thien et al., 2000; Ziemer & Ross, 1970) to changes in the quality of life (Thien et al., 2000)). The description of positive impacts on patients' mood and staff-patient relationship (Beumont et al., 1994), the lack of any negative impact on patients' weight gain and the preliminary evidence for positive outcomes of the programmes justifies their use and further investigation into their implementation in treatment is therefore warranted.

1.4.2. Body-orientated therapy (BOT) and physical activity

A slightly different approach to manage hyperactivity in patients with dieting disorders, known as body-orientated therapy (BOT) has been advocated by some (Probst et al.,

305

1995). Rather than focusing on activity and exercise per se, this approach focuses on the body experience of the patients. Body experience comprises all individual and social experiences: the affective and the cognitive, the conscious and the subconscious (Probst et al., 1995). Specifically, the term 'body experience' refers to the neurophysiological aspect (body scheme, body orientation, body size estimation, body knowledge) and the psychological-phenomonological aspect (body image, body awareness, body boundary, body attitude).

It was only in the last decade that a growing interest for the incorporation of body experience in treatment was formulated (Probst et al., 1995). The approaches differ in terms of the role of body experience in dieting disorders; one group sees the disturbed body experience as a secondary symptom caused by another factor. Accordingly, it is assumed that once the cause is resolved, the body experience will normalise. Another group sees the disturbed body experience as a primary and essential aspect of the dieting disorder, which requires specific therapeutic intervention (Laumer et al., 1997; Probst et al., 1995). As a direct approach to influence body experience, BOT in the form of a multidimensional approach has emerged. BOT is mentioned in the context of the management of physical activity, as one of its major objectives is to curb hyperactivity. In fact, it incorporates parts of the graded exercise programmes mentioned in table 1. In order to get an understanding of the aims and characteristics of BOT, the major components, objectives and its evaluation are summarised in table 2.

While BOT is a multidimensional approach, Laumer, Bauer, Fichter and Milz (1997) have investigated the potential benefits of movement groups such as Feldenkrais-method in the context of dieting disorders. Feldenkrais (1949) published his method in 1949 with the particular aim to increase body awareness and psychological well-being

306

through consciousness of body movements. The Feldenkrais-method is described as a form of somatic education and is designed to improve function in activities of daily living, work and recreation (Buchanan & Ulrich, 2001). It is assumed that more effective and efficient actions emerge from guided exploration of movements that promote improved attention and awareness, and refines the ability to detect information and make perceptual discriminations. Teaching of the Feldenkrais-method aims to enhance people's awareness of their habitual solutions to motor problems and the sensations accompanying those habits, demonstrating other solutions and helping students select easier, more efficient and more effective movement options (Buchanan & Ulrich, 2001). Advocating the unity of body and mind, Feldenkrais (1949) suggested that through re-organising body movement, changes in behaviour can occur and last. The Feldenkrais-method has been used in older adults, patients with multiple sclerosis and adults with chronic pain (for a review see (Buchanan & Ulrich, 2001)). As the Feldenkrais-method aims to change a person's habits and personality –focussing on the unity between body and mind - and as disturbance of body experience is one of the core features of dieting disorders, Laumer et al. (1997) have suggested using the method in the treatment of dieting disorders. They hypothesised that the method might impact on patients' body-perception, body image and self-esteem. In contrast to curbing hyperactivity, the method makes use of physical activity and body movement to improve body-perception and psychological well-being in patients with dieting disorders. The Feldenkrais-method for dieting disorder is summarised in table 2 together with BOT.

As another body-orientated strategy or body movement group, Yoga has been suggested for treatment of dieting disorders. Giles and Chng (1984), whose work focus was on occupational therapy and activity-orientated approaches to cognitive restructuring, suggest that Yoga has several advantages over simple relaxation in patients with dieting disorders. It provides the much-needed body-conditioning when all other activities are restricted. Further, the nature of Yoga might help patients to control their hyperactivity. Scheduling Yoga sessions before and after meals might reduce the anxiety and feelings of discomfort well known in patients with dieting disorders. Despite these useful suggestions, studies into the effectiveness of Yoga for treatment of dieting disorders are lacking. Rani and Krishna Rao (1994) demonstrated improvements in body awareness in healthy adults undergoing a Hatha Yoga class, thus indicating potential benefits for its use in dieting disorders.

Table 2: Body-orientated therapy (BOT)

	Probst, Van Coppenolle and Vandereycken (1995) Belgium
Patient group	(semi)-inpatients group-therapy
Criteria for attendance	Not specified
Components	- Relaxation and breathing techniques (Jacobson's progressive relaxation method and autogenic training by Schulz) - Massage (relaxing and/or activating massage) - Role playing ('doubling': initiate patient non-verbal posture; role reversal: patient impersonates a real or imaginary person to increase awareness of the self) - Physical activities, sports and games (fitness, aerobics, callanetics, sports and gymnastics; integration of components of Graded Exercise Programmes (Beumont et al., 1994) - Dance and creative movement (dance and movement forms which focus on expression through the body for example rhythmic exercises, dance, aerobics; patient can express feeling experiences) - Sensory awareness training (exploration focuses on breathing, heartbeat, feeling of hunger and fatigue) - Self-perception and body-perception (awareness of one's own body and its external appearance through mirror exposure and video feedback) - Guided imagery (to discover negatively loaden body parts)
Objectives	Three starting points for BOT: Distorted body experience Hyperactivity Fear of losing self-control Four objectives: 1. Rebuilding a realistic self image 2. Curbing hyperactivity into more controlled movement; learning how to limit physical activity through rest and relaxation; sustaining a good physical condition 3. Developing social skills 4. Learning how to enjoy the body
Evaluation	Probst, Vandereycken, Van Coppenolle and Pieters (1999) Follow-up study with patients with AN and BN over three time points (admission, after 6 months, after one year) N-AN-R=177 N-AN-P=126 N-BN=157 N-total=460 N-completed treatment=306 (67%) N-drop outs=154 (33%) Measures Body Attitude Test (BAT) Eating Disorder Inventory (EDI) Eating Disorder Evaluation Scale (EDES) Results

58% who finished treatment had a positive evolution regarding body experience
Negative value at admission decreased significantly after therapy and remained
consistent after one year.

	Laumer et al. (1997) Germany
Patient group	Inpatients with AN, BN and obesity
Criteria for attendance	Not specified
Components	9 sessions Themes during the sessions Movements of lips, eyes, head Movements of the back Movements during breathing, rhythmic, exploration of own breathing rhythm Movements of the legs Posture improvements and related emotions
Objectives	Improvement of body-perception, body image and general well-being through increased awareness of body and its movement
Evaluation	Laumer et al. (1997) Follow-up study with patients receiving Feldenkrais-training and patients without Feldenkrais-training (5-weeks) N=30 Group Feldenkrais: N=15 (2 AN, 9 BN, 4 obesity) Control-group: N=15 (2 AN, 9 BN, 4 obesity) Measures 34 items of the Body Cathexis Scale and Body Parts Satisfaction Scale Questionnaire on body experience Questionnaire on psychological well-being Self-evaluation of anorexic symptoms (ANIS) EDI Results In the Feldenkrais-group greater satisfaction with body parts such as the hips, thighs, upper torso Higher acceptance of own body Higher scores in scales of spontaneity (but no improvement for general well being) No improvement in terms of body image but in scales assessing feelings of being overwhelmed No changes in dieting disorder symptoms

From the study of Probst et al. (1999), no information is available on a reduction of
patients' physical activity. It remains open if BOT primarily addresses the distorted
body experience or is able to counteract hyperactivity as well. However, the follow-up
conducted by Probst et al. (1999) showed that BOT and its techniques seem appropriate
to balance and modify negative body experience with a possible impact on patients'

activity. Thus, further investigation into the use of BOT by clinical specialists is warranted.

The study of Laumer et al. (1997) supports the notion that with the help of body movement groups such as Feldenkrais, improvements in patients' body experience can be achieved. Further evaluation studies are necessary to determine the specific benefits of the Feldenkrais-method for the various dieting disorders. However, the improvements in body perception and in specific aspects of well-being justify its use in the treatment of patients with dieting disorders and potentially, in the management of physical activity. Yoga as a useful strategy for body-conditioning and reduction of anxiety seems promising in the context of management of physical activity and future studies should evaluate its use in treatment.

1.4.3. Heat treatment for patients with AN

Extrapolating from animal models, researchers have recently suggested supplying external heat to patients with AN, in order to prevent them from hyperactivity.

In his review, Lambert (1992) mentions the role of thermogenesis to account for the increased activity in emaciated rats, suggesting an inverse relationship between body temperature and running (see also part 2, chapter 4.1.3.). Rats on a restricted feeding schedule are forced to cope with a core temperature outside the thermoneutral zone (27-31°C, where food intake is not needed in order to maintain core body temperature) and they therefore run to heat themselves. However, Morrow et al. (1997) showed in their study that rats increased their activity before their body temperature dropped, resulting in an assumption that the initial increase in activity relates to factors other than temperature regulation. As weight loss progresses, thermal needs would then become

311

prominent (Gutierrez, Vazquez, & Boakes, 2001b). The hypothesis that hyperactivity is linked to hypothermia, predicts that activity will be lower at higher ambient temperatures. Gutierrez, Vazquez and Boakes (2001b) list indirect evidence (from a re-analysis of data from experiments that have been concerned with other factors) summarising several studies and point out the various ambient temperatures used in the studies along with differences in rats' survival. Morrow et al. (1997) studied the impact of various ambient temperatures on rats' survival using the activity-based anorexia (ABA) -paradigm (Epling & Pierce, 1996) (see also part 2, chapter 1.6.2.) and found that warming animals with a heat lamp (increasing the ambient temperature from 21°C to 37°C) significantly increased the likelihood and length of survival.

It is therefore suggested that a high ambient temperature plays a protective role in the ABA-paradigm, evidenced by the fact that it increased survival of the rats. Reduction in rats' activity at higher ambient temperature with an interruption of the decrease in food intake and a possible direct effect of high ambient temperature on food intake (Gutierrez et al., 2001b) were discussed as possible causes for the rats' survival rates.

Extrapolated to humans with AN, restless hyperactivity and fidgeting may play a similar thermoregulatory role to that of running in ABA rats. Accordingly, warming of the patients might decrease activity levels. Further, studies into the relationship between physical activity and energy intake (for a review see (Blundell & King, 1999)) suggest that engaging in physical activities does not automatically generate an increase in the drive to eat, which would compensate for the energy expended. In fact, Blundell and King (1999) argue that it would be more difficult for individuals to increase their energy intake above the expended energy the greater the individual's level of the physical activity and thus, the energy expenditure. Gutierrez et al. (2001b) therefore argued that rewarming not only helps the patient to decrease her activity but also to increase her food intake.

Rewarming as a therapeutic approach is not entirely new. In fact, as early as 1874, Gull recommended application of external heat to patients with AN. His recommendation was based on reports by the Swiss physiologist Chossat who made careful observations of the consequences of starvation in different species. Recently, Gutierrez and Vazquez (2001a) described the use of heat treatment in a case-study. They implemented setting the thermostat at 25°C, use of an electrical pad and sauna sessions in three patients with AN. In all three patients, they found a reduction in patients' activity level and extreme exercising from the onset of the treatment. Furthermore, as activity receded patients did not report anxiety, depression or any other unpleasant effects; on the contrary, they repeatedly stressed the calming and relaxing effect of heat. Improvement of other symptoms (such as calorie counting and fat phobia) was also observed. As they did not employ any specific psychotherapeutic techniques, they assumed that the reported changes were brought about by heat treatment. The study can be criticised in terms of its design and methodology (small sample of patients, different age and gender; use of three different heating strategies; lack of control-group; compliance to heating in outpatients). However, the positive findings warrant further investigation into the potential impact of heat treatment.

Bergh, Brodin, Lindberg and Soedersten (2002) identified two risk factors for anorexia: dieting and increased physical activity. Extrapolating from animal studies, they argued that anorexia develops because it is initially rewarding to eat less and move more, as both these risk factors have shown to activate the mesolimbic dopaminergic reward system (see also (Casper, 1998)). They argue that the psychopathology of anorexia is a

313

consequence of starvation, and hypothermia and a further increase in physical activity emerges in the state of starvation. Using this framework they developed a treatment directed at the disordered eating and altered perception of satiety, hypothermia, physical hyperactivity and disordered social life. The treatment comprised training to initiate eating, feedback on eating and satiety (patients ate from a plate situated on a scale; the scale was connected to a computer, which stored the weight loss of the plate; rating scales appeared on the monitor, and the patient recorded his/her level of satiety), supply of external heat (patients rested in a room in which they could set the temperature at up to 40°C) and restriction of physical activity (patients were placed in wheel chairs or were allowed to walk slowly within the clinic).

In a randomised-controlled trial with 19 patients with AN and 13 patients with BN, Bergh et al. (2002) investigated the efficacy of their treatment approach. Outcome criteria included patients being in a state of remission, where they no longer met the criteria for a dieting disorder (i.e., body weight normalised, a normal psychiatric profile and normal laboratory tests). They found a significant effect of their treatment on remission rates. Fourteen of 16 patients (87.5%) in treatment were considered in remission after a median of 14.4 months (range: 4.9-26.5 months). Only one of the 16 controls went into remission during the 21.6-month observation period. Although their results are impressive, the impact of heat supply on remission rates remains unclear. The suggested treatment approach (incorporating initiation of eating, feedback on satiety level, supply of external heat and restriction of physical activity) improved remission rates in the patient group, but to what extent warming affected patients' activity and weight gain can not be extrapolated.

314

In another randomised-controlled study, Birmingham, Gutierrez, Jonat and Beumont (2004b) investigated the impact of warming on patients' weight gain. They used thermal vests in a group of 21 patients with AN. Ten patients were randomised to the treatment, 11 were randomised to the control group. Both groups wore the vests but only in the treatment group were the vests set on a medium heat for 3 hours per day over a 21-day period. BMI was the main measure of outcome. No difference emerged in the increase in BMI between the treatment and control group. However, patients described positive effects and the majority of the treatment and control group (66.7% of the treatment group and 87.5% of the control group) preferred to continue or start the warming-procedure. Those patients who had been warmed noticed improved digestion, a calming effect and a decreased parotid size. Birmingham et al. (2004b) concluded despite the negative finding regarding the BMI that methodological problems (such as the lack of blinding and possible warming of the control group through wearing the vests) might explain the non-significant result. Also, because of the positive effects mentioned by the patients and requests from staff, the authors decided to use warming as and adjunctive treatment in patients with AN.

In conclusion, while researchers have recently advocated the use of warming patients with AN to counteract hyperactivity and enable weight gain, research into warming patients is still at a preliminary stage. Potential positive effects on patients' mood, digestion and possibly on the parasympathetic nervous system via a decrease in hypothermia are desired outcomes in the treatment of inpatients with AN. Also, the fact that patients themselves use various warming strategies (such as drinking hot liquids, leaning close to heaters and covering themselves with hot blankets) and were not opposed to the new treatment strategy as described by Birmingham et al. (2004b) warrants further investigation into the potential benefits of its inclusion in treatment. The current study investigates to what extent clinical specialists are aware of the recent research into physical activity and heating and hence, to which degree they incorporate heating strategies into their treatment.

1.4.4. Summary of suggested treatment strategies

Various components of physical activity - excessive exercising, restless hyperactivity and commitment to exercise – were described. Negative effects of each of the components have been listed that necessitate an incorporation of management of physical activity into treatment of dieting disorders. Five strategies for management of physical activity in patients with dieting disorders have been presented. These were response prevention, physical activity as an incentive for weight gain, exercise programmes, body-orientated strategies (BOT, Feldenkrais and Yoga) and the use of heat treatment. It has yet to be determined to what extent the suggested programmes and strategies affect the various components of physical activity in patients with dieting disorders.

However, positive outcomes have been reported from the exercise programmes, BOT, Feldenkrais-method and heat treatment. Exercise programmes and body-orientated strategies in particular showed positive effects on patients' body composition, body image and psychological well-being. Unfortunately, none of the researchers used decrease of physical activity as an outcome criterion, probably due to difficulties in assessing changes in physical activity and the lack of a clear definition of hyperactivity (Katz, 1996). In one of the few studies that addressed separate components of physical activity as an outcome-measure, Long and Hollin (1995) found decreases in the compulsion to exercise after attendance at a two-phase program (see table 1). The presented review suggests incorporating strategies such as specific exercise programmes, BOT and heat treatment into the treatment of dieting disorders.

An analysis of treatment guidelines from different countries gives an understanding of how the role of physical activity is perceived and what treatment strategies are recommended. The following chapter examines suggestions from treatment guidelines (from USA, Australia, Canada and Germany) for the management of physical activity in patients with dieting disorders.

1.5. Treatment guidelines for dieting disorders and the issue of physical activity

The role of physical activity in dieting disorders is acknowledged as important in the guidelines from the USA, Australia, Canada and Germany although to varying degrees. The guidelines were published from various disciplines such as pharmacy, dietetics and psychiatry. It can be assumed that the perspective on the treatment of physical activity varies according to the authors' professional background. Certainly, the interest in the role of physical activity has grown amongst experts in the field of dieting disorders, in particular when comparing the 1993 guidelines of the with the latest version (American Psychiatric Association, 2000). This latest version of the guidelines entails the role of nonexercise activities (fidgeting; NEAT) in dieting disorders, expands on the discussion regarding motives for physical activity and increases awareness of the link between activity and dieting disorders in athletes.

As far as the assessment of physical activity is concerned, the RANZCP guidelines (Wakefield, 2004) and the treatment protocols of the WHO (1997) call for a more comprehensive assessment of the various components of physical activity. The RANZCP guidelines (Wakefield, 2004) recommend a thorough assessment of activity patterns, including premorbid exercise patterns, current levels of exercise (type, frequency and duration), reasons for exercising and relationship to eating patterns (e.g.,, debting behaviour) and the use of exercise as a leisure pursuit. The Eating Behaviour Assessment Interview of the WHO (1997) assesses motives for exercises, frequency, duration and type of exercise and associated attitudes and feelings. The Canadian guidelines (1998) recommend a thorough assessment of the history of overexercising whereas the German guidelines (Fichter et al., 2000) focus on assessing compulsive behaviours and attitudes regarding physical activity.

Suggestions for management strategies of physical activity in patients with dieting disorders range from using physical activity as negative reinforcement for weight gain (American Psychiatric Association, 1993; American Psychiatric Association, 2000; Fichter et al., 2000), restricting patients' activity (Wakefield, 2004), including supervised low weight strengthening activities (American Dietetic Association, 2001) and using psychoeducation around exercise (World Health Organisation Collaborating Centre for Mental Health and Substance Abuse, 1997).

In conclusion, despite the increasing interest in the issue of physical activity, the guidelines are lacking necessary information and fail to suggest comprehensive strategies to manage activity in patients. Even though the latest APA guidelines mention the role of nonexercise activity, the various components of physical activity need to be pointed out more clearly, and assessment tools need to be advocated (such as the use of accelerometers for restless hyperactivity). The use of self-monitoring of physical activity might be discussed and investigated in the future and proposed in treatment guidelines. Proposed treatment strategies (such as exercise programmes, BOT and heat treatment) for physical activity need to be incorporated into the guidelines. None of the guidelines mention the use of exercise programmes, nor do any of the guidelines quote research in terms of body orientated strategies or heat treatment.

1.6. Aim of the study

Physical activity has been recognised as fundamental to the pathogenesis of dieting disorders and models to explain the link between the two phenomena have been suggested. Various treatment strategies have recently been advocated such as the use of exercise programmes, BOT and heat treatment. The guidelines from four different countries did not incorporate all of these strategies to their full extent. The following study therefore aimed to determine how clinical specialists perceive the role of physical activity in dieting disorders and which treatment strategies they incorporate in treatment. A survey with an international cohort of 33 clinical specialists was conducted. Clinical specialists from USA/Canada, Europe, Japan/China and Australia/New Zealand were administered a specially designed survey via e-mail, on physical activity and its management in dieting disorders. The following areas were investigated:

1. Clinical specialists' understanding of the role of physical activity in dieting disorders.

2. Clinical specialists' estimates of the number of patients presenting with overactivity.

3. Clinical specialists' views regarding the components of physical activity in AN.

4. Strategies used by clinical specialists in their assessment and management of physical activity in in- and outpatients with AN.

2. Methods

2.1. Respondents

In March 2003, a group of 53 'clinical specialists' from 13 different countries was contacted via e-mail (see Appendix A) and asked to complete the attached survey. The clinical specialists were identified as experts in the field of dieting disorders based on recent publications in international journals of dieting disorders. Codes were assigned to each respondent, assuring confidentiality. The study aimed to include both research and clinical specialists to participate in the survey. Therefore clinical specialists were asked to forward the survey on to their colleagues, both clinicians and researchers working in the field of dieting disorders. A reminder was sent to non-respondents in May 2003.

Of the 53 clinical specialists that were contacted, 33 replied (62.3%). Five respondents (15.2%) came from USA/Canada, six (18.2%) from Europe (including UK), nine (27.3%) from Japan/China and 13 (39.4%) from Australia/New Zealand. The majority of the respondents were psychiatrists (n=16, 48.5%), but also psychologists, exercise/motor-therapists, nurses, medical doctors and dieticians participated. Participants' professions are listed in table 3.

Table 3: Professions of respondents

	USA/Can n=5	Europe n=6	Japan/China n=9	Australia/NZ n=13	Total N=33
Psychiatrist n (%)					
	3	2	6	5	14
	60.0	33.3	66.7	38.5	48.5
Psychologist n (%)					
	1	1	2	2	5
	20.0	16.7	22.2	15.4	18.2
Exercise therapist [1] n (%)					
		1		2	3
		16.7		15.4	9.1
Nurse n (%)					
				2	2
				15.4	9.1
Dietician n(%)					
				1	1
				7.7	3.0
Medical doctor n(%)					
	1	2	1	1	4
	20.0	33.3	11.1	7.7	12.1

Can= Canada
[1] Including physiotherapists and psychomotor therapists.

Sixteen (48.5%) of the respondents were working within a university setting, 17 (51.5%) were working in specialised therapy centres. Respondents had on average 15 years experience in the field of dieting disorders (range: 1-26 years).

Fifteen (45.5%) worked predominantly with outpatients, six (18.2%) predominantly with inpatients and twelve (36.4%) worked with both in- and outpatients. Respondents were subdivided into two groups according to the patient group they were working with. Respondents who worked with in- and outpatients were included in the analysis for both groups. Twenty-seven respondents (15 primarily working with outpatients, 12 working with in- and outpatients) formed the outpatient group, and 18 respondents (six primarily working with inpatients, 12 working with in- and outpatients) formed the inpatient group.

2.2. The Eating Disorder Specialist/Clinician Survey (EDSCS)

The EDSCS (see Appendix B) was specially designed for this study as a semi-structured eight-page survey to address the issue of physical activity and its management in dieting disorders. Physical activity was defined as any bodily movement produced by skeletal muscles that results in energy expenditure (Caspersen, Powell, & Christenson, 1985). The qualitative aspect of physical activity (i.e., commitment to exercise (Beumont et al., 1994; Davis et al., 1993a), see part 2 chapter 1.4.1.2.) was included in the definition. The survey aimed first to assess clinical specialists' understanding of the role of physical activity in dieting disorders. Five options (three adapted from Eisler and LeGrange (1990)) were presented. These were:

- Option 1: Activity is fundamental to the pathogenesis of the dieting disorder.

- Option 2: There is a direct relationship between activity and dieting disorders, i.e., overactivity can lead to the development of a dieting disorder (adapted from Eisler and LeGrange (1990)).

- Option 3: There is an indirect relationship between overactivity and dieting disorder, in that both are related to some third variable, i.e., another disorder or a predisposing condition, and thus will occur together by more than chance frequency (adapted from Eisler and LeGrange (1990)).

- Option 4: The two phenomena are essentially variants of each other. Etiological factors (such as genetic, personality, familial and social factors) can lead in some cases to a disorder that is superficially different to dieting disorders but is in effect the same disorder with different manifestations (adapted from Eisler and LeGrange (1990)).

- Option 5: Physical activity plays a minor role in dieting disorders.

323

Participants were asked to select only one of the five options. They were also asked if they considered physical activity to be an important component of AN (dichotomous variable, yes/no) and for estimates of patients presenting with overactivity in their unit. The remainder of the survey was divided into two parts: a) questions focusing on physical activity and its management in inpatient-settings and b) questions focusing on outpatient-management. The respondents answered the questions depending on which patient group they were predominantly treating.

To determine their views regarding the components of physical activity in inpatients and outpatients with AN, respondents were asked to rate the four problematic components of physical activity for in- and outpatients separately. These were

1. Excessive exercising

2. Obsessive-compulsive attitudes towards exercising

3. Contrived activity

4. Restless hyperactivity.

Respondents were asked to rank the four problematic components on a 4-point scale (with 1=most problematic and 4=least problematic). As 23 respondents (69.7%) used the same ranking number more than once, a categorical variable for the 'most-problematic' answers of the respondents (option 1 chosen) was created (1=excessive exercising as most problematic, 2= obsessive attitudes as most problematic etc). If a participant for example ranked excessive exercise as most important, she/he would then obtain number 1 in the categorical variable. Options for 'none of the four options seen as most important' and 'more than one component most important', were included, resulting in six categories.

Questions around assessment and management included a list of assessment and intervention strategies suggested in the literature already described (chapters 1.3. and 1.4.). Six aspects of physical activity were presented to the respondents in the assessment section. These were

1. History of physical activity

2. Current activity patterns

3. Patients' beliefs surrounding activity

4. Motivation to engage in physical activity

5. Commitment/Obsession with the activity of exercising

6. Willingness to reduce activity.

Respondents were asked to select which items they addressed in their routine assessment.

In terms of management of physical activity, components of published exercise programmess (Beumont et al., 1994; Carraro et al., 1998; Long & Hollin, 1995; Thien et al., 2000; Ziemer & Ross, 1970) were presented in the survey. Respondents were asked to indicate the therapeutic techniques they used in their program. The intervention-strategies were subdivided as follows:

1) management of activity on the ward,

2) components of an exercise program,

3) treatment of physical activity as part of body-orientated therapies (BOT)

4) strategies to counteract restless hyperactivity (fidgeting).

1) Management of activity on the ward

Respondents were asked to indicate the point at which they would consider actively discouraging of activity and at what point they would prohibit activity. Three options were listed: a) discouragement at a certain amount of body weight/body mass index (e.g., at a low BMI), b) at a certain percentage of ideal body weight and c) at a certain percentage of body fat. Respondents were also asked to describe how activity was monitored, restricted and used as part of an exercise program (e.g., supervision by nurses, the use of bed-rest or exercise as an incentive to weight-gain).

2) Components of an exercise program

Components of reported exercise programmes (see table 1) were presented in the survey and included whether patients were seen individually or in a group-setting, and which disciplines were involved in the exercise program. Disciplines listed included

- Psychomotor therapists
- Physiotherapists
- Psychologists
- Psychiatrists
- Art therapists
- Nurses.

Respondents could select more than one professional group. Respondents were then asked to indicate the therapeutic techniques they were using in their program such as psychoeducation, challenging patients' beliefs, group games and movement groups.

3.) Treatment of physical activity as part of body-orientated therapies

Six body-orientated techniques were listed in the survey and respondents were asked which, if any, they included:

1. Relaxation and breathing techniques

2. Massage

3. Role-playing

4. Physical activity, sports and games

5. Dance and creative movement

6. Self-perception and body-perception.

4.) Strategies to counteract restless hyperactivity (fidgeting)

Respondents were asked whether they utilised heating strategies to counteract restless hyperactivity (eg the use of thermal vests and /or sauna baths) as part of treatment.

The last question asked respondents to indicate whether the issue of physical activity warrants funds being allocated into its research, assessing the perceived importance of research into physical activity and dieting disorders. Respondents were asked to provide a list of research areas into activity and dieting disorders they might be interested in.

2.3. Statistical analysis

Due to the small sample size per country no statistical differences between respondents from the four country-groups could be computed. However, frequency tables are presented to show differences between countries on a descriptive level. The four country-groups were USA/Canada (USA/Can), Europe, Japan/China and Australia/New Zealand (NZ). The statistical package SPSS version 10.0 was used to compute the frequency tables.

Presentation of the results was structured according to the objectives of the study rather than according to the structure of the EDSCS. Thus, the following structure emerged:

- Understanding the role of physical activity in patients with AN

- The importance of physical activity in AN

- Estimates of the number/proportion of patients with dieting disorders who are overactive

- Most problematic components of physical activity as perceived by the respondents

- Assessment and management of physical activity in inpatients

- Assessment and management of physical activity in outpatients.

3. Results

3.1. Understanding the role of physical activity in patients with dieting disorders

Of the 33 respondents, the majority (n=13, 39.4%) agreed that physical activity and dieting disorders are directly related and one may be a risk factor for developing the other. Twenty-four percent (n=8) of the respondents believed that the two phenomena were indirectly related through a third factor or that they were variants of each other (n=8, 24%). Around 15% (n=5) perceived physical activity as fundamental to the pathogenesis of dieting disorders. Two clinical specialists from Japan/China and one from Europe indicated that physical activity plays a minor role in ED (option 5; 9%). Table 4 shows the distribution of the responses for respondents from each country-group.

Table 4: Understanding the role of physical activity in dieting disorders

Link between Physical activity and dieting disorder: Six options

	USA/Canada n=5	Europe n=6	Japan/China n=9	Australia/NZ n=13	Total N=33
Physical activity fundamental to pathogenesis of dieting disorders n (%)					
		1		4	5
		16.7		30.8	15.2
Two phenomena directly related n (%)					
	2	3	2	6	13
	40.0	50.0	22.2	46.2	39.4
Two phenomena indirectly related n (%)					
		2	3	3	8
		33.3	33.3	23.1	24.0
Two phenomena variants of each other n (%)					
	3	2	2	1	8
	60.0	33.3	22.2	7.7	24.0
Physical activity plays minor role n (%)					
		1	2		3
		16.7	22.2		9.1

Respondents who chose more than one option (n=3) were included.

3.2. The importance of physical activity in AN

Of 33 respondents, 28 (84.8%) agreed that physical activity was an important component of AN. Four (12.1%) did not see it as an important component and one (3.0%) did not respond. The four respondents who did not see physical activity as an important component were all from Japan and China. One Japanese respondent stated: [I found that] *Japanese dieting disorder patients exercise more than controls,* [although] *the number of patients with hyperactivity* [defined through a specified amount of time per week] *was less compared to Western countries* (Japanese respondent, e-mail, March 2003).

330

3.3. Estimates of the patients presenting with hyperactivity/overexercising

The treatment units/practices differed in size. Number of admissions per year ranged from 15-800 patients. Twenty-four respondents stated that on average, 40.3% (range: 10.0-100.0%) of the patients presented with hyperactivity/overexercising. The highest number of hyperactive patients was reported in Australia/ NZ (51.7%, SD=25.2%), followed by Europeans who noticed hyperactivity/overexercising in 49.7% of their patients (SD=28.2%). Respondents from USA/Canada found overexercising in about 37.5% of their patients (SD=22.2%) and Japanese/Chinese respondents in only 15.5% (SD=6.1%). Figure 1 illustrates these findings.

Respondents' estimates of patients presenting with hyperactivity/overexercising

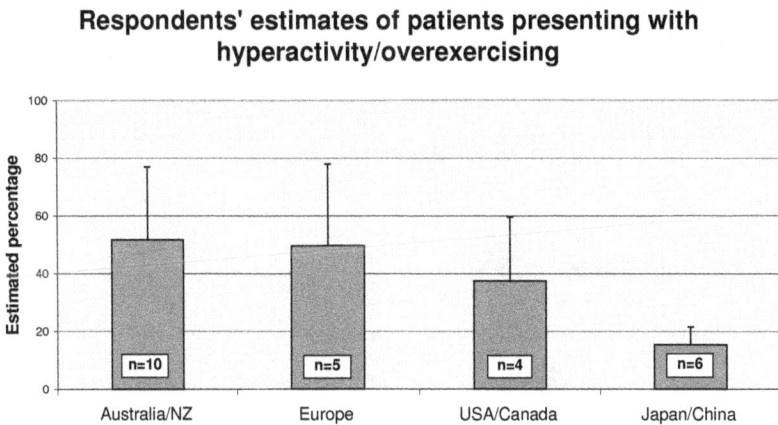

Figure 1: Respondents' estimates of patients presenting with hyperactivity/overexercising

3.4. Most problematic components of physical activity as perceived by the respondents

3.4.1. Inpatients

Eighteen respondents (six primarily working with inpatients, 12 working with in- and outpatients) formed the inpatient group. The majority of respondents either considered obsessive-compulsive attitudes in inpatients as most problematic or did not perceive any of the components as most problematic. Table 5 summarises the frequency and percentage.

Table 5: Physical activity-components perceived as most problematic in inpatients

	Frequency	%
Excessive exercising	4	22.2
Obsessive-compulsive attitude	6[1]	33.3 [1]
Contrived activity	1	5.6
Restless hyperactivity	2 [1]	11.1 [1]
None	6	33.3
Total	18	100.0

[1] Respondent who selected more than one component was included.

3.4.2. Outpatients

A group of 27 respondents (15 primarily working with outpatients, 12 working with in- and outpatients) formed the outpatient group. The majority of respondents (33.3%) considered excessive exercising as most problematic component in outpatients. A third selected the obsessive-compulsive attitude and another third selected restless hyperactivity. Table 6 shows the frequency and percentage.

Table 6: Physical activity-components perceived as most problematic in outpatients

	Frequency	%
Excessive exercising	9[1]	33.3[1]
Obsessive-compulsive attitude	8[1]	29.6[1]
Contrived activity	5[1]	18.5[1]
Restless hyperactivity	8[1]	29.6[1]
None	8	29.6
Total	27	100.0

[1] Respondents who chose more than one component (n=5) were included.

3.5. Assessment and management of physical activity in inpatients and outpatients

3.5.1. Inpatients

Results from 18 respondents (six primarily working with inpatients, 12 working with in- and outpatients) were included in the analysis for assessment and management of physical activity in inpatients with AN.

3.5.1.1. Assessment

In the inpatient group, 17 (94.4%) of the respondents stated that they assessed patients' history of activity and current activity patterns, 16 (88.9%) assessed patients' beliefs surrounding activity, 14 (77.8%) assessed commitment to exercise, 12 (66.7%) expressed interest in patients' willingness to reduce activity and nine (50.0%) assessed patients' motivation to engage in physical activity. Four respondents (22.2%) suggested further assessment areas not included in the provided list: assessment of future career and ambition, neurological assessment, palpation of muscles, evaluation of muscles' tone and weakness, physical side effects and considerations, influences on activity behaviour through family and the Eating and Exercise Examination-Computerised (EEE-C (Abraham & Lovell, 1999)). Six respondents reported the time they spent on the assessment ranging from 7min to 1.5hrs (Mean=37min, SD=31min).

3.5.1.2. Discouraging and prohibiting physical activity in inpatients

Sixteen (88.9%) of the respondents actively discouraged inpatients' physical activity, only two (11.1%) did not. Twelve (66.7%) prohibited inpatients' physical activity when patients were at a certain BMI, percentage of ideal body weight and/or percentage body fat. Three respondents listed further criteria for discouraging activity, particularly where the patient is medically compromised (i.e., with regard to blood pressure and electrolyte balance, diagnosis of bradycardia, hypothermia, and/or dizziness). Two respondents mentioned medical factors as criteria for activity-prohibition, namely blood chemistry or cardiac abnormalities.

3.5.1.3. Activity-intervention on ward

Nursing staff supervision was the most common inpatient-strategy for management of physical activity selected by 12 respondents (67%). Bedrest to prevent patients from exercising or exercise as a motivation factor (incentive) was utilised by eight respondents (44% each). Table 7 displays the respondents' selection. Nine respondents listed further strategies to manage physical activity on an inpatient-ward such as allowing supervised prescribed exercise to help diffuse compulsion, encouraging playful activities, encouraging rest after meals, keeping patients in their rooms, teaching stretching exercises, offering physiotherapy and psychoeducation on pros and cons of continuing activity at a low body weight.

Table 7: Selection of intervention strategies on an inpatient ward

	USA/Can n=3	Europe n=3	Japan/China n=3	Australia/NZ n=10	Total N=18
Bedrest n (%)					
	1		1	6	8
	33.3		33.3	60.0	44.4
Exercise as a motivation factor n (%)					
		2	1	5	8
		66.6	33.3	50.0	44.4
Staff supervision n (%)					
	3	2	1	6	12
	100.0	66.6	33.3	60.0	66.7

3.5.1.4. Components of an exercise program for management of physical activity in inpatients

Two respondents did not answer the question regarding individual or group sessions, resulting in a sample size of 15. Of these, 10 (55.6%) dealt with the issue of physical activity either during individual or group sessions. Five (27.8%) dealt with the issue in individual sessions only.

With regards to the type of professionals involved, physiotherapists were most frequently involved in the development and delivery of structured activity/exercise programmes (n=12, 70.6%), followed by psychiatrists (n=9, 52%), nurses (n=9, 52.9%), psychologists (n=8, 47.1%) and psychomotor therapists (n=2, 11%). One respondent (6%) indicated that an art therapist would be responsible.

Regarding treatment strategies, psychoeducation, challenging patients' beliefs and the use of self-monitoring were most frequently selected for management in inpatients. Ten (58.8%) respondents of the inpatient group provided movement groups. Respondents from USA/Canada (n=1) and Europe (n=1) incorporated the Feldenkrais-method in their treatment, whereas respondents from Australia/NZ (n=5) used Yoga. Further movement groups mentioned by the respondents were dance-therapy, "Konzentrative

335

Bewegungstherapie" (concentrative movement therapy), Pilates, swimming, progressive-muscle-relaxation, behaviour restriction therapy and self-defence. Table 8 summarises the therapeutic techniques offered by the respondents.

Table 8: Selection of therapeutic techniques to manage physical activity in inpatients

	USA/Can n=2	Europe n=3	Japan/China n=2	Australia/NZ n=10	Total N=17[1]
Psychoeducation n (%)					
	2	3	2	9	16
	100.0	100.0	100.0	90.0	94.1
Challenging patients' beliefs n (%)					
	2	1	2	9	14
	100.0	33.3	100.0	90.0	82.4
Self-monitoring n (%)					
		2	2	7	11
		66.6	100.0	70.0	64.7
Group games n (%)					
	1	3		3	7
	50.0	100.0		30.0	41.2
Sessions at gym n (%)					
		2		6	8
		66.6		60.0	47.1
Movement groups n (%)					
	1	3		6	10
	50.0	100.0		60.0	58.8

[1] One expert stated not to include a structured program for the issue of physical activity.

3.5.1.5. Body-orientated strategies in inpatients

Fourteen (77.8%) of the respondents included body-orientated therapy strategies in their treatment approach. Relaxation, massage and self- and body perception were the most frequently implemented body-orientated strategies. Table 9 summarises the selection of the implemented strategies.

Table 9: Selection of body-orientated strategies in inpatients

	USA/Can n=3	Europe n=3	Japan/China n=2	Austr/NZ n=10	Total N=18
Integration of BOS n (%)					
	3	3	2	8	14
	100.0	100.0	100.0	80.0	77.8
Relaxation n (%)					
	3	3		8	14
	100.0	100.0		100.0[1]	100.0[1]
Massage n (%)					
	1	2		8	11
	33.3	66.6		100.0[1]	78.6[1]
Role playing n (%)					
	1	1		1	3
	33.3	33.3		12.5[1]	21.4[1]
Sports and games n (%)					
		3		3	6
		100.0		37.5[1]	42.9[1]
Dance n (%)					
	1	3		2	6
	33.3	100.0		25.0[1]	42.9[1]
Self- and body perception n (%)					
	2	3		3	8
	66.6	100.0		37.5[1]	57.1[1]

[1] Of those respondents who integrated BOS in their treatment.

3.5.1.6. Strategies to counteract restless hyperactivity (fidgeting) in inpatients

None of the 18 respondents used heat treatment to counteract restless hyperactivity. Seven respondents (38.9%) listed other treatment approaches to prevent inpatients' restless hyperactivity. Of those, four (57.1%) mentioned medication such as Olanzapine. Other suggested strategies were bed rest (n=1, 14.3%), meditation/relaxation (n=1, 14.3%) and refeeding (n=1, 14.3%).

3.5.1.7. Treatment time spent on the issue of physical activity

Five respondents did not respond to the question of how much time they spent on the issue of physical activity during treatment. Six respondents reported the number of sessions. As the number of sessions varied between the respondents, percentage of time spent on the issue of physical activity during treatment was computed. They spent on average 39.4% (range: 16.7-80.0%) of the total treatment time on the issue of physical activity.

3.5.2. Outpatients

A group of 27 respondents (15 primarily working with outpatients, 12 working with in- and outpatients) formed the outpatient group.

3.5.2.1. Assessment

In the outpatient group, all respondents (100.0%) stated that they included patients' current activity patterns in their assessment. Twenty-four (88.9%) assessed patients' beliefs surrounding activity, 23 (85.2%) assessed patients' motivation to engage in physical activity, 22 (81.5%) asked about the patients' history of activity, 21 (77.8%) assessed patients' willingness to reduce activity and 20 (74.1%) covered patients' commitment to/obsession with the activity of exercising. Three respondents suggested further assessment areas not included in the list provided, namely assessment of ambition (particularly related to physical activities), palpation of muscles, evaluation of muscle tone and weakness, physical side effects of exercise and the patients' thoughts about their future activity.

Eight respondents (29.6%) reported the time they spent on the assessment of physical activity. On average, they spent around 34 minutes (range: 5 minutes-2.5 hours) assessing physical activity in outpatients.

3.5.2.2. Discouraging and prohibiting physical activity in outpatients

Twenty-four (88.9%) of the respondents actively discouraged activity in the management of outpatients, three (11.1%) did not. Sixteen (59.3%) prohibited physical activity when the patient reached a certain BMI (n=11, 40.7%) and/or percentage of ideal body weight (n=10, 37.0%). Three respondents (11.1%) stated that it would be impossible to prohibit outpatients' physical activity.

3.5.2.3. Prescription of bedrest in outpatients and alternative suggestions

Five respondents (18.5%) indicated prescribing bedrest for their outpatients in the hope of preventing them from exercising. However, the majority (81.5%) did not prescribe bedrest. Thirteen respondents (48.1%) listed further options how to deal with the issue of activity in outpatients. These were actively encouraging the patient to stay home and rest in front of the TV (n=3), use of cognitive-behavioural strategies such as psychoeducation (n=3), restrict activity to stretching (n=2), hospitalisation (n=1), heat treatment (n=1) and introduction of activity logs and self-monitoring (n=3).

3.5.2.4. Components of an exercise program for management of physical activity in outpatients

Seven respondents did not answer the question regarding provision of treatment in individual or group format, resulting in a sample size of 20. Of these, 14 (70.0%) dealt with the issue of physical activity during individual sessions, six (30.0%) made physical activity part of both individual and group treatment.

Twenty participants (74.1%) responded to the question regarding staff involvement in managing physical activity in outpatients. With regards to the type of professionals involved, psychiatrists were most frequently involved in the development and delivery of structured activity/exercise programmes (n=13, 65.0%), followed by psychologists (n=11, 55.0%), nurses (n=6, 30.0%) and physiotherapists (n=5, 25.0%). Three respondents listed further staff - dietitians, exercise therapists, physicians at sports clinics and general practitioners.

One respondent did not answer the questions on treatment strategies, resulting in a sample size of 26. Psychoeducation, challenging patients' beliefs and the use of self-monitoring were the most frequently therapeutic strategies used in outpatients. Five respondents (19.2%) provided movement groups, i.e., Yoga. These were all from Australia/NZ. Additional movement groups listed by the respondents were aquacise, hydrotherapy and stretching. Table 10 displays the selection of the therapeutic techniques for the management of activity in outpatients.

Table 10: Selection of therapeutic techniques to manage physical activity in outpatients

	USA/Can	Europe	Japan/China	Australia/NZ	Total
	n=4	n=3[2]	n=9	n=11	N=26[1]
Psychoeducation n (%)					
	3	2	8	9	22
	75.0	66.6	88.8	81.8	84.6
Challenging patients' beliefs n (%)					
	4	2	6	10	22
	100.0	66.6	66.6	90.9	84.6
Self-monitoring n (%)					
	3	1	8	9	21
	75.0	33.3	88.8	81.8	80.8
Group games n (%)					
	1			3	4
	25.0			27.2	15.4
Sessions at gym n (%)					
	2			3	5
	50.0			27.2	19.2
Movement groups n (%)					
				5	5
				45.4	19.2

[1] One expert did not answer questions regarding therapeutic techniques.

3.5.2.5. Body-orientated strategies in outpatients

Thirteen (50.0%) of the respondents included body-orientated therapy strategies in their treatment approach. Of these, the majority used psychoeducation followed by implementing sports and games and self- and body perception strategies. Table 11 displays the selection of the body-orientated strategies.

Table 11: Selection of body-orientated strategies in outpatients

	USA/Can N=4	Europe n=3[2]	Japan/China n=9	Australia/NZ n=11	Total N=26[1,2]
Integration of BOS n (%)	3 75.0		2 22.2	8 72.7	13 50.0
Relaxation n (%)	2 50.0[1]		2 100.0[1]	8 100.0[1]	12 92.3[1]
Massage n (%)				5 62.5[1]	5 38.5[1]
Role playing n (%)	1 33.3[1]		1 11.1[1]	1 9.0[1]	3 23.1[1]
Sports and games n (%)	2 66.6[1]		1 11.1[1]	5 62.5[1]	8 61.5[1]
Dance n (%)				3 37.5[1]	3 23.1[1]
Self- and body perception n (%)	1 33.3[1]		2 100.0[1]	5 62.5[1]	8 61.5[1]

[1] Of those respondents who integrated body-orientated strategies in their treatment.
[2] One expert did not answer the question regarding body-orientated treatment strategies.

3.5.2.6. Strategies to counteract restless hyperactivity (fidgeting) in outpatients

One respondent (3.7%) from Europe used heat treatment to counteract restless hyperactivity in outpatients by prescribing sauna baths and/or wearing thermal vests. Another respondent (3.7%) from Japan stated that patients often choose to take long hot baths. One respondent reported that restless hyperactivity generally resolved with refeeding.

3.5.2.7. Treatment time spent on the issue of physical activity

Nine respondents (56.3%) reported the number of sessions they spent on the issue of physical activity. As the number of sessions varied between the respondents, percentage of time spent on the issue of physical activity during treatment was computed, resulting in a mean of 32.0% (range: 0-100.0%) of treatment time spent on the issue of physical activity.

3.6. Suggestions for future research into physical activity and AN

Twenty-eight of the 33 respondents (84.8%) agreed that the issue of physical activity was important enough to warrant funds allocated to its research. Three respondents (9.1%) were unsure whether the issue was important enough and two (6.1%) disagreed. Twelve respondents (36.4%) suggested research ideas into activity and dieting disorders. Research ideas ranged from issues regarding assessment of physical activity to its treatment and evaluation. They are summarised in table 12.

Table 12: Research ideas into physical activity and its management in dieting disorders

Country-group (Number of respondents)	Research ideas
USA/ Canada (n=1)	- At what point in weight restoration should exercise be reintroduced - What type of exercise would be most beneficial for patients with dieting disorders
Europe (n=3)	- Influence of ambient temperature - Research on specific treatment interventions - Specialised therapy programmes on hyperactivity and body acceptance
Japan/China (n=1)	- How much hyperactivity can cause how much weight loss at what weight level; why are some patients more vulnerable to more weight loss
Australia/NZ (n=7)	- Effectiveness of treatment modalities from medication to heat - Planned exercise - Alternative exercises - How to control/modify activity levels to healthy levels - Effect of olanzapine on restless hyperactivity - Specialised training programmes for physical therapists - Development of specific treatment approach for dieting disordered patients - Motivating factors to engage in physical activity - Patient's history, when did they start exercising, family history - Type of activity and motivation to stop/control activity levels

4. Discussion

Surveys with clinical specialists are rare in the field of dieting disorders. However, they give an insight into the link between research results and clinical practice. This study aimed to assess clinical specialists' understanding of and management strategies regarding physical activity in patients with dieting disorders, with special focus on AN.

4.1. Summary of major findings

In this survey, the majority of clinical specialists acknowledged the importance of physical activity. However, respondents from four different country-groups perceived the link between dieting disorder and physical activity differently, with specialists from an Asian background perceiving the role of physical activity to be minor. One third of the respondents (33.3%) perceived the obsession with the activity of exercising as most problematic components of physical activity in inpatients and one third did not perceive any of the components as most problematic. The excessive exercising was perceived as most problematic in outpatients by the majority of the respondents (33.3%). Despite the fact that the majority of the clinical specialists stated incorporating a comprehensive assessment of physical activity in both in- and outpatients, objective monitoring and self-monitoring tools were rarely used. Overall, only a few of the exercise programmes/strategies described in recent publications were utilised.

4.2. Understanding the role of physical activity in patients with AN

More than one third of clinical specialists in this survey appear to concur with current research into physical activity and AN that suggests that physical activity is seen as a factor that can lead to the development of a dieting disorder, particularly AN (Casper, 1998; Davis et al., 1999; Favaro, Caregaro, Burlina, & Santonastaso, 2000). The position of the majority of clinical specialists thus reflects recent findings into childhood activity and a personality profile of obsessive and addictive traits that are assumed to predispose for the development of weight concerns and obsessive and pathological attitudes towards the activity of exercise (Davis et al., 1999). These attitudes in turn foster further exercise and weight loss, resulting in biological changes, for example in the serotonin turnover (Favaro et al., 2000), that maintain the physical activity and the dieting disorder (see also part 2, chapter 4.3.1.).

Responses of respondents were spread evenly between two further options describing the link between physical activity and dieting disorder (24% each). These were 'the two phenomena are indirectly related' and 'the two phenomena are variants of each other'. Accordingly, no option stood out in terms of frequency of respondents. It could therefore be speculated that there is still no agreement between international clinical specialists as to the link between the two phenomena and as a consequence, the role of physical activity in dieting disorders is not clear.

A clear majority perceived physical activity as playing a major role in dieting disorders (90.9%). A minority of clinical specialists who disagreed with this were mostly from Japan or China, perhaps reflecting cultural differences in the understanding of physical activity in dieting disorders, or in the clinical presentation of patients from those countries. Investigating activity-levels in the general population in China (Tianjin), Hu et al. (2002) found a higher percentage of female inactive Chinese compared to results from studies in the USA (US Department for Health and Human Services, 1997) and Europe (see also part 1, chapter 4.2.1.2.). These results suggest that engaging in leisure-time physical activity is not common in Asian populations, and the assumption therefore arises that physical activity may be a less significant clinical feature in Asian patients with dieting disorders. Supporting this notion, Nakamura (2000) found that fewer patients with dieting disorders in Japan engaged in strenuous exercise to lose weight, while more patients dieted or fasted. Similarly, one Japanese respondent in this study commented that *'Japanese dieting disorder patients exercise more than controls, but the number of patients with hyperactivity* (defined through a specified amount of time per week, eg 6 times/week for at least one hour*) was less compared to Western countries'* (personal communication, March 2003). There is growing interest in cross-cultural similarities and differences in the presentation of dieting disorders (Soh, Beumont, Touyz, Surgenor, & Lee, 2003), and in this context the issue of physical activity warrants further investigation.

4.3. Clinical specialists' estimates of the number of patients presenting with overactivity

The fact that the majority (87.5%) agreed that physical activity is an important issue in dieting disorders correlates with recent descriptions of dieting disorders, whereby activity is described as characteristic a behaviour as dieting (Birmingham & Beumont, 2004a; Katz, 1996). The respondents' average estimated percentage of overactive patients (40%) is at the lower end of estimated percentages of overactivity in AN reported in the literature. The range of estimated percentages from the respondents in the current study (10-100%) is in line with obtained frequency ranges from current investigations into the frequency of excessive exercising (Beumont, Booth, Abraham, Griffiths, & Turner, 1983; Davis et al., 1994; Kron et al., 1978; Penas-Lledo et al., 2002; Sharp, Clark, Dunan, Blackwood, & Shapiro, 1994) (see part 2 chapter 1.4.1.1.). The low average percentages of patients presenting with hyperactivity/overexercising from respondents from Japan and China (15.5%) might reflect cultural differences in the presentation of dieting disorders, particularly with regard to overactivity. This notion is supported by the observation that only clinical specialists from Japan and China, contrary to their colleagues from Westernised countries, perceived the role of physical activity as being minor in dieting disorders. Due to the small sample size in the current study, statistical tests to investigate significant cross-cultural differences regarding the perception of physical activity in patients with dieting disorders could not be computed. Recent studies into the link between physical activity and dieting disorders suggest that it is the obligatory attitude towards exercising, rather than the quantity of exercise per se, that is associated with dieting disorder-related symptoms (Mond, Hay, Rodgers, Owen, & Beumont, 2004; Seigel & Hetta, 2001) (see also part 2, chapter 1.4.1.2.). Penos-Lledo et al. (2002) found that compulsive exercise is more commonly found in AN but excessive exercise (defined through frequency, intensity and motivation to lose weight rather than by its compulsive nature) is found equally in AN and BN. These results highlight the importance of a clear definition of the components of physical activity such as excessive exercising, restless hyperactivity and commitment to exercise. The use of different definitions impacts on frequency estimates of patients engaging in the various types of behaviour.

4.4. Clinical specialists' view regarding the components of physical activity in inpatients and outpatients

Clinical descriptions of patients' activity pattern have suggested that activity develops from being organised, planned and structured at the commencement of the disorder, to becoming more intensified, driven and titrated against caloric intake over the course of the dieting disorder (Beumont et al., 1994). With further weight loss patients tend to experience a diffuse restlessness where they experience progressive insomnia (Katz, 1996) and are unable to sit still (see part 2 chapter 1.4.2.). One would assume from these descriptions, that restless hyperactivity should be the most striking component seen in inpatients.

In contrast to these descriptions, restless hyperactivity was not perceived as the most problematic component of physical activity in inpatients. There are three possible explanations for the finding. First, the obsessive-compulsive attitudes towards exercising are perceived by clinicians as the most problematic characteristic. Researchers recently showed that it is the obsessive attitude towards physical activity, rather than the quantity of activity that differentiated dieting disorder patients from the general population (Mond et al., 2004; Seigel & Hetta, 2001). Davis et al. (1997; 1999) have done extensive research into compulsive physical activity and have discussed the role of obsessive and pathological attitudes towards exercise. With these concepts in mind, respondents' selection of the obsessive-compulsive attitudes as one of the most problematic issues in inpatients seems not only justified, but might express the need for further management strategies to be developed in this area.

Second, the question regarding the 'most problematic components of physical activity' did not specify for whom it would be most problematic. Various interpretations are thus possible, i.e., is the behaviour problematic for the patient or for the management of the patient? It might be due to this ambiguity, that restless hyperactivity was not perceived as most problematic.

Third, in the survey restless hyperactivity was defined as "little fidgeting movements of which the patient is not aware". The link to animal models was mentioned. It could be that this definition of restless hyperactivity was too restrictive. Inclusion of characteristic behaviours such as pacing along the corridor or the inability to sit still and read for even a few minutes might have lead to a broader perception of patients' restlessness, and hence, to a higher number of respondents indicating restless hyperactivity to be problematic.

The perception of excessive exercise as being the most problematic component of activity in outpatients is in line with clinical descriptions (Beumont et al., 1994; Katz, 1996). Clinical specialists encounter reports of excessive exercising from outpatients, where the quantity of the exercise is the most striking characteristic. It can be assumed that outpatients who overexercise are either at the beginning of the obsessive spiral towards excessive exercise (Davis et al., 1999) or they have weight-recovered but are still obsessed with the activity of exercise, as shown by Windauer, Lennerts, Talbot, Touyz and Beumont (1993). Excessive exercising is difficult to manage in outpatients. Clinical specialists rely on patients' reports (or under-reports) about duration and intensity of exercise. Excessive exercising can trigger and reinforce dieting disorder related symptoms, and as such is a serious and problematic component of activity in outpatients.

4.5. Assessment and management of physical activity

4.5.1. Assessment of physical activity in inpatients and outpatients

More than 70% of the respondents assessed activity in inpatients from a broad perspective (including a history of activity, patients' beliefs and the commitment to exercise) rather than solely focusing on the frequency dimension. In outpatients, the assessment tended to be even more comprehensive, with more than 70% of the respondents assessing at least four to five aspects of physical activity.

Clinical specialist therefore are aware of the issue of physical activity and include it in their initial assessment. This finding is in line with observations from Shelton and Klesges (1995). They pointed out that physical activity assessment in dieting disorders is less clear than in obesity, however clinicians assess it at the commencement of their treatment. The finding also corresponds to suggestions from treatment guidelines to broadly assess physical activity (Wakefield, 2004; World Health Organisation Collaborating Centre for Mental Health and Substance Abuse, 1997). Accordingly, clinicians are aware of the growing interest in the issue of physical activity and the fact that physical activity in patients with dieting disorders comprises more than just exercise behaviour.

Respondents were not asked if they used questionnaires regarding physical activity. The question therefore remains as to what extent clinical specialists make use of recently developed questionnaires such as the Commitment to Exercise Scale (Davis et al., 1993a) or the semi-structured interview developed by Seigel and Hetta (2001). Tools such as pedometers or accelerometers that estimate body movement and energy expenditure are powerful instruments that deliver an accurate and objective assessment of physical activity, especially with regard to restless hyperactivity. In this survey, only one respondent (from USA/Canada) reported using activity-logs (for inpatients). Therefore, even though a majority of clinical specialists conducted a comprehensive assessment of physical activity in in- and outpatients, further research into useful assessment tools (such as objective monitoring) is needed to provide clinicians and patients with improved ability to accurately assess and understand physical activity patterns and related energy expenditure.

4.5.2. Management of physical activity in inpatients and outpatients

Regarding management strategies of physical activity for inpatients, nearly 90% of the respondents discouraged their patients from activity, using BMI-cut off as a criterion in the majority of cases. Prohibition of activity was less commonly used but still incorporated by more than 60% of the respondents. The majority of respondents of the current survey used staff supervision on the ward as the main strategy to counteract inpatients' activity. Similarly with outpatients, around 90% of the respondents discouraged their patients from physical activity and nearly 60% prohibited activity. Prescription of bed rest was not prescribed for outpatients.

The fact that the majority of clinicians in this survey discouraged or restricted patients' physical activity is in line with recommendations from treatment guidelines (Wakefield, 2004). Further, prohibition of physical activity was less commonly reported and reflects the tendency to follow lenient rather than strict treatment approaches (Touyz, Beumont, Glaun, Philips, & Cowie, 1984).

Touyz et al. (1993) and Beumont et al. (1994) have discussed the role of staff, particularly nurses to supervise patients' activity. Beumont et al. (1994) pointed out that after the introduction of a graded exercise program for inpatients, staff reported higher compliance in the patients and presumably, improvements in the relationship between staff and patients.

The difficult role of the nurse in the management of dieting disorders has been analysed using a qualitative approach by King and Turner (2000). They observed that caring for patients with dieting disorders/AN is particularly challenging for nurses because they have the greatest contact with patients. Resistant behaviour, interpreted as non-compliance, leads to frustration in the nurses and increases the likelihood of nursing staff distancing themselves from the patients. Strategies that enable an easing of the tension between nurses and patients could significantly improve the therapeutic relationship and the patients' compliance. It is likely that patients' urge to exercise may be counteracted more fruitfully when they are encouraged to engage in certain activities and at the same time educated regarding the role of physical activities in the onset and maintenance of the disorder rather than prohibiting any type of activity.

Touyz et al. (1993) have demonstrated that this strategy does not interfere with weight gain. In summary, the majority of respondents discouraged and prohibited physical activity in patients and incorporated staff supervision in their treatment approach despite the negative impact on patient and staff-relationship. It is important to incorporate treatment alternatives that reduce tensions between patients and staff. Supervised exercise, in an exercise program, might prove to be an appropriate alternative.

4.5.2.1. Strategies from graded exercise programmes

Three graded exercise program strategies stood out as the strategies most commonly used by respondents for inpatients and outpatients: psychoeducation, challenging patients' belief and self-monitoring. Particularly in terms of psychoeducation, clinicians follow recommendations from treatment guidelines. The World Health Organisation (1997) recommended to use psychoeducation around exercise in the management of patients with dieting disorders. Generally, all three techniques stem from a cognitive-behavioural approach. Only one respondent (from Japan/China) indicated using psychoanalytic strategies to counteract physical activity. A discussion of all strategies is beyond the scope of this paper, thus the use of self-monitoring and movement groups as two promising management strategies that warrant further investigation will be discussed.

Self-monitoring

Self-monitoring was utilised as a treatment strategy by more than 60% of the respondents. The survey did not ask respondents which technique they used for self-monitoring physical activities (e.g., questionnaires, diaries or motion sensors). Therefore further investigation into which self-monitoring devices clinical specialists use in their patients and how beneficial self-monitoring of physical activities is for the treatment of dieting disorders would be useful.

Research into self-monitoring of physical activity in dieting disorders is rare, although self-monitoring is most commonly used in patients with obesity to promote increases in physical activity (Leermakers, Dunn, & Blair, 2000). Self-monitoring of food intake in the assessment and treatment process of dieting disorders has been a common practice for some time and was recently reviewed by Wilson and Vitousek (1999). The advantages of self-monitoring (despite its lack of agreement on energy expenditure with tools such as the doubly labelled water method) are that behaviour is described in real time and hence less vulnerable to inaccuracy caused by distortions related to simple forgetting, current status or cognitive schemata for self-relevant events. Wilson and Vitousek (1999) concluded that self-monitoring remains a useful and versatile method of examining eating patterns and their correlates in the natural environment. Similar to self-monitoring of food intake, self-monitoring of physical activity could provide useful information for the assessment and treatment of patients who present with overactivity.

Movement groups

Respondents from Europe, USA/Canada and Australia/NZ stated that they incorporate strategies such as movement groups into treatment plans for inpatients. They made use of various movement groups: respondents from Europe and USA/Canada utilising the Feldenkrais-method, and those from Australia/NZ utilising Yoga in their treatment. Feldenkrais (1949) published his method in 1949 with the particular aim of increasing body awareness and psychological well being through consciousness of body movements. Even though Laumer, Bauer, Fichter and Milz (1997) have investigated the potential benefits of the Feldenkrais-method in the context of dieting disorders, it is yet to be clarified to what extent the Feldenkrais-method can impact on physical activity levels in patients with dieting disorders. However, the positive relationship with body perception indicates that it could be useful in the treatment of dieting disorders and the question arises as to why respondents from Australia/NZ and Japan/China did not use it in their treatment.

In contrast, 30% (n=5) of Australian/NZ respondents utilised Yoga as a movement group. The effectiveness of Yoga has not been studied extensively in patients with dieting disorders and therefore research into its effectiveness in this particular population is necessary. It is therefore of interest a) to investigate the effectiveness of

Yoga in the treatment of dieting disorders with special focus on physical activity and b) to understand why this technique is commonly implemented in treatment despite lacking scientific evidence.

The small sample size in this study does not allow any conclusions to be drawn as to why respondents from some countries seem to prefer one body movement strategy above another. Larger surveys investigating cultural differences might answer this question.

Interestingly, movement groups were not commonly recommended or used in outpatients by respondents of this survey. Only 19% (n=5) of the respondents (all from Australian/NZ) incorporated movement groups (predominantly Yoga) into treatment. If body movement groups represent an effective strategy for patients with dieting disorders, future research needs to look into recommendations from clinical specialists for outpatients. Even though movement groups might not form part of the outpatients treatment itself due to time-constraints, therapists might recommend that participation in certain movement groups might encourage patients to engage in healthier and more relaxing physical activities.

In summary, the majority of respondents in this study incorporated only three exercise strategies into their treatment for dieting disorder patients (psychoeducation, challenging of patients' beliefs and self-monitoring). Stretching exercises, posture improvement and or scheduled aerobic exercise were rarely incorporated. Follow-up studies have suggested that comprehensive exercise programmes provide additional benefits to patients' physical health, i.e., preventing a decrease in muscle mass and bone mass and decreasing the risk of arteriosclerosis (Thien et al., 2000), improving the therapeutic relationship between patients and staff (Beumont et al., 1994), and increasing patients' compliance (Touyz, Lennerts, Arthur, & Beumont, 1993). Further investigation as to why clinical specialists do not incorporate more of these strategies into their treatment plans is therefore warranted.

4.5.2.2. Body-orientated strategies

Body-orientated strategies were incorporated in inpatient-treatment by around 80% of the respondents. Relaxation was the most commonly used strategy. In outpatients, only 50% of the respondents incorporated body-orientated strategies, mainly using relaxation, sports and games, and self- and body-perception strategies.

It is of interest that the strategy of self- and body-perception (where patients' awareness for their own body is increased through mirror or video exposure) is used by around 60% of respondents working with inpatients and more than 60% of respondents working with outpatients. Recent studies demonstrated that mirror exposure produced a significant and sustained reduction in body dissatisfaction (Key et al., 2002). In this survey, the form of self- and body-perception intervention was not specified, and it remains unclear as to which strategies were used. It warrants further investigation however, to investigate how widespread the use of mirror exposure is, given its potential benefits on the one hand, and its negative side effects (such as creating intolerable anxiety (Key et al., 2002)) on the other. It also needs to be investigated to what extent a decrease in negative body experience through mirror exposure impacts on the amount of physical activity.

4.5.2.3. Heat treatment

Respondents of this survey did not use heat treatment very often. Only one respondent (from Europe) reported utilising it in outpatients. Research into the use of heat treatment and its potential benefits on patients' overactivity is still in its early stages. More studies into its usefulness and effectiveness are needed. However, the described calming effect on the patients (Gutierrez & Vazquez, 2001a) and hence, possible impact on the therapeutic relationship between staff and patients (Birmingham et al., 2004b), suggests that it might become an adjunctive strategy of treatment in the near future as already pursued by Bergh et al. (2002). Also, the observation of patients warming themselves as described by Birmingham et al. (2004b) and in this survey by one of the respondents - *"They developed the method themselves. The temperature of Japanese bath water is normally high so it may constitute a natural heat treatment"* (e-mail, May 2003) - shows the need to further investigate this behaviour.

4.5.3. Summary regarding assessment and management of physical activity

This study is the first survey into clinical specialists' understanding of and management of physical activity in patients with dieting disorders. The results of the survey converged with the recognition of physical activity as being an important symptom in dieting disorders that needs to be carefully assessed and addressed during treatment. Results also demonstrated a discrepancy between latest research studies into physical activity (e.g., suggestions for exercise programmes, BOT, heat treatment and assessment tools) and the degree to which these were incorporated into treatment.

It appears that clinical specialists use a more comprehensive assessment and incorporate more treatment strategies for physical activity than suggested in published treatment guidelines. They are however, still lacking incorporation of useful tools such as objective monitoring and incorporation of published exercise programmes into treatment plans. Future research needs to address the discrepancy between treatment guidelines, research results and clinical specialists' use in practice. The research ideas suggested by the clinical specialists in the current study reflect the need for further research into areas around physical activity such as the impact on weight loss and when it should be introduced as part of the treatment, specialised therapy programmes and their effectiveness and restlessness and its management through heat treatment and/or medication. The treatment of dieting disorders with special attention to physical activity can only be improved by further research into the efficiency of treatment programmes and their implementation into treatment plans by clinical specialists.

It also appears that clinical specialists from different countries perceive the role of physical activity in dieting disorders differently. In particular, Asian clinical specialists perceive it as less important. In this paper, possible cultural differences in the presentation of dieting disorders, with special focus on physical activity, have been discussed and it is suggested that cultural differences and the role of physical activity should be further investigated. It can be speculated that if patients from an Asian background present with overactivity to a lesser degree, different treatment strategies would have to be established. Or, as suggested by Soh et al (2003), there might not necessarily be lower prevalence rates of overactivity in Asian patients with dieting disorders but instead an ignorance as to the role of physical activity and exercising in cultures where a low percentage of people engage in leisure-time activities. Future studies into cross-cultural presentation of dieting disorders need to include the aspect of physical activity to identify prevalence rates.

4.6. Methodological concerns

Specialist surveys have been conducted in the field of obesity (Bray, York, & DeLany, 1992), but no survey of clinical specialists in dieting disorders could be found in a literature search using Pubmed, Medline and PsycInfo. Respondents to this study were too few to conduct statistical analysis, for instance on cultural differences. The findings can therefore only be interpreted on a descriptive level. Future studies with larger sample sizes are needed to address the question of cultural differences in the management of physical activity in dieting disorders.

Clinical specialists from various professional backgrounds (psychiatrists, psychologists, and physiotherapists) were included in the survey, with the majority of respondents being psychiatrists. It is therefore likely that the current survey captured the understanding and management of physical activity from a psychiatric point of view and cannot be generalised to all health professionals. Studies analysing understanding and management of physical activity in dieting disorders for various professional groups would highlight different approaches from different disciplines. After obtaining a comprehensive understanding of the approaches of different disciplines regarding the management of physical activity, various approaches could then be integrated into a multi-disciplinary treatment plan which is usually recommended in the treatment of dieting disorders (American Dietetic Association, 2001; American Psychiatric Association, 1993; American Psychiatric Association, 2000; Beumont, Hay, &

Beumont, 2003; Canadian Paediatric Society, 1998; Fichter et al., 2000; Rock, 1999; Wakefield, 2004).

The respondents also differed in their experience with dieting disorders, ranging from one to 26 years of working in the field. In a larger sample, experience (defined as years of working in the field) could be integrated in the analysis as a possible confounding variable.

In addition, it could be speculated that those specialists that responded to this survey (33 out of 53) had a special interest in the issue of physical activity in dieting disorders. As a result, the findings of this survey probably reflect the views of a selected group of specialists with a special interest in physical activity, rather than giving a broad overview of current points of view among specialists in the field of dieting disorders. Surveys conducted at research meetings or conferences, similar to Bray, York and DeLany (1992), where experts with a variety of research interests are gathered, might overcome this selection bias. Also, as the surveys were sent out via e-mail, technical problems due to the form of communication might have occurred resulting in a reduction in the response rate.

For some of the questions in the survey, more extensive definitions might have been beneficial. It was not assessed, for example, which self-monitoring devices were used to monitor activity. Ideally, different surveys would be designed for different aspects of assessment and management of physical activity, bearing in mind that there is a 'maximum' number of questions that a group of specialists will answer (Karceski, Morrell, & Carpenter, 2002).

The survey aimed to assess clinical specialists' understanding of the link between physical activity and dieting disorders. A focus on AN was obvious in the assessment and management section. Future surveys should delineate the patient groups by designing separate surveys for each type of dieting disorder (AN, BN, EDNOS) and obesity.

4.7. Conclusion

In this study, the majority of clinical specialists perceived physical activity as an important component of AN and assumed that there is a direct link between dieting disorder and physical activity. Those respondents who considered physical activity to be less important were all from Japan and/or China, perhaps indicating cross-cultural differences in the presentation and/or perception of eating disorders that warrant further investigation. This survey suggests that a comprehensive assessment of patients' physical activity is part of the routine assessment for the majority of specialists. However, formal assessment tools such as objective monitoring were rarely used. The majority of respondents incorporated only three strategies of published exercise programmes into treatment (psychoeducation, challenging patients' beliefs and self-monitoring). Published treatment approaches for the management of physical activity will only be incorporated into clinical practice if clinical specialists consider that the strategies will be useful and/or effective. Accordingly, future research needs to more closely evaluate various physical activity treatment strategies, address issues of cultural significance or difference, and report clinical specialists understanding and experience of the issues at hand.

We wish to thank Professor Toro Uehara, University of Gunma, Faculty of Medicine, Japan, for putting us into contact with colleagues from Japan and China.

361

5. References

Abraham, S. & Lovell, N. (1999). Research and clinical assessment of eating and exercise behavior. *Hospital Medicine, 60,* 481-485.

American Dietetic Association (2001). Position of the American Dietetic Association: Nutrition intervention in the treatment of anorexia nervosa, bulimia nervosa, and eating disorders not otherwise specified (EDNOS). *Journal of the American Dietetic Association, 101,* 810-838.

American Psychiatric Association (1993). Practice Guideline for Eating Disorders. *American Journal of Psychiatry, 150,* 212-228.

American Psychiatric Association (2000). Practice guideline for the treatment of patients with eating disorders (revision). *American Journal of Psychiatry, 157,* 1-39.

Bergh, C., Brodin, U., Lindberg, G., & Soedersten, P. (2002). Randomized controlled trial of a treatment for anorexia and bulimia nervosa. *Proc Natl Acad Sci (PNAS), 99,* 9486-9491.

Beumont, P. J. V., Booth, A. L., Abraham, S., Griffiths, D. A., & Turner, T. R. (1983). A temporal sequence of symptoms in patients with anorexia nervosa: A preliminary report. In P.L.Darby, P. E. Garfinkel, D. M. Garner, & D. V. Coscina (Eds.), *Anorexia nervosa: Recent devlopments in research* (pp. 129-136). New York: Liss.

Beumont, P. J., Arthur, B., Russell, J. D., & Touyz, S. W. (1994). Excessive physical activity in dieting disorder patients: Proposals for a supervised exercise program. [Review] [48 refs]. *International Journal of Eating Disorders, 15,* 21-36.

Beumont, P., Hay, P., & Beumont, R. (2003). Summary Australian and New Zealand clincial practice guideline for the management of anorexia nervosa. *Australasian Psychiatry, 11,* 129-133.

Biadi, O., Rossini, R., Musumeci, G., Frediani, L., Masullo, M., Ramacciotti, C. E. et al. (2001). Cardiopulmonary exercise test in young women affected by anorexia nervosa. *Italian Heart Journal: Official Journal of the Italian Federation of Cardiology, 2,* 462-467.

Birmingham, C. L. & Beumont, P. (2004a). *The medical management of eating disorders: A textbook with manuals for health care professionals.* Cambridge.

Birmingham, C. L., Gutierrez, E., Jonat, L., & Beumont, P. Randomized controlled trial of warming in anorexia nervosa. *International Journal of Eating Disorders,* (in press).

Blinder, B. J., Freeman, D. M. A., & Stunkard, A. J. (1970). Behavior therapy of anorexia nervosa: Effectiveness of activity as a reinforcer of weight gain. *American Journal of Psychiatry, 126,* 77-82.

Blundell, J. E. & King, N. A. (1999). Physical activity and regulation of food intake: Current evidence. *Medicine & Science in Sports & Exercise, 31,* S573-S583.

Bouten, C. V., van Marken Lichtenbelt, W. D., & Westerterp, K. R. (1996). Body mass index and daily physical activity in anorexia nervosa. *Medicine and Science in Sports and Exercise, 28,* 967-973.

Bray, G. A., York, B., & DeLany, J. (1992). A survey of the opinions of obesity experts on the causes and treatment of obesity. *American Journal of Clinical Nutrition, 55,* 151S-154S.

Buchanan, P. A. & Ulrich, B. D. (2001). The Feldenkrais method: A dynamic approach to chaning motor behavior. *Research Quarterly for Exercise & Sport, 72,* 315-323.

Canadian Paediatric Society (1998). Eating disorders in adolescents: Principles of diagnosis and treatment. *Paediatrics and Child Health, 3,* 189-192.

Carraro, A., Cognolato, S., & Bernardis, A. L. (1998). Evaluation of a programme of adapted physical activity for ED patients. *Eating & Weight Disorders: EWD, 3,* 110-114.

Casper, R. C., Schoeller, D. A., Kushner, R., Hnilicka, J., & Gold, S. T. (1991). Total daily energy expenditure and activity level in anorexia nervosa. *American Journal of Clinical Nutrition, 53,* 1143-1150.

Casper, R. (1998). Behavioral activation and lack of concern, core symptoms of anorexia nervosa? *International Journal of Eating Disorders, 24,* 381-393.

Caspersen, C. J., Powell, K. E., & Christenson, G. M. (1985). Physical activity, exercise, and physical fitness: Definitions and distinctions for health-related research. *Public Health Reports, 100,* 126-131.

Davis, C., Fox, J., Cowles, M., Hastings, P., & Schwass, K. (1990). The functional role of exercise in the development of weight and diet concerns in women. *Journal of Psychosomatic Research, 34,* 563-574.

Davis, C., Brewer, H., & Ratusny, D. (1993a). Behavioral frequency and psychological commitment: Necessary concepts in the study of excessive exercising. *Journal of Behavioral Medicine, 16,* 611-628.

Davis, C. & Fox, J. (1993b). Excessive exercise and weight preoccupation in women. *Addictive Behaviors, 18,* 201-211.

Davis, C., Kennedy, S. H., Ravelski, E., & Dionne, M. (1994). The role of physical activity in the development and maintenance of eating disorders. *Psychological Medicine, 24,* 957-967.

Davis, C. (1997). Eating disorders and hyperactivity: a psychobiological perspective. [Review] [78 refs]. *Canadian Journal of Psychiatry - Revue Canadienne de Psychiatrie, 42,* 168-175.

Davis, C., Katzman, D. K., & Kirsh, C. (1999). Compulsive physical activity in adolescents with anorexia nervosa: a psychobehavioral spiral of pathology. *Journal of Nervous & Mental Disease, 187,* 336-342.

De Coverley Veale, D. M. W. (1987). Exercise dependence. *British Journal of Addiction, 82,* 735-740.

de Zwaan, M., Aslam, Z., & Mitchell, J. E. (2002). Research on energy expenditure in individuals with eating disorders: a review. [Review] [40 refs]. *International Journal of Eating Disorders, 31,* 361-369.

Eisler, I. & le Grange, D. (1990). Excessive exercise and anorexia nervosa. *International Journal of Eating Disorders, 9,* 377-386.

Epling, W. F., Pierce, W. D., & Stefan, L. (1983). A theory of activity based anorexia. *International Journal of Eating Disorders, 3,* 7-46.

Epling, W. F. & Pierce, W. D. (1996). An overview of activity anorexia. In W.F.Epling & W. D. Pierce (Eds.), *Activity anorexia. Theory, research, and treatment* (pp. 3-12). Mahwah, N.J.: Lawrence Erlbaum Associates.

Exner, C., Hebebrand, J., Remschmidt, H., Wewetzer, C., Ziegler, A., & Herpertz, S. (2000). Leptin suppresses semi-starvation induced hyperactivity in rats: Implications for anorexia nervosa. *Molecular Psychiatry, 5,* 476-481.

Favaro, A., Caregaro, L., Burlina, A., & Santonastaso, P. (2000). Tryptophan levels, excessive exercise, and nutritional status in anorexia nervosa. *Psychosomatic Medicine, 62,* 535-538.

Feldenkrais, M. (1949). *Body and mature behaviour.* London: Routledge and Kagan.

Fichter, M., Schweiger, U., Krieg, C., Pirke, K. M., Ploog, D., & Remschmidt, H. (2000). *Praxisleitlinien in Psychiatrie und Psychotherapie. Band 4: Behandlungsleitlinie Essstoerungen.* Darmstadt: Steinkopff.

Giles, G. M. & Chng, C. L. (1984). Occupational therapy in the treatment of anorexia nervosa: A contractual-coping approach. *British Journal of Occupational Therapy, 47,* 138-141.

Goebel, G., Schweiger, U., Kruger, R., & Fichter, M. M. (1999). Predictors of bone mineral density in patients with eating disorders. *International Journal of Eating Disorders, 25,* 143-150.

Grinspoon, S., Herzog, D., & Klibanski, A. (1997). Mechanisms and treatment options for bone loss in anorexia nervosa. *Psychopharmacology Bulletin, 33,* 399-405.

Gull, W. W. (1874). Anorexia nervosa (apepsia hysterica, anorexia hysterica). *Transactions of the Clinical Society of London, 7,* 22-28.

Gutierrez, E. & Vazquez, R. (2001a). Heat in the treatment of patients with anorexia nervosa. *Eating and Weight Disorders, 6,* 49-52.

Gutierrez, E., Vazquez, R., & Boakes, R. A. (2001b). Ambient temperature: a neglected factor in Activity-based Anorexia.
Ref Type: Unpublished Work

Herrin, M. (2003). Exercise management. In M.Herrin (Ed.), *Nutrition counseling in the treatment of eating disorders* (pp. 181-188). New York: Brunner-Routledge.

Hu, G., Pekkarinen, H., Hanninen, O., Tian, H., & Jin, R. (2002). Comparison of dietary and non-dietary risk factors in overweight and normal-weight Chinese adults. *British Journal of Nutrition, 88,* 91-97.

Karceski, S., Morrell, M., & Carpenter, D. (2002). The expert consensus guideline series: Treatment of epilepsy. *Epilepsy & Behavior, Vol 2,* -A50.

Katz, J. L. (1996). Clinical observations on the physical activity of anorexia nervosa. In W.F.Epling & W. D. Pierce (Eds.), *Activity anorexia: Theory, research and treatment* (pp. 199-207). Mahwah N.J.: Lawrence Erlbaum Associates.

Key, A., George, C. L., Beattie, D., Stammers, K., Lacey, H., & Waller, G. (2002). Body image treatment within an inpatient program for anorexia nervosa: the role of mirror exposure in the desensitization process. *International Journal of Eating Disorders, 31,* 185-190.

King, S. J. & de Sales, T. (2000). Caring for adolescent females with anorexia nervosa: registered nurses' perspective. *Journal of Advanced Nursing, 32,* 139-147.

Krahn, D. D., Rock, C., Dechert, R. E., Nairn, K. K., & Hasse, S. A. (1993). Changes in resting energy expenditure and body composition in anorexia nervosa patients during refeeding. *Journal of the American Dietetic Association, 93,* 434-438.

Kron, L., Katz, J. L., Gorzynski, G., & Weiner, H. (1978). Hyperactivity in anorexia nervosa: a fundamental clinical feature. *Comprehensive Psychiatry, 19,* 433-440.

Lambert, K. G. (1992). The activity-stress paradigm: Possible mechanisms and applications. *The Journal of General Psychology, 120,* 21-32.

Lasègue, C. H. (1964). De l'anorexia hysterique. In M.Kaufman & M. Heiman (Eds.), *Evolution of a psychosomatic concept: Anorexia nervosa* (pp. 141-155). New York: International Universities Press.

Laumer, U., Bauer, M., Fichter, M., & Milz, H. (1997). [Therapeutic effects of the Feldenkrais method "awareness through movement" in patients with eating disorders]. [German]. *Ppmp Psychotherapie Psychosomatik Medizinische Psychologie, 47,* 170-180.

Leermakers, E. A., Dunn, A. L., & Blair, S. N. (2000). Exercise management of obesity. [Review] [40 refs]. *Medical Clinics of North America, 84,* 419-440.

Levine, J. A., Eberhardt, N. L., & Jensen, M. D. (1999). Role of nonexercise activity thermogenesis in resistance to fat gain in humans. *Science, 283,* 212-214.

Long, C. G. & Hollin, C. R. (1995). Assessment and management of eating disordered patients who over-exercise: A four-year follow-up of six single case studies. *Journal of Mental Health, 4,* 309-316.

Mavissakalian, M. (1982). Anorexia nervosa treated with response prevention and prolonged exposure. *Behaviour Research & Therapy, 20,* 27-31.

Mehler, P. S. (2003). Osteoporosis in anorexia nervosa: Prevention and treatment. *International Journal of Eating Disorders, 33,* 113-126.

Melchior, J. C., Rigaud, D., Rozen, R., Malon, D., & Apfelbaum, M. (1989). Energy expenditure economy induced by decrease in lean body mass in anorexia nervosa. *European Journal of Clinical Nutrition, 43,* 793-799.

Mond, J. M., Hay, P. J., Rodgers, B., Owen, C., & Beumont, P. J. V. Relationships between exercise behaviour, eating-disordered behaviour and quality of life in a community sample of women: When is exercise 'excessive'? *European Eating Disorders Review,* (in press).

Montoye, H. J., Kemper, H. C., Saris, W. H. M., & Washburn, R. A. (1996). *Measuring physical activity and energy expenditure.* Champaign, IL: Human Kinetics.

Morrow, N. S., Schall, M., Grijalva, C. V., Geiselman, P. J., Garrick, T., Nuccion, S. et al. (1997). Body temperature and wheel running predict survival times in rats exposed to activity-stress. *Physiology and Behavior, 62,* 815-825.

Nakamura, K., Yamamoto, M., Yamazaki, O., Kawashima, Y., Muto, K., Someya, T. et al. (2000). Prevalence of anorexia nervosa and bulimia nervosa in a geographically defined area in Japan. *International Journal of Eating Disorders, 28,* 173-180.

Nudel, D. B., Gootman, N., Nussbaum, M. P., & Shenker, I. R. (1984). Altered exercise performance and abnormal sympathetic responses to exercise in patients with anorexia nervosa. *Journal of Pediatrics, 105,* 34-37.

Penas-Lledo, E., Vaz Leal, F. J., & Waller, G. (2002). Excessive exercise in anorexia nervosa and bulimia nervosa: Relation to eating characteristics and general psychopathology. *International Journal of Eating Disorders, 31,* 370-375.

Pirke, K. M., Trimborn, P., Platte, P., & Fichter, M. (1991). Average total energy expenditure in anorexia nervosa, bulimia nervosa, and healthy young women. *Biological Psychiatry, 30,* 711-718.

Platte, P., Pirke, K. M., Trimborn, P., Pietsch, K., Krieg, J. C., & Fichter, M. (1994). Resting metabolic rate and total energy expenditure in acute and weight recovered patients with anorexia nervosa and in healthy young women. *International Journal of Eating Disorders, 16,* 45-52.

Platte, P., Lebenstedt, M., Rueddel, H., & Pirke, K. M. (2000). Energy cost of physical activity in patients with anorexia nervosa. *European Eating Disorders Review, 8,* 237-244.

Polito, A., Fabbri, A., Ferro-Luzzi, A., Cuzzolaro, M., Censi, L., Ciarapica, D. et al. (2000). Basal metabolic rate in anorexia nervosa: Relation to body composition and leptin concentrations. *American Journal of Clinical Nutrition, 71,* 1495-1502.

Probst, M., Van Coppenolle, H., & Vandereycken, W. (1995). Body experience in anorexia nervosa patients: An overview of therapeutic approaches. *Eating Disorders: the Journal of Treatment & Prevention, 3,* 145-157.

Probst, M., Vandereycken, W., Van Coppenolle, H., & Pieters, G. (1999). Body experience in eating disorders before and after treatment: a follow-up study. *European Psychiatry: the Journal of the Association of European Psychiatrists, 14,* 333-340.

Rani, N. J. & Krishna Rao, P. V. (1994). Body awareness and Yoga training. *Perceptual & Motor Skills, 79,* 1103-1106.

Ravussin, E. (1995). Energy expenditure and body weight. In K.D.Brownell & C. G. Fairburn (Eds.), *Eating disorders and obesity. A comprehensive handbook* (pp. 32-37). New York: The Guilford Press.

Rock, C. L. (1999). Nutritional and medical assessment and management of eating disorders. *Nutrition in Clinical Care, 2,* 332-343.

Schebendach, J., Golden, N. H., Jacobson, M. S., Arden, M., Pettei, M., Hardoff, D. et al. (1995). Indirect calorimetry in the nutritional management of eating disorders. *International Journal of Eating Disorders, 17,* 59-66.

Seigel, K. & Hetta, J. (2001). Exercise and eating disorder symptoms among young females. *Eating & Weight Disorders: EWD, 6,* 32-39.

Sharp, C. W., Clark, S. A., Dunan, J. R., Blackwood, D. H. R., & Shapiro, C. M. (1994). Clinical presentation of anorexia nervosa in males: 24 new cases. *International Journal of Eating Disorders, 15,* 125-134.

Shelton, M. L. & Klesges, R. C. (1995). Measures of physical activity and exercise. In D.B.Allison (Ed.), *Handbook of assessment methods for eating behaviors and weight-related problems. Measures, theroy, and research* (pp. 185-201). Thousand Oaks: Sage Publications.

Soh, N., Beumont, P., Touyz, S., Surgenor, L., & Lee, E. L. (2003). Eating disorders in East Asia - is there a difference? *Newsletter: Pacific Rim college of Psychiatrists, March/April,* 5.

Strober, M., Freeman, R., & Morrell, W. (1997). The long-term course of severe anorexia nervosa in adolescents: Survival analysis of recovery, relapse and outcome predictors over 10-15 years in a prospective study. *International Journal of Eating Disorders, 22,* 339-360.

Thien, V., Thomas, A., Markin, D., & Birmingham, C. L. (2000). Pilot study of a graded exercise program for the treatment of anorexia nervosa. *International Journal of Eating Disorders, 28,* 101-106.

Touyz, S., Beumont, P., Glaun, D., Philips, T., & Cowie, I. (1984). A comparison of lenient and strict operant conditioning programmes in refeeding patients with anorexia nervosa. *British Journal of Psychiatry, 144,* 517-520.

Touyz, S. & Beumont, P. J. V. (1985). A comprehensive, multidisciplinary approach for the management of patients with anorexia nervosa. In S.Touyz & P. J. V. Beumont (Eds.), *Eating disorders: Prevalence and treatment* (pp. 11-22). Sydney: Williams and Wilkins.

Touyz, S., Beumont, P. J., & Hook, S. (1987). Exercise anorexia: A new dimension in anorexia nervosa? In P.J.Beumont, G. D. Burrows, & R. C. Casper (Eds.), *Handbook of eating disorders. Part 1: Anorexia and bulimia nervosa* (pp. 143-157). Amsterdam: Elsevier.

Touyz, S., Lennerts, W., Arthur, B., & Beumont, P. J. V. (1993). Anaerobic exercise as an adjunct to refeeding patients with anorexia nervosa: Does it compromise weight gain? *European Eating Disorders Review, 1,* 177-182.

Touyz, S. & Beumont, P. J. (1999). Anorexia nervosa: New approaches to management. *Modern Medicine of Australia, June,* 95-110.

US Department for Health and Human Services (1997). Guidelines for School and Community Programs to promote lifelong physical activity among young people. *Morbidity and Mortality Weekly Reports, 46,* 1-36.

Vaisman, N., Rossi, M. F., Corey, M., Clarke, R., Goldberg, E., & Pencharz, P. B. (1991). Effect of refeeding on the energy metabolism of adolescent girls who have anorexia nervosa. *European Journal of Clinical Nutrition, 45,* 527-537.

van Marken Lichtenbelt, W. D., Heidendal, G. A., & Westerterp, K. R. (1997). Energy expenditure and physical activity in relation to bone mineral density in women with anorexia nervosa. *European Journal of Clinical Nutrition, 51,* 826-830.

Wakefield, A. Nutrition management of anorexia nervosa. *Australian Journal of Nutrition and Dietetics,* (in press).

Wilson, G. T. & Vitousek, K. M. (1999). Self-monitoring in the assessment of eating disorders. *Psychological Assessment, 11,* 480-489.

Windauer, U., Lennerts, W., Talbot, P., Touyz, S., & Beumont, P. (1993). How well are 'cured' anorexia nervosa patients? An investigation of 16 weight-recovered anorexic patients. *British Journal of Psychiatry, 163,* 195-200.

World Health Organisation Collaborating Centre for Mental Health and Substance Abuse (1997). Dieting Disorders. In World Health Organisation Collaborating Centre for Mental Health and Substance Abuse (Ed.), *Management of*

Mental Disorders. Treatment Practice Protocols (pp. 464-525). Darlinghurst NSW: World Health Organisation Collaborating Centre for Mental Health and Substance Abuse.

Ziemer, R. R. & Ross, J. L. (1970). Anorexia nervosa: A new approach. *American Corrective Therapy Journal, 24,* 34-42.

6. Appendices

6.1. Appendix A: Email to clinical specialists

Dear _____

Physical activity in eating/dieting disorders has been studied extensively over a number of years. We have a fairly good understanding of what constitutes 'overexercising' in people with eating/dieting disorders and we are discussing terms such as 'hyperactivity'. We are aware that there is a relationship between exercise/activity and eating/dieting disorder. However, studies into treatment of physical activity in people with eating/dieting disorders are very rare. As you know, activity has a major impact on energy expenditure (and on weight gain) therefore strategies are needed to help people with eating/dieting disorders balance and modify activity levels as part of the treatment process. We also need to look at counteracting the obsessionality that accompanies activity in many people with eating/dieting disorders.

In this preliminary survey we would like to ask the advice of experts and clinicians in the field of eating/dieting disorders from Australia, Japan, Singapore, USA, Canada and Europe. What is your understanding of, and treatment approach towards, the physical activity of patients with eating/dieting disorders? **We would very much appreciate it if you could complete the attached questionnaire and forward it on to clinicians (eg psychiatrist, psychologists, dietitians) you are working with.** It is our intention that by gathering experts' and clinicians' international opinion on this issue, we may be able to develop some draft guidelines for the treatment of over-activity in this patient group in the future. Your participation is greatly appreciated.

The questionnaire consists of 4 questions and is mainly centred on the management of physical activity in anorexia nervosa. Please return the completed questionnaire to Ms Tanja Hechler (PhD-student and research coordinator: tanja.hechler@email.cs.nsw.gov.au) at the University of Sydney, Australia. You can either complete the questionnaire via e-mail or print it out and send/fax it back to me. If you choose to fill it out via e-mail, please use the tab-key to move between questions. Depending on the questions, you either just tick the respective box or fill in numbers. If you choose for example other treatment approaches than the ones we have listed, please specify your approach by briefly describing it in the respective field. If you choose to mail or fax the survey, please address your answer to the following address:

> Ms Tanja Hechler (PhD-student)
> C/o Experts' and clinicians' survey
> Department of Psychological Medicine
> Royal Prince Alfred Hospital
> Bldg. 92/ Level 2
> Camperdown NSW 2050
> Australia
> Ph: 02-9515-5844; Fax: 02-9515-7778

It would be greatly appreciated if you could return the survey by the **15th of May 2003**. We will send you a reminder on the 20th of April 2003. If you are not interested in participating please return the survey regardless, writing 'no comment' on the front page. Please do not hesitate to contact us if you require any additional information, if you would like a copy of the references quoted, or if you would like to discuss these issues further. Thank you very much for your help.

Yours sincerely,
Tanja Hechler

In collaboration with Prof Pierre Beumont (Psychiatrist), Prof Stephen Touyz (Psychologist), Peta Marks (Mental Health Nurse)

6.2. Appendix B: The Eating Disorder Specialist/Clinician Survey (EDSCS)

EATING DISORDER SPECIALIST/ CLINICIAN SURVEY
Activity and its management

Demographics

A. General information
Professional discipline (eg psychiatrist, psychologist etc):
Number of years working in the Eating Disorder Field:
Country: City: Institution you work at :

B. Is your work with
☐ Predominantly inpatients (Please, answer questions 1a, 1b, 3 and 4.)
☐ Predominantly outpatients/day patients (Please, answer questions 2a, 2b, 3 and 4.)
☐ Mixture of both inpatients and outpatients (Please, answer all questions.)

C. Do you believe that activity is an important component of anorexia nervosa?
☐ Yes
☐ No

D. Approximately how many patients receive treatment in your unit each year?

During 2002, approximately how many of the patients you treated presented with (or developed) hyperactivity/overexercising?

Physical activity does not merely mean exercising, but is defined as ANY bodily movement produced by skeletal muscles resulting in energy expenditure (Caspersen et al., 1985). Attempts have been made to subdivide physical activities in patient with eating/dieting disorders (Beumont et al., 1994; Bouten, van Marken Lichtenbelt & Westerterp, 1996) as well as examining motivational factors (Beumont et al., 1994).

Question 1a)

Which of the following **activity-issues do you consider problematic** in **INPATIENTS** with anorexia nervosa?
(Please rank: 1 = most problematic, 4 = least problematic. Please use each number once only.)

Excessive exercise [____] (1=most problematic, 4=least problematic)

> *Exercising at least six times/week for at least 1 hr per session in one of the following activities: swimming, bicycling, running, skating, home exercise, dance classes, aerobics or weight training* (defined by Davis et al., (1993a).

Obsessive-compulsive attitude towards exercising [____] (1=most problematic, 4=least problematic)

> *Feelings of well-being are influenced by exercising. Adherence to exercise is maintained in the face of various adverse conditions. Patient's exercise regime interferes with social commitments* (Commitment to Exercise Scale; Davis et al., (1993a).

Contrived activity [____] (1=most problematic, 4=least problematic)

> *Activity is deliberately structured to maximise energy expenditure, e.g. through domestic work, walking instead of taking the bus, standing* (Beumont et al., 1994).

Restless hyperactivity [____] (1=most problematic, 4=least problematic)

> *Little fidgeting movements of which the patient is not aware, probably occurring as a result of malnutrition as shown in animal models* (Epling & Pierce, 1996).

Others [____] (Please, specify.)

Question 1 b)

In terms of management, which of the following elements (A-E) best describe components of your treatment approach regarding physical activity in INPATIENTS with anorexia nervosa? (Please tick all that apply.)

A. Assessment

☐ *history of activity*

☐ *current activity patterns*
☐ patient's beliefs surrounding activity
☐ motivation to engage in physical activity
☐ commitment/obsessionality with the activity of exercising
☐ willingness to reduce activity as per your recommendations
☐ other   (Please, specify.)

How much time on average do you spend on the assessment of physical activit

B.I.) Active discouragement of activity, if...
☐ patient is at a low body weight   (please, specify)
☐ patient is at a low % of ideal body weight   (please specify)

☐ *patient is at a low % of body fat   (please specify)*
☐ other   (Please, specify.)

B.II.) Prohibition of activity, if...
☐ patient is at a low body weight   (please, specify)
☐ patient is at a low % of ideal body weight   (please specify)

☐ *patient is at a low % of body fat   (please specify)*
☐ other   (Please, specify.)

C. Activity-intervention on ward
☐ Bedrest to prevent patient from exercising (response prevention; (Touyz Beumont, 1985)
☐ Exercise as a motivation factor (incentive) in an operant-conditioning progra (Blinder, Freeman, & Stunkard, 1970)
☐ Staff supervising patient's general activity
☐ Other   (Please, specify.)

D. Structured program for the issue of physical activity
Characterised by (please tick all that apply.)

☐ Individual sessions (eg with psychologist, dietitian, psychomotor therapist)
☐ Group sessions

D.I.) Who is involved with developing and/or supervising structured activity/exercise programmes?
☐ Psychomotor therapists (PMT: professional who helps people with psychological problems in the area of movement and body experience (see also www.pmtinfosite.nl/home-I-e.shtml))
☐ Physiotherapists
☐ Psychologists
☐ Psychiatrists
☐ Art therapists
☐ Nurses
☐ Other   (Please, specify.)

D.II.) Do you utilise any of the following?
☐ Psychoeducation
        (about integrating a healthy pattern of activity into one's lifestyle)

☐ Challenging the patient's belief and attitudes
        (around activity and exercise)

☐ Self-monitoring
        (using diaries and/or mechanical devices (eg pedometers, accelerometers) to increase their awareness of their activity-level)

☐ Group games, team sports, role games
        (to tackle socialising problems;(Carraro et al., 1998))

☐ Supervised sessions with gym equipment
        (providing moderate muscular toning, stretching, weight training and posture improvement (Beumont et al., 1994; Carraro et al., 1998).

☐ Movements groups (Laumer et al., 1997)
        ☐ Tai Chi (one of three fighting arts to develop inner strength through paying attention to internal sensations and their causes, see also www.chessnut.demon.co.uk/neichia/tcc_intro.html)
        ☐ Yoga
        ☐ Feldenkrais (an educational system which uses movement exercises to increase body awareness and improve ease, balance, grace and effectiveness of   action,   see   also www.bonnernet.com/users/aoc/disciplines/feldenkrais/index.php   and (Laumer et al., 1997)

☐ Autogenic training
☐ Other   (Please, specify.)

☐ Other treatment approaches   (Please, specify.)

D.III.) Do you utilise one of the following to counteract restle hyperactivity?

☐ **Use of heat treatment to address restless hyperactivity using (Bergh, Brodin, Lindberg, & Soedersten, 2002; Gutierrez & Vazquez, 2001a):**

　　☐ *Thermal vests*
　　☐ Sauna baths
　　☐ Other heat treatments   (Please, specify.)

☐ Other treatment approaches for restless hyperactivity   (Please, specify.)

E. Treatment of physical activity is part of body-orientated therapies *(Probs et al., 1995)*. (Please tick all that apply.)

☐ Relaxation and breathing techniques
☐ Massage
☐ Role playing
☐ Physical activity, sports and games
☐ Dance and creative movement
☐ Self-perception and body perception
☐ Other   (Please, specify.)

How many sessions on average do you spend on the issue of physical activity per **inpatient** during her treatment? (eg. 4 out of 12 sessions) ☐

Question 2a)

Which of the following **activity-issues do you consider problematic** in **OUTPATIENTS** with anorexia nervosa?
(Please rank; 1 = most problematic, 4 = least problematic. Please use each number once only.)

Excessive exercise [＿＿] (1=most problematic, 4=least problematic)

Exercising at least six times/week for at least 1 hr per session in one of the following activities: swimming, bicycling, running, skating, home exercise, dance classes, aerobics or weight training (defined by Davis et al., (1993a)

Obsessive-compulsive attitude towards exercising [＿＿] (1=most problematic, 4=least problematic)

Feelings of well-being are influenced by exercising. Adherence to exercise is maintained in the face of various adverse conditions. Patient's exercise regime interferes with social commitments (Commitment to Exercise Scale; (Davis et al., 1993a))

Contrived activity [＿＿] (1=most problematic, 4=least problematic)

Activity is deliberately structured to maximise energy expenditure, e.g. through domestic work, walking instead of taking the bus, standing (Beumont et al., 1994)

Restless hyperactivity [＿＿] (1=most problematic, 4=least problematic)

Little fidgeting movements of which the patient is not aware, probably occurring as a result of malnutrition as shown in animal models (Epling & Pierce, 1996)

Others [＿＿] (Please, specify.)

Question 2b)

In terms of management, which of the following elements (A-E) best describes components of your treatment approach regarding physical activity in OUTPATIENTS with anorexia nervosa? (Please tick all that apply.)

A. Assessment

☐ *history of activity*

☐ *current activity patterns*
☐ patient's beliefs surrounding activity
☐ motivation to engage in physical activity
☐ willingness to reduce activity as per your recommendations
☐ commitment/obsessionality with the activity of exercising
☐ other   (Please, specify.)

How much time on average do you spend on the assessment of physical activity
☐

B.I.) Active discouragement of activity, if...
☐ patient is at a low body weight   (please, specify)
☐ patient is at a low % of ideal body weight   (please specify)

☐ *patient is at a low % of body fat   (please specify)*
☐ other   (Please, specify.)

B.II.) Prohibition of activity, if...
☐ patient is at a low body weight   (please, specify)
☐ patient is at a low % of ideal body weight   (please specify)

☐ *patient is at a low % of body fat   (please specify)*
☐ other   (Please, specify.)

C. Activity-intervention with outpatients
☐ Prescription of bedrest to prevent patient from exercising (response prevention (Touyz & Beumont, 1985))
☐ Other   (Please, specify.)

D. Structured program for the issue of physical activity
Characterised by (please tick all that apply.)

☐ Individual sessions (eg with psychologist, dietitian, psychomotor therapist)
☐ Group sessions

D.I.) Who is involved with developing and/or supervising structured activity/exercise programmes?
☐ Psychomotor therapists
☐ Physiotherapists
☐ Psychiatrists
☐ Psychologists
☐ Art therapists
☐ Nurses
☐ Other   (Please, specify.)

D.II.) Do you utilise any of the following?
☐ Psychoeducation
    (about integrating a healthy pattern of activity into one's lifestyle)

☐ Challenging the patient's belief and attitudes
    (around activity and exercise)

☐ Self-monitoring
    (using diaries and/or mechanical devices (eg pedometers, accelerometers) to increase their awareness of their activity-level)

☐ Group games, team sports, role games
    (to tackle socialising problems;(Carraro et al., 1998))

☐ Supervised sessions with gym equipment
    (providing moderate muscular toning, stretching, weight training and posture improvement (Beumont et al., 1994; Carraro et al., 1998)).

☐ Movements groups (Laumer et al., 1997)
    ☐ Tai Chi
    ☐ Yoga
    ☐ Feldenkrais
    ☐ Autogenic training
    ☐ Other   (Please, specify.)

☐ Other treatment approaches   (Please, specify.)

D.III.) Do you utilise one of the following to counteract restless hyperactivity?

☐ **Use of heat treatment to address restless hyperactivity using (Bergh et al 2002; Gutierrez & Vazquez, 2001a)**

    ☐ *Thermal vests*
    ☐ Sauna baths
    ☐ Other heat treatments   (Please, specify.)

☐ Other treatment approaches for restless hyperactivity   (Please, specify.)

E. Treatment of physical activity as part of body-orientated therapies *(Probst et al., 1995)* (Please, tick all that apply.)
☐ Relaxation and breathing techniques
☐ Massage
☐ Role playing
☐ Physical activity, sports and games
☐ Dance and creative movement
☐ Self-perception and body perception
☐ Other   (Please, specify.)

How many sessions on average do you spend on the issue of physical activity per **outpatient** during her treatment? (eg. 4 out of 12 sessions)

Question 3)

How do you see **the role of physical activity** in eating/dieting disorders?
(Please tick only one.)

(Adapted from Eisler and LeGrange, (1990))

☐ activity is fundamental to the pathogenesis of the disorder

☐ the two phenomena are directly related in that one may be a risk factor for developing the other

☐ the two phenomena are indirectly related in that they are both related to some third variable (eg obsessive-compulsive tendencies) and thus will occur together with more than chance frequency

☐ the two phenomena are essentially variants of each other with developmental, gender, familial and cultural factors accounting for why one or the other expression of the underlying vulnerability occurs in a given person

☐ Physical activity plays a minor role in eating/dieting disorders. More important are factors such as   (Please specify.)

Question 4)

Do you believe that the issue of activity is important enough to warrant funds allocation into its research?
☐ No
☐ Yes

If YES, what specifically would you find most clinically beneficial as far as research into activity would be concerned?

Thank you very much for your help!

General conclusions

After analysing the results according to the assumptions described in the general introduction, the following conclusions can be stated:

Assumption 1: Australians and Germans will not differ in their perception and understanding of seasonal changes in physical activity, food choice and dieting.

Assumption 1 was partly supported in that the majority of both Australians and Germans perceived seasonal changes, particularly in various aspects of physical activity. Thus, physical activity appears to be a behaviour which varies considerably with the seasons, a variation which is perceived similarly by residents from different climates. However, Australians and Germans differed in the reported causes for the perceived changes. A detailed discussion of this finding was presented in Part 1.

Results of Part 1 justified an investigation into seasonal variation in physical activity in Australian patients with anorexia nervosa and a control group.

Assumption 2: Seasonal variation in physical activity (i.e., duration, frequency and body movement) and body composition will be detected in patients with anorexia nervosa and a negative relationship between physical activity and body composition variables will emerge in the patient group.

Results from Part 2 offered partly support for assumption 2. Similar to controls, patients' reported time spent in moderate intensity activities varied across the seasons, with decreases in winter and increases in summer. However, for patients, body movement remained elevated across all seasons compared to controls. In terms of exercise behaviour, the number of patients engaging in exercise increased during summer. Hence, the results demonstrated seasonal variation in some aspects of physical activity (i.e., moderate intensity activities and exercise) in patients with anorexia nervosa. It appears that summer, in particular, may represent a 'high-risk' season for increased physical activity in patients with anorexia nervosa.

In terms of physical activity and body composition variables, a trend for a negative correlation between percentage body fat and the amount of time spent in strenuous intensity body movement emerged in the patient group further highlighting the need for management strategies for physical activity to prevent patients from relapsing into the weight-loss and exercise cycle.

Accordingly, management strategies for physical activity were presented in Part 3 and a survey of clinical specialists on their understanding and management of physical activity in patients with anorexia nervosa was conducted. The majority of clinical specialists acknowledged the importance of physical activity in anorexia nervosa. However, the literature review and results from the survey demonstrated a discrepancy between published articles on assessment and management strategies for physical activity, and their use in clinical practice. Further, Asian clinical specialists appear to perceive the role of physical activity differently compared to Australian, European, American and Canadian specialists.

Future research should replicate and extend the current findings on seasonality in physical activity in anorexia nervosa. If these results are replicated, management strategies which are mindful of the aspect of seasonality may need to be included in future studies. Also, additional surveys of clinical specialists regarding physical activity and anorexia nervosa are needed to optimise the implementation of published assessment and management strategies for physical activity into the treatment process, including an investigation into cultural differences.

Originality of Thesis

I hereby declare that the work embodied in this thesis is he result of my original research, that no part of it has been submitted for any degree or diploma of any other university or institution, and that to the best of my knowledge no material published or written by another person has been included, except where due acknowledgement has been indicated.

_____

Tanja Hechler

_____

Date

www.ingramcontent.com/pod-product-compliance
Lightning Source LLC
Chambersburg PA
CBHW020452270326
41926CB00008B/573